BUILDING A
GREAT LIBRARY

BUILDING A
GREAT LIBRARY

The Coolidge Years
at Harvard

by
William Bentinck-Smith

Harvard University Library

CAMBRIDGE · MASSACHUSETTS

1976

Composition by The Harvard University Printing Office
Printed by The Stinehour Press

Copyright © 1973, 1974, 1976 by the President and Fellows of Harvard College

Reprinted, with additions, from the *Harvard Library Bulletin*,
volumes XXI (1973) and XXII (1974)

Library of Congress Catalog Card Number 75–27901

ISBN: 0–674–08578–7

To the long line of devoted individuals — librarians, faculty, staff, and donors — who through more than three centuries have labored, and continue to labor, to make the Harvard Library a great resource for scholarship.

Contents

"Gone the sarcophagus known as Gore —
The Library's longer and Widener now . . ."

From "Kitty and Copey and Bliss"
by Laurence McKinney, A.B. 1912

Preface

ARCHIBALD CARY COOLIDGE had a lingering youthful dread that he might end his days as a dilettante. Perhaps he had reason to worry, for he was born into fortunate circumstances and could easily have spent his years in respectable indolence. In his formal boyhood schooling in a variety of educational institutions he showed no particular early promise of orderly thought and study. But he came alive at Harvard College. Harvard suited him to his boot-tops, and through a chain of not unsurprising circumstances he returned to his college, after rigorous study and stimulating travel in Europe, to make a memorable career as a professor of history and international affairs, as a teacher of scholars, as an academic man of affairs, and as the director of a great library.

From childhood an instinctive, voracious reader, Coolidge early converted his enthusiasm for books into a deep concern for their use in the world of learning. As a young instructor and assistant professor, he searched out and bought scarce and important titles in his fields of interest and gave them to Harvard. His disciplined mind could not tolerate the crowding and disorder imposed on the Harvard Library by a combination of years of forced economy and haphazard growth. President A. Lawrence Lowell made no mistake in selecting his cousin Archibald Coolidge to help him find a solution to the library crisis Lowell had inherited from his predecessor.

Coolidge took over with characteristic energy and enthusiasm. Whether he could have succeeded so completely had not tragedy struck the Widener family is problematical. With the great Widener gift the question of space was settled for a generation, and Coolidge could bring his common sense to bear on the library's administrative problems and concentrate his acquisitive talents on the strategy of scholarly collecting.

Unsparing of himself and unfailingly generous in the cause of books and scholarship, Coolidge built wisely on the solid foundations of the past. He vastly extended the scope of the library's collections and left a heritage of strength to the next generation, making possible the bold new departures in historical and international studies which followed the second World War.

Originally this study was intended to be a straightforward account of Coolidge's library career — in one easy installment — for the *Harvard Library Bulletin*. At least that is what the editors suggested, thinking that some work I had been doing on Coolidge in another context could be adapted for the *Library Bulletin*'s pages. However, the extensive Coolidge papers in the Harvard University Archives, relatively unexplored, invited more extensive treatment. From the beginning of the story's enlargement, Edwin E. Williams, Editor, and Rene Kuhn Bryant, Associate Editor, have been enthusiastic and indispensable advisors and wonderfully generous in allotting space in their journal to a chronicle which has gone on and on and on. Throughout its development Douglas W. Bryant, Director of the Harvard University Library, has given the project warm support, strong encouragement, and official sanction.

From the nieces and nephews of Professor Coolidge has come ready help. They recognized a life-size figure, not a mythical genius, in the uncle they remember, and their contributions helped to define the man with that keen insight that comes from childhood observations recollected in maturity. John P. Coolidge started me on the right course and helped me get my bearings among the very numerous Coolidge clan. Archibald C. Coolidge II of Cambridge, Maryland, spent hours recording lively, witty, appreciative comments on his intimate association with his uncle. Jane Revere Coolidge Whitehill saved me from a number of errors and incorrect assumptions and passed on some invaluable recollections of her uncle's character and family relationships. Harold J. Coolidge Jr. put me on the track of the photographs of the five brothers which Hamilton Richards and J. Gardner Coolidge generously lent as illustrations. In addition to a number of other pictures, Gardner Coolidge also shared his own recollections of "Uncle Arch" and brought Coolidge names and faces into sharper focus. J. Randolph Coolidge IV furnished the two lovely photographs of the Stone House and its view and contributed some anecdotes. Anne Richards Preedy loaned the fine picture of the Coolidge family. I am grateful to Professor William L. Langer, Gertrude M. Shaw, Margaret Currier, and the late Helen G. Powers for ready help in submitting to lengthy questioning about Professor Coolidge. Miss Currier, daughter of T.

Franklin Currier, lent a number of valuable documents and photographs from her father's files. Harley P. Holden and Clark A. Elliott, Curator and Associate Curator respectively of the Harvard University Archives, together with their friendly and ever willing staff, have always patiently and efficiently provided answers to countless inquiries.

Above all, thanks are due to my associate Jill Radcliffe Norton, who with unflagging zeal searched, numbered, indexed, read copy and proof — and shared her counsel. Archibald Cary Coolidge has become her friend as well as mine.

WILLIAM BENTINCK-SMITH

BUILDING A
GREAT LIBRARY

ARCHIBALD CARY COOLIDGE
1866–1928

The Education of a Director

Ｉ N THE PREFACE to his biography of Suleiman the Magnificent, Roger Bigelow Merriman, the Gurney Professor of History, acknowledged that the book was "only partially my own," that it originated in an unfinished manuscript written more than forty years before by the late Archibald Cary Coolidge (1866–1928). Mr. Merriman then went on to summarize in a long paragraph — probably as well as anyone has ever said it — what Archibald Cary Coolidge had done for Harvard in his lifetime:

I trust that the publication of this life of one of the greatest yet least known sovereigns of the sixteenth century will serve among other things to remind Harvard men all over the world of the immense debt which the University owes to Professor Coolidge. To one who, like myself, has studied and taught here for over half a century, that debt looms larger and larger as the years go by. Others have already written of his unfailing kindness, humor, and tact, of his boundless generosity and unselfishness. Here, however, I want especially to emphasize the greatness of his achievement in broadening the University's horizon. The Widener Library and the collections which he gave or obtained for it are perhaps the most conspicuous monument to his success in this respect; but the Corporation records and the University Catalogues of the last fifty years tell a no less notable tale for the curriculum. When Professor Coolidge came back to Harvard in 1893, the only undergraduate instruction given in modern history outside of the United States consisted of two general courses on Western Europe in the seventeenth, eighteenth, and nineteenth centuries; the Scandinavian, Slavic, Ottoman, and Iberian worlds were left practically untouched; the African, Asiatic, and Latin-American ones wholly so. Two years later we find Professor Coolidge himself offering two half courses, to be given in alternate years, on the history of the Scandinavian lands and on the Eastern Question, and in 1904–05 another on the Expansion of Europe since 1815. In 1896 he persuaded the Corporation to embark on an even more daring adventure, and invite "Mr." (later Professor) Leo Wiener to give instruction in Slavic Languages and Literature, with the understanding that he was also to assist at

3

the Library in cataloguing Slavic and Sanskrit books; and in 1907–08 Professor Coolidge himself offered a full course on the history of Russia. All this was the entering wedge for greater things to come, not only at Harvard but elsewhere; it deserves, in fact, to be regarded as the origin of the scientific study of Slavic history, languages, and literatures in America. A half course in Spanish history was first given in 1903, and a professorship of Latin-American history and economics was endowed a decade later. Instruction in the history of Asia and of the African colonies was to follow in the succeeding years. For every one of these and for many other advances, Professor Coolidge was directly or indirectly responsible. Invariably he foresaw and pointed out the need. Often he gave generously to meet it, and his judgment of men was sound and keen. It has been well said of him that he was far more interested in the production of scholars than in the products of scholarship itself. To him more than to any other man is due what the Harvard History Department was able to accomplish in the days of its greatness. To us who have been brought to open our eyes to wider horizons by the tragic events of the past five years, his visions of a half-century ago seem prophetic.[1]

Mr. Merriman's laudatory list of Archibald Coolidge's accomplishments — particularly Coolidge's contributions to the growth and strengthening of the University Library, which are central to the whole story — have been only partially revealed in previously published accounts, even in the biography, *Archibald Cary Coolidge, Life and Letters*, published in 1932 by his brother, Harold Jefferson Coolidge, and his former student and long-time associate, Professor Robert Howard Lord.[2] It is an axiom of university life, as Professor Paul H. Buck (writing just twenty years after Mr. Merriman) pointed out, that possession of a great library, emphasizing new areas of scholarship,

[1] Roger Bigelow Merriman, *Suleiman the Magnificent* (Cambridge, Harvard University Press, 1944), pp. vi–vii.

[2] Harold Jefferson Coolidge and Robert Howard Lord, *Archibald Cary Coolidge, Life and Letters*, Boston, Houghton Mifflin Company, 1932. Harold Jefferson Coolidge (1870–1934), younger brother of Archibald Coolidge and a graduate of Harvard (A.B. *magna cum laude* 1892), was a Boston trustee and a partner in the firm of Loring, Coolidge. Robert Howard Lord (1885–1954), who graduated from Harvard *magna cum laude* in 1906 and took his A.M. in 1907, and Ph.D. in 1908, was Coolidge's most able student of the early years. He became an expert on the countries of Eastern Europe, particularly Poland, was Coolidge's substitute for Eastern Europe on The Inquiry (1917–1919) and an adviser at the Peace Conference in Paris in 1918–1919. Lord served as Instructor in History (1910–1916), Assistant Professor of History (1916–1922), Associate Professor (1922–1924), and Professor (1924–1926). He left Harvard to study for holy orders in the latter year and in 1929 entered the Roman Catholic priesthood. For much of the rest of his life he taught church history at St. John's Seminary, Brighton, Mass.

enables a university "to build programs on solid foundations of research materials." A great library attracts to its university scholars and funds for scholarship. "Slavic studies could not have forged ahead at the rapid pace of the past decade," Mr. Buck declared, "if Archibald Cary Coolidge had not anticipated Faculty needs by fifty years and built up major collections in the area at a time when only a handful of American scholars were prepared to use them. It would not be easy to estimate how greatly the University and the nation have benefited from his vision." [3]

Archibald Cary Coolidge was born in Boston, 6 March 1866, third of five surviving sons of Joseph Randolph and Julia Gardner Coolidge. His father graduated from the Law School (LL.B. 1854), and all five sons attended Harvard College. "His ancestors on both sides," his biographers state, "were generally well-to-do and often rich, according to the standards of the day, with the result that, although some of them may have worked hard at their occupations, they did not as a rule have to do so for a living. They were therefore able to avail themselves of the best that American education had to offer, with unusual opportunities for work, study, and travel in Europe and the Far East." [4]

Harold Coolidge points out that their father was a student for ten years in Switzerland and Germany before going to the Harvard Law School. The family tradition was of travel, foreign scenes, the China trade, and a world view exemplified by their ancestor Thomas Jefferson, a great-great-grandfather through the Randolphs and a moulding influence on young Archibald Coolidge. "With such antecedents, it is not strange that Archy Coolidge should from his earliest childhood have shown an intense and all-absorbing interest in intelligent travel, in the development of institutions of learning, and in the study and history of the making of nations." [5]

The relationship with the Virginia branch of the family, Harold Coolidge reflected, "was of marked influence on Archy Coolidge's early education and on his thought throughout his whole life. He harked back constantly to Virginia in his day-dreams and conversation, and one of his strongest, though always unfulfilled personal ambitions, was

[3] Paul Herman Buck, *Libraries and Universities, Addresses and Reports*, Edited by Edwin E. Williams, with an Introduction by Howard Mumford Jones (Cambridge, Harvard University Press, 1964), p. 74.

[4] Coolidge and Lord, *op. cit.*, p. 2.

[5] *Ibid.*, p. 3.

the repurchase of Monticello and its restoration to the family line . . ."

The Coolidge family circle was "serious and elevating." The father was "a man of wide reading and stimulating conversation," handsome, aristocratic, very conscious of his social and intellectual standing; the mother "a quiet, home-loving, religious woman whose devoted care, always tempered with a happy dry humor, was of infinite importance in moulding the character, and compelling and holding the love of all her sons." Yet, some of the parental influence was oddly conceived and shared. The father and mother "conscientiously" experimented with different theories of discipline and shifted the children's schools according to their changing ideas about education, and their own convenience. At the age of four (in 1870–71), little Archibald Coolidge spent the winter in Nice and Switzerland. In subsequent years he then attended three different boys' schools in Boston and finally was sent in 1875 to a school in Shadwell, Virginia, run by his cousin, Charlotte Randolph, where he stayed until 1877. There followed four winters in two private schools in Boston. Harold Coolidge felt that this period "did not produce much in the way of education, but . . . gave opportunity for winning declamation prizes, which pleased the family relatives, and for omnivorous reading on any subjects bearing on the intrigues of foreign courts, statesmen, and generals, with the resulting wars and dynastic and territorial changes . . . So far as the ordinary sports and amusements of a healthy growing boy among his fellows went, they were practically crowded out by the greater interest in reading and day-dreaming. Archy never learned to skate, seldom rode a horse," played baseball only well enough to lose two front teeth. For summer fun the Coolidges dispatched Archy to "camp" in the Adirondacks, Kennebago Lake, or King and Bartlett Ponds in Maine. After his final year of two at Adams Academy in Quincy, young Coolidge traveled to San Francisco with his uncle and aunt, Mr. and Mrs. John L. Gardner [6] of Boston, and then entered Harvard with the Class of 1887. He lived for all four years in Wadsworth House, and distinguished himself for high scholarship, graduating with a *summa cum laude* in history and membership in Phi Beta Kappa. But college was not all work, for Coolidge joined the Hasty Pudding and Alpha Delta Phi (now the Fly Club), and became a fairly successful featherweight boxer and wrestler.

The next six years Archibald Cary Coolidge (he always signed his

[6] See note 18 below.

name in full) spent traveling, studying at the Ecole des Sciences Politiques in Paris and getting his doctorate with von Holst at Freiburg.[7] He even tested out his inclinations toward the Foreign Service with seven months in Russia, mainly as the unauthorized Acting Secretary of the American Legation in St. Petersburg, but with a month as Secretary to his uncle, Thomas Jefferson Coolidge, the American Minister to France, and a short stint as Secretary to the American Legation in Vienna.

By the time he returned to Cambridge in 1893,[8] he had visited China, Japan, India, Russian Central Asia, Egypt, and most of Europe. He could speak French fluently, German quite well, and was moderately acquainted with Italian and Russian. His interest in the history and cultures of the nations of the world, in the relations among the nations, and in the development and administration of United States foreign policy had been whetted to a keen edge.

His first Harvard teaching post was as Instructor in History, helping Professor Edward Channing with History 1, the great survey course in European history. In his second year he assumed full charge of this course and also assisted Professor Silas Macvane with his course on Continental Europe since the Middle of the Eighteenth Century. In 1899 he was appointed Assistant Professor. He became a full Professor in 1908 and served as Director of the University Library from 1910 to 1928. Early in his teaching years he introduced his famous course on the history and expansion of Russia (growing out of his teaching of the history of Northern and Eastern Europe) and he was instrumental in spurring the development of courses on the history of

[7] Hermann Eduard von Holst (1841–1904), an Estonian by birth, was professor of modern history and a specialist in American studies at Freiburg. He "dominated the academic scene" there for twenty years and, after the establishment of the University of Chicago in 1891, became chairman of its history department. He was the author of a biography of Calhoun and two works on American constitutional history. The title of Coolidge's thesis was "Theoretical and Foreign Elements in the Constitution of the United States."

[8] The family story is that "Uncle Archy" gave up his ambitions for the Foreign Service because of a broken love affair. Coolidge and Lord only say that "compelling family reasons brought him back to Boston" in April 1893. Beyond this hint that the love of Coolidge's life left him for another during his absence in Europe, Coolidge and Lord provide no further details. For more on this episode see note 252. Coolidge's travel letters to his family are now in the University Archives and are liberally quoted in the chapter "Preparation for a Busy Life" in Coolidge and Lord, *op. cit.*

Latin America, Northern Europe, the Far East, and the Ottoman Empire as well as Slavic countries other than Russia.

During his years of Harvard teaching, Coolidge was known initially for History 1 (the introductory course in European history), and History 15 (history of Russia). To these he added History 48, an advanced course on the history of Russia, History 19 (a course on the Eastern Question), History 30B, on the Expansion of Europe since 1815, and a seminar, History 29, "Selected Topics in the History of the Nineteenth Century." At one point he even taught a course (History 18) on the Far East in the Nineteenth Century because he could not find anyone else to teach it and thought the subject so important. Most of these additional courses were begun before his Library appointment, and he continued to give the half courses and seminar course, from time to time, even while serving as Director of the Library. Meanwhile others, like Charles Homer Haskins, Robert Howard Lord, Michael Karpovich, and Samuel Hazzard Cross, assumed the teaching load which Coolidge had to forsake.

As a teacher Coolidge was undramatic, precise, sober, businesslike, clear in thought and expression. "He was," his biographers record, ". . . fairness and impartiality personified . . . his task . . . not to mete out praise or blame . . . but to understand and explain." History 1 was a kind of mob scene, and as his friend Merriman remembered, "It would be affectation to pretend that the teaching of a class as large as that was Coolidge's forte; his manner and intonation were peculiar, and he often packed his lectures with more facts than freshmen could possibly assimilate. On the other hand, he gave his pupils an excellent foundation . . . "[9] Coolidge's teaching method, style of presentation, and tendency to lisp and mispronounce the initial "r" made him an object of friendly student satire. The *Harvard Lampoon* suggested that his effigy might be placed outside Gore Hall, sculptured in Indian war garb standing on the bodies of freshmen whom he was hacking to pieces with Putzger's historical atlas.[10] On another occasion the *Lampoon* burlesqued a Coolidge lecture as follows:

Chawlemagne (S–H–A–W–L–M–O–R–N, Chawlemagne), so incweased the powew of the Fwancs that one fwanc was worth a dollar duwing his weign. Pleath turn to the Puth-ger — page one hundwed. Thpwot colored wed ith

[9] R. B. Merriman, "Archibald Cary Coolidge," *Harvard Graduates' Magazine*, XXXVI (June 1928), 551–552.
[10] *Harvard Lampoon*, XLIII (5 June 1902), 129.

where he had his houth. Notith, pleath, how the wiver wuns awound the houth. Quiet!! (Q–U–I–T, quiet.) No pwimary-school twicks, or thewe will be an hour-exam. on Fwiday. Will the gentleman in the fwont wow pleath wake up or leave the woom? . . . There will be no lecture yesterday, ath usual, but for Fwiday I shall expect a M–AP of the wandewings of the Iswaelites, and I shall NOT accept blank space as a wepwesentation of the lost twibes.[11]

Throughout his academic life, despite his library responsibilities, his outside lecturing, and his abiding concern with "foreign relations," Coolidge continued to play an active role in the History Department, which he served as Chairman from 1 September 1907 until 23 February 1910. Ephraim Emerton, Edward Channing, and Albert Bushnell Hart were then the surviving veterans, while Coolidge's contemporaries and colleagues through his three decades of association with the department included such men as William Scott Ferguson, Charles Homer Haskins, Charles Howard McIlwain, Roger Bigelow Merriman, Frederick Jackson Turner, Edwin Francis Gay, and George Foot Moore. Although there was some overlapping of careers, Coolidge's days of Harvard teaching were associated with these men rather than with Samuel Eliot Morison, Arthur Meier Schlesinger, Sr., Frederick Merk, or William Leonard Langer, who belong to the generation of Coolidge's pupils.

The first part of Coolidge's Harvard career was oriented toward undergraduates, both through teaching and through social contacts. He was instrumental for example in obtaining family financing to build on the Gold Coast the then private dormitory Randolph Hall (now part of Adams House) where he lived for many years and maintained an open door to students. He was a devoted final club man in a time when the lack of university housing and social centers for students made the clubs very important. Finally he served for a time as a member of the Administrative Committee (1896–1905) and as a member and chairman of the Committee on Athletics (1899–1905) of the Faculty of Arts and Sciences.

His Library responsibilities and attention to the development of scholarly resources for Harvard gradually moved him from an inclination toward the College toward a concern for the whole University.

The tradition of Archibald Cary Coolidge persists today as strongly as ever. He is rightfully and generally regarded as a pioneer in the establishment and development of Slavic studies in the United States

[11] *Harvard Lampoon*, XLV (21 May 1903), 94.

and as the mentor of a generation of scholars in international studies; even more important, perhaps, he is remembered as the tireless proponent of the principle that every venture into a new area of scholarship and teaching has to be backed up with library materials.

When Archibald Cary Coolidge first began taking an active interest in the fortunes of the Harvard Library, as a young Instructor in History, the Library was in a very serious plight. Twenty years before the Harry Elkins Widener Memorial Library was built, Justin Winsor, the Librarian, was reiterating in his annual report for 1894, with renewed emphasis, "the utter inadequacy" of Gore Hall. "I have exhausted the language of warning and anxiety," he said. "Each twelve months brings us nearer to a chaotic condition. The Library goes on with its natural accessions, and friends of learning give us the means to add more and more to our growth. We have as yet no assurance to give them that their gifts can be properly cared for and the use of their books properly regulated for the general good." [12]

By the mid-nineties, Gore Hall was used to its fullest capacity, and the least circulated books — to the number of 15,000 — had to be removed and stored in the basement of the Chapel in order to make room for new accessions of greater general interest. The condition of the shelving and the stacks was "fast becoming chaotic." Faculty and students could not be permitted free use of the inadequate card catalogue because of the limited space available. The main reading room was "daily overcrowded . . . badly ventilated, imperfectly lighted, and generally unfitted for its purposes." [13] Despite these disadvantages and despite the reading rooms that were set up in Harvard Hall and various classrooms and laboratories, the use of Gore Hall had more than doubled in a five-year period. It was more and more difficult to find books there and just as difficult to use them. At this point in the Library's history Archibald Coolidge walked on the scene and sensed the importance of increasing the Library's holdings in the history and cultural background of those areas of the world which most interested him.

[12] Seventeenth *Report* (1894) of Justin Winsor, Librarian of Harvard University, p. 16.
[13] *Ibid.*, statement of Thomas J. Kiernan, quoted p. 17. Thomas J. Kiernan (1837–1914) was connected with the Library for fifty-nine years, beginning in March 1855 and ending with his death on 31 July 1914. From 1877 he was Superintendent of Circulation. The Governing Boards conferred on him the honorary degree of Master of Arts in 1892.

With his experience in the St. Petersburg legation and travels to
Samarkand and Tashkent behind him, he was full of fire to teach a
course on the history of northern and eastern Europe, in addition to
his work with History 1, the historical survey course bringing Europe
to the eve of the French Revolution. In retrospect, he was fond of
relating how amazed and deprecating were the reactions to his suggestion of a new course when he introduced the subject at a departmental meeting in the academic year 1893–94.

When Coolidge's History 15 first appeared in the Harvard catalogue in 1894–95, its scope was Denmark, Sweden, Poland, Russia, and
Turkey from 1453 to 1795. In the same year Coolidge announced his
intention of helping the Library to augment its Slavic collections. His
first large contribution was a group of 1,371 titles — almost the entire
contents of a catalogue from Harrassowitz of Leipzig [14] which he purchased for Harvard's benefit. Even in these days of large numbers, this
would seem a very substantial gift. In a year when the total acquisitions
of the Library were 15,000 volumes, to receive nearly ten percent of
them in one field, and that a field lightly represented, was a master
stroke. The following year there came 415 volumes and 180 pamphlets
of Slavic origin from "the same gentleman," who also secured (quite
likely from his own pocket or that of his father) $300 to spend on
Slavic books.

The love affair with the Harvard library continued from that time
and hardly a year passed when there was not some acknowledgement
of Coolidge's concern. A spur to progress was the advent to Cambridge (at Coolidge's instigation) of Leo Wiener, who arrived in 1896

[14] Otto Harrassowitz, *Antiquarischer Catalog 202: Slavica; Sprachwissenschaft,
Literatur, Geschichte u. Ethnographie der Slavischen Völker*, Leipzig, 1895. Otto
Harrassowitz of Leipzig began to be the chief continental agent for the Harvard
Library about 1885. His son, Hans Harrassowitz, joined the firm in 1911, and commenting on this event and on the long association with Harvard, Otto wrote in
1912, "Allow me to draw your attention to the fact that it is now almost 30 years
since we received the first orders from the Harvard Library. Your order numbers
during this long space of time have run from 1–10,000 and again from 1–39,000, and
I think that an estimated figure of 150,000 volumes supplied to your Library is not
too high, including all serials and continuations and periodicals." In 1909–10, for
example, the Library spent more than $9,000 with Harrassowitz to get 3,029 volumes,
of which 65% were catalogue orders or "old books" ordered. Although the connection suffered during the first World War, it resumed when peace returned to
Europe. Now located in Wiesbaden, the firm is still a major source of supply for
the Library. See Richard W. Dorn, "Otto Harrassowitz, Buchhandlung-Verlag-
Antiquariat: The First Century," *Harvard Library Bulletin*, XXI:4 (October 1973),
365–374.

as Instructor in Slavic Languages [15] and was set to work arranging and helping to catalogue thc Coolidge collection. By the summer of 1897 all the books had been catalogued, and Wiener and two assistants began dealing with the hundreds of pamphlets in the collection. Justin Winsor died in November and was succeeded in April 1898 by William Coolidge Lane,[16] who reported to the President that in the year in question "Dr. A. C. Coolidge has continued to make large additions to our Slavic collection at his own expense." This was the beginning of a professional association between Coolidge and Lane which was to last three decades, until Coolidge's death and Lane's retirement, both of which occurred in 1928.

By 1898–99 the Slavic collection had grown to 4,509 volumes, a major part of them Coolidge's contributions, and the eager young Assistant Professor began branching out into books relating to Turkey with "constant advice and watchfulness." He also contributed 322 volumes relating to the history of Poland. It was no coincidence that the Librarian noted in that same year a gift of $3,000 from J. Randolph Coolidge (Archibald Coolidge's father) for books on the history of Turkey and the Eastern question.

The chief reason for this new development was the sudden availability of the library of M. Charles Schefer of Paris, a distinguished student of Eastern history and editor of many volumes of early travel in the Levant. This library included "a rich collection of works relating to the history of Turkey, and much contemporary material of the 16th and 17th centuries bearing on the conflicts between the Turks and the nations of Europe." Remarked the hard-pressed Lane, for whom a real bargain was worth a comment, "A substantial part of this collection, amounting to 445 volumes, was bought at a cost of a little under $1,000, and the balance of the gift remains to be used for future purchases in the same field." Then in a footnote, he announced with pride, that through the generosity of the Coolidges, father and son, Harvard had been able to purchase "the great library of Count Riant,

[15] Leo Wiener (1862–1939) met Coolidge through Professor Francis James Child, for whom Wiener had been doing some research work on the South Slavic manifestations of Scottish ballads. It was through Coolidge's influence that Wiener became Instructor in Slavic Languages and Literatures in 1896 — the first such appointment in any American university. Coolidge also provided the College with funds to help underwrite Wiener's salary. Wiener became a full professor in 1911 and served until his retirement in 1930.

[16] Mr. Lane was no immediate kin to Archibald Cary Coolidge.

relating mainly to the history of the Crusades and of the Latin East." Lane termed this gift "the most valuable which the Library has ever received, with the possible exception of the Ebeling Library, given . . . by Israel Thorndike." [17]

Seventy percent of the purchase price of this great collection was borne by the Coolidges, most of the remainder from College book funds. The $10,735 which it cost was a large sum at the time, but in present-day terms, when such collections are no longer available, it seems an incredible bargain. Yet the library's "friends" were then so few and so lacking in appreciation of the importance of the University's collection to scholarship, that the benefactions of the Coolidges assume vast proportions. [18]

Count Riant's library comprised 7,649 volumes and nearly 1,200 pamphlets — about 25 percent of Harvard's total acquisitions in 1899–

[17] Second *Report* (1899) of William Coolidge Lane, Librarian of Harvard University, pp. 215–216. The Ebeling collection, made by a Hamburg professor, gave Harvard at one stroke in 1818 at a cost to the donor of $6,500, one of the most complete collections of books, pamphlets, and newspapers on American history up to that point. Israel Thorndike (1755–1832) of Beverly and Boston, was in younger years a privateer, later a very successful merchant, and long a member of the state legislature.

[18] Coolidge's private income, when he first began teaching at Harvard, was $8,000. (Statement of John P. Coolidge, 30 January 1973.) Archibald Coolidge's capital may have increased somewhat over the years as a result of shrewd investment advice from his brother Harold, or from his personal business counselor, John Farwell Moors, A.B. 1883, Lecturer in Business Administration (1908–1918) and Fellow of Harvard College (1918–1931). Nevertheless, Coolidge did not have really substantial outside income until a fifth of his mother's estate came to him in 1925. His Library salary was never more than $4,000, and since he was technically on a half-time basis the balance of his salary derived from History Department funds. Before the substantial faculty salary increase resulting from the Harvard Endowment Fund campaign of 1919, Coolidge was paid $2,000 by the History Department, $2,500 by the Library. After the war his total salary went to $8,000, the faculty maximum, shared equally by the Department and the Library. John Coolidge points out that his grandfather, J. Randolph Coolidge, inherited no substantial fortune, that most of the family wealth came from the Salem and Boston shipping fortune of the Peabodys and Gardners through Randolph Coolidge's wife, Julia Gardner Coolidge. Mrs. Coolidge was the sister of John Lowell Gardner and sister-in-law and intimate of the famous Isabella Stewart Gardner (Mrs. Jack Gardner). (See Louise Hall Tharp, *Mrs. Jack*, Boston, Little, Brown and Company [1965].) Randolph Coolidge's brother, T. Jefferson Coolidge, was a different kind of man. He "was ambitious and decided to devote [himself] to the acquisition of wealth." (*T. Jefferson Coolidge 1831–1920, An Autobiography*, Boston, Massachusetts Historical Society, 1923.) Randolph's other brother, Algernon, became a doctor and married a Lowell, which helped the family fortune of that Coolidge branch.

1900. The major areas of interest represented were historical chronicles and source books bearing on the "Latin East," the Crusades, and the traces of the Crusades in Constantinople and the Holy Land. Included were literary history and bibliography, geography, ecclesiastical history and theology, military and religious orders, and the Turkish wars. With the Schefer and Riant collections came more than a hundred manuscripts and a similar number of incunabula.

In the summer of 1900 Professor Leo Wiener (probably at Coolidge's expense) visited various towns in Southern Europe where Slovak literature had flourished and found the library of Lombardini of Sollein, a Slovak writer who had died three years before. Wiener made arrangements to purchase this collection, as well as additional material, until the total prospective purchase totaled 123 volumes and 1,567 pamphlets. The Librarian, Lane, recorded that this collection included "many rare periodicals, and much folklore material, a collection of this literature probably larger and more complete than any other in existence, except that owned by L. Rizner, a prominent Slovak bibliographer. The books came to the Library as the gift of Professor A. C. Coolidge." Also in 1900–01 Coolidge gave the Library $3,750 "to pay for books bought at his desire relating to the history of Poland and other Slavic countries, and to the history of the Ottoman Empire, including over three hundred of the Zeitungen or contemporary accounts of the Turkish wars in the seventeenth century." With the backing of Lane and Coolidge, the Library Council made a special appropriation for "expensive books" and thus was able to fill out a number of valuable sets of Italian learned publications and rare serials which were not in the Riant collection. Further acquisitions from the Riant library and purchases to complete gaps in Count Riant's valuable holdings followed for the next several years — 700 volumes in 1901–02, and from other sources several editions of Tasso. Coolidge's hand was evident here as well as in his own pet field of Russian and Eastern European printed materials.

A collection of Russian pamphlets issued in Geneva, relating to Nihilism, arrived in 1901–02, as well as the 100-volume set of the *Russkaya Starina* of St. Petersburg, the 56-volume set of the *Monumenta Hungariae historica*, and Cantemir's manuscript history of the Ottoman Empire. In his report for 1902–03, Lane wrote: "From Assistant Professor Coolidge we have continued to receive abundant additions to our collections on the Ottoman Empire, Morocco, China, and

Slavic countries, subjects in which he has long been specially interested." The harvest that year yielded "a number of incunabula and . . . a collection of thirty Spanish pamphlets of the early seventeenth century giving contemporary notices of Turkish affairs."

In the following year (1903–04) came the third major acquisitional triumph which Coolidge made possible — the purchase of the von Maurer library, a collection of books related to the northern Germanic countries, which Lane called "the greatest gift of the year, and one of the most valuable the Library has ever received." The von Maurer library was the product of a father and son — Georg Ludwig von Maurer (1790–1872) and Konrad von Maurer (1823–1902). The elder, a jurist by profession, had been regent of Greece and a minister of Bavaria and had long had a special interest in the history of German government and law. The younger became particularly interested in Old Norse law. Yet the library was by no means limited to these subjects. It was rich in old manuscripts and early printed books, both historical and literary, and amounted to about 10,000 titles, a third of them related to Scandinavian literature (nearly 2,700 volumes and about 2,900 pamphlets).

Not content with this magnificent donation, not content with his earlier pledges to help the Library with Slavic and Eastern European materials, not content with donations of books on South America, Coolidge made a public announcement on the occasion of the opening of the Germanic Museum (now the Busch-Reisinger Museum of Germanic Culture) on 10 November 1903, that he intended to acquire and present to the University Library ten thousand volumes on German history, to be known as the Hohenzollern Collection in honor of the visit of Prince Henry of Prussia to Harvard.[19] This was to be a project of some years standing and to help carry it out Coolidge employed Walter Lichtenstein, a gifted and energetic young bibliophile, to order, receive, and "check off" the books for this collection.[20] The process

[19] Prince Henry of Prussia came to Harvard on 6 March 1901, to announce a gift to the University from his brother, the German Emperor, of twenty-five reproductions of German works, dating from the eleventh to the eighteenth century. These were eventually to be housed in the new Germanic Museum. It was a gala occasion on a dazzlingly bright day. After a procession from Boston with thirteen carriages and two troops of cavalry through new-fallen snow, the Prince received an honorary LL.D. in Sanders Theatre, attended a luncheon of notables in University Hall, and spoke to the student body in the Union in the afternoon.

[20] Walter Lichtenstein, A.B. 1900, Ph.D. 1907, born in 1880 in Braunschweig,

of looking up books in the Library's holdings was a very time-consuming one, partly because of the several systems of cataloguing and huge backlog of uncatalogued books, partly because of the dispersion of the Library into reading rooms and storage spaces, and partly because of the weeks that had to pass between the dispatch of an order and the receipt of the wanted book. Since the Harvard Library had only Alfred C. Potter [21] and his few assistants in the Ordering Department, Coolidge paid the entire cost of the additional help needed to accession the von Maurer collection and to select and purchase titles for the Hohenzollern Collection. Not only did this mean Lichtenstein's salary but also the expense of sending Lichtenstein abroad and maintaining him there for fourteen months, beginning in the spring of 1905, so that he could seek "desirable additions for the Hohenzollern Collec-

---

Germany, began his work with the Hohenzollern Collection in 1903 and, as its Curator, spent fourteen months in Europe in 1905–1906, purchasing and checking titles for Coolidge in Germany, Austria, Hungary, Serbia, Italy, Holland, and England. In 1906 he became assistant-in-charge of the European history collections in the Library, a post he retained until September 1908, when he was appointed librarian at Northwestern University. He received the title of full professor in 1911. Lichtenstein, however, still maintained his connection with the Harvard Library and was "more out of the country than in it," until 1915, working principally for Harvard and Coolidge. "The most interesting experiences in my life are those connected with my travels in behalf of the Library . . . " he remarked retrospectively in 1925 in the Twenty-Fifth Anniversary Report of the Class of 1900.

In 1918, to "earn sufficient money" to pay for the education of his two daughters, he left Northwestern for the First National Bank of Chicago, and severed his connection with the Harvard Library. He eventually became vice-president of the bank and, at retirement in 1945, when General Lucius D. Clay became Military Governor of the American Sector of Germany, Lichtenstein was placed in charge of financial institutions for the American Military Government. (The Federal Republic of Germany conferred upon him its Order of Merit in 1962 for his accomplishments in promoting a knowledge of German culture in the United States as well as for his work with General Clay.) He returned to Cambridge in 1954, served as Honorary Curator of German History in the Harvard College Library, and was a familiar figure in the Cambridge community until shortly before his death in 1964. An intellectually gifted and very sensitive man, Lichtenstein left his private papers to Harvard under the restriction that they not be open to scholars until 1985. His letters to Coolidge, however, may be found in the Coolidge Papers in the University Archives.

[21] Alfred Claghorn Potter was connected with the Harvard Library for nearly forty-eight years. He went to work in Gore Hall in the fall of 1889, a few months after his graduation from Harvard College, became in 1904 Assistant Librarian in charge of ordering (i.e., acquisitions) and directed the book-purchasing of the Library until his appointment as Librarian, upon the retirement of Lane in 1928. He retired in 1936.

tion" in Germany, Holland, and Italy and do other book-buying and book-trading for the Library.

This experiment proved to be a tremendous success. The total cost of the purchases, including the commission for the principal dealer, Otto Harrassowitz of Leipzig, Lichtenstein's salary and expenses, and the cost of binding and shipping, came to $8,622 — or $1.83 per volume — according to Potter. "In no other way," he remarked, "could we have procured so many books on this subject in so short a time." There was the additional advantage that Lichtenstein could examine and select for himself on the spot, without the problem of analyzing catalogues and searching bibliographies. "In a remarkably short time and at a surprisingly low cost," the Hohenzollern Collection reached 8,000 volumes, and the Library planned to attain the promised 10,000 by purchasing "continuations," such as reports, journals, papers, and sets in progress.

Lichtenstein's own comment about his trip illustrates the richness and variety of Coolidge's gifts — principally in books termed "second-hand." Lichtenstein, who was given the title of Curator of the Hohenzollern Collection in 1905 and made assistant in charge of European history, wrote:

Being on the spot I was often able to purchase large sets at much cheaper rates from dealers whose catalogues rarely reach us, or who often have no regular catalogues at all. Another advantage I enjoyed in that I had a choice of books to an extent one never has from catalogues; in no other way than by going to Germany itself could the Hohenzollern collection have been completed for years; and even when completed, many of the best sets now a part of the collection most likely would have been lacking. I purchased many books, the titles of which are too obscure to have been purchased from catalogues, and, on the other hand, I refrained from buying many volumes, the titles of which would have proved very attractive in a catalogue. I bought a part of the Pfister collection, which purchase was only made possible by my presence in Munich; and in this collection there are many treasures, which, I trust, will prove of great value to students of German History and Economics in the years to come.

In all, I visited about 300 German bookdealers, purchasing books from fifty of them. As for the actual books obtained, the fact is worth mentioning that we have now nearly every German historical periodical, general as well as local, large as well as small. The same is true of the expensive sets of Urkundenbücher.

The works on the history of Bavaria alone number 1,500 volumes, and include a special collection of material relating to King Louis II and his tragic end. Among the many interesting single volumes may be mentioned a manuscript economic survey of Bavaria, made at the end of the sixteenth century, not hitherto printed (the famous Sahl: Stüfft und Grundtpuech), and several volumes of manuscript records of the early Bavarian diets. The Nürnberg manuscripts include three volumes of Müllner's 'Relationes,' a history of Nürnberg families of the seventeenth century, and a history of the Nürnberg guilds, adorned with water-color illustrations of the implements used by the guilds.

In the field of German history outside of Bavaria, I obtained a complete collection of the original dispatches issued by the Prussian and Bavarian governments during the Franco-Prussian War; a collection of 157 contemporary pamphlets bearing upon the questions discussed in the Frankfort Parliament of 1849; and a small collection of broadsides bearing on the Berlin Revolution of the 18th of March, 1848, including the famous proclamation of Frederick William IV, 'An meine lieben Berliner,' in which this Prussian king forgives his subjects the riots which they had caused.[22]

While the librarians expressed some concern as to how it would be possible to finance "continuations" and other purchases for the Hohenzollern collection when Coolidge's promised gift was completed, the indefatigable Coolidge continued to pay for books in his other fields of interest, such as France, Morocco, and Turkey. He pledged $1,000 in 1906 for books on French history, provided the Corporation would appropriate a similar amount. This they did, and the result was important purchases in early and local French history. One can also assume that Coolidge's hand was prominent in the acquisition in 1906–07 of the documents and proceedings of the Russian Duma, the publications of Russia's first census (that of 1897), and statistics of Russian railroads — all of which were received from the Russian Government through the good offices of the American Ambassador, George von L. Meyer.[23] Also, from N. V. Tschaikovsky, a Russian exile in London, came 162 volumes and pamphlets, everything published by the Socialist-Revolutionary Party since 1902.

The following year, in addition to helping the Library to acquire 1,000 volumes in French history and 500 on the history of Germany (plus others on India and Morocco), Coolidge began to interest himself in the practical problems of making the Harvard collections more

[22] Ninth *Report* (1906) of William Coolidge Lane, Librarian of Harvard University, pp. 222–223.

[23] George von Lengerke Meyer (1858–1918), an intimate of Theodore Roosevelt and Henry Cabot Lodge, served as American Ambassador to Italy (1900–1905), Ambassador to Russia (1905–1907), Postmaster General of the United States (1907–1909), and Secretary of the Navy (1909–1913). He was a member of the Harvard Board of Overseers from 1911 to 1917 and President of the Board from 1914 to 1917.

That's Prof. Coolidge, the histry teacher. Joe got him just when he wuz noticin' how much he looked like Napoleon. It's astonishin', ain't it, how much these great men look like each other.

Text and drawing from "Harvard Inside-Out," by Elmer E. Hägler, Jr. (Boston, 1916).

Coolidge as a Harvard Senior, 1887.

"Uncle Arch" (right) with his nephew Oliver Coolidge
at Manchester, Massachusetts, about 1905.

Coolidge at his desk in Gore Hall, 1912.

readily and easily available to readers. He offered to bear the expense of integrating Francis Parkman's valuable collection of Canadiana with Harvard's books on the same subject. He also promised to bear the expense of reclassifying Harvard's books on Mexico, Central America, and the West Indies. This was the commencement of a series of annual donations for cataloguing and classification which continued on a regular basis until Coolidge's death.

In the period from 1906 to 1907 Coolidge spent two terms as Hyde Lecturer in France.[24] It was during this period at the Sorbonne that Archibald Coolidge found Edith Wharton and her husband (Edward Robbins Wharton, A.B. 1873) living in the large apartment at No. 53 rue de Varenne, which was for many years her home abroad. *The House of Mirth* had just begun to appear in French in the *Revue de Paris*, two years after its publication in England and America. "As soon as he found we were in Paris he decided that I must be made known to his friends in the University," Mrs. Wharton recorded in *A Backward Glance* (1934). "So indefatigable was this kindly being in bringing to the house the most agreeable among his colleagues, as well as other acquaintances, that my husband and I christened him 'the retriever'."

From Paris, on 8 February 1907, he wrote a chatty letter to W. C. Lane about Library problems, which showed his keen interest in all aspects of the institution.

Dear Lane:

How goes everything in the good town of Cambridge and its most interesting spot, the Harvard Library? The object of this letter is to get you to send me your annual report if you have not already done so, and it is out. I hear the Corporation has cut down the book buying funds sadly this year. I almost feel as if they were getting even with me for extracting money from them for French history. However, if you have fewer orders to send out you can catch up better with back work on classification etc. By the way, has Kearney [Carney[25]] got his So. African rearrangement finished by this time? I have

---

[24] "For a number of years James Hazen Hyde [A.B. 1898] maintained at his own expense an exchange with France whereby an American professor lectured at the French universities for half a year, and a Frenchman delivered a course of public lectures at Harvard . . . The interchange has been highly profitable." A. Lawrence Lowell, President's *Report* for 1910–1911.

[25] Frank Carney (1861–1949) grew up and grew old with the Harvard Library. Irish born, he came to work for the Harvard Library in May 1875 at the age of thirteen as an errand boy and stack assistant in his after-school hours. He was appointed Assistant in the Library in 1894. He served as Superintendent of the Build-

bought a few odd books here for the library myself, mostly on the French colonies in Africa. How is the Lichtenstein arrangement working? Shall you be able to get round to your American history classification this winter as you have been so anxious to do? I very much hope that in your new addition [26] you will give every inch to book room that is possible. It is a pity that the whole basement can not be devoted to it. Of course the present accom[m]odation for unpacking boxes etc. is very bad, but I believe we should put up with it such as it is, rather than have no room for our books . . . and, of course, we volunteers who are trying to get outside gifts are not going to slacken up even if the books have to go on the floor. All told I am glad that I have not your job. Time passes away for me in Paris here rapidly and pleasantly. I am more than half though my lectures, and my departure is beginning to appear not far away. I shall not get home to make life a burden to you until some time in July so you can escape to the mountains in due season.

With best wishes
Sincerely yours
Archibald Cary Coolidge

During Coolidge's absence in Europe, Lichtenstein was beginning to get restless and, seeing himself at somewhat of a dead end at Harvard, was casting about for fresh opportunity. Coolidge heard about it from W. C. Lane and sent the following comments from Bordeaux on 29 April 1907:

Dear Lane:

When I reached here this afternoon I found a batch of letters waiting for me including a welcome one from you . . . Some time ago I received a short note from Lichtenstein saying that he had handed in his resignation. It did not sound absolutely final, and I waited till I should hear from you. I do not know whether L. expected me to get excited and to argue the matter out with him. At any rate I answered coolly that at this distance I was not capable of having an opinion. Like you, I am not quite sure the change will be to his advantage for I am not sure that he can either teach or write successfully, but I do not wonder that he wants to try. Even if the New York thing amounts to nothing, I think he will jump at whatever comes along for he is evidently restless. The worst of it is I do not see anything we can do. We can not, as the President pointed out last year, raise his salary any more out of justice to the others . . . The thing seems insolluble [sic]. Of course, I am a good deal disappointed. Lichtenstein has done valuable work for me and there was more I wanted him to do. The experiment we have been trying is interesting, and in several ways he is par-

---

ings of the College Library from 1911 to 1932. Carney was the acknowledged hero of the great move out of Gore in 1912 and into Widener in 1915.

[26] The major addition to Gore Hall in 1907 was the only considerable enlargement of central Library space since the erection of the original building in 1841 and its two-story wing of 1877.

ticularly fitted for the job. One thing I particularly regret. I wanted him to go to Europe again to buy French books. He knew this and had asked if there was any chance of next year. I said no and that the matter was indefinite, and indeed I should have preferred waiting a while, but if he does not go to New York and remains restless I should like to despatch him abroad again next winter, in order to get this done before we lose his services, for I believe he would be better than any one else we could get for it. To be sure he does not know French history as he does German, but he knows a good deal, and he has just gone through the same sort of preliminary training in reclassifying the collection and adding to it. It would be a much simpler matter than his previous trip. Very likely, all he would need to do would be to go straight to Paris and nowhere else. In some ways it is an unusually good time to buy French works for, I have been told that a good many convent libraries have come on the market. I therefore authorize you at your discretion to broach the matter to Lichtenstein, if circumstances appear to make it worth while. I suppose the terms would be the same as before — he called them liberal then, but marriage may have changed his views of such things. He ought to agree to stay with us three months after he gets back in order to get his stuff into order. Where the money will come from I do not know, but I shall have to find it somehow or other. The expedition ought not to take more than six months at the utmost.

As for the question of a successor to Lichtenstein in the Library, frankly I do not feel inclined to assume the expense. Although, as you know I am interested in the experiment as such. I was willing to pay for it chiefly because the person in question was particularly well fitted to do things I wanted done. If he goes, I may put the money into some other hobby or in buying more books or keep it, as I have been spending lately at a pace which rather frightens me. I am sorry to leave the Library in the lurch and I don't know what my plan of campaign will be, but I am afraid it is not safe for you to build on my continuing this particular subsidy to some one else . . .

I am glad your new addition promises to be good looking, and I don't wonder it takes up your time. If you lock up the Library this summer you will have to give me a key or I shall go in as a floor layer. Tell Carney that he had better have his odds and ends all cleared by the time I get back, so that I can spring some new classification on him after convincing you of its urgent necessity . . .

> Very sincerely yours
> Archibald Cary Coolidge

Although "the New York thing" apparently fell through, Lichtenstein ultimately resigned as of 1 September 1908 to become Librarian of Northwestern University. In the years ahead he continued, until the end of World War I, to play an important role for Coolidge and the Library, but (as the Librarian reported) temporarily his resignation "interrupted so far as European history is concerned, the newly

introduced method of organizing the work of the Library by departments of knowledge, instead of by administrative processes."

A two-story addition to Gore Hall went up on the north side of the
east stack in the summer of 1907 and provided important relief in the
desperate search for space, thanks to a timely bequest of $300,000 from
Mrs. Amey Richmond Sheldon and help from the balance of a gift for
construction from William Amory Gardner, A.B. 1884. The Librarian hailed the achievement, wishfully, "as part of a possible series of
enlargements of the present Library which should result in a great
building adequate to the needs of the University for many years to
come."

The new space was, however, only a very temporary respite. Books
continued to flow in, largely attributable to Coolidge's energy and
generosity. His own contribution, shared with Clarence L. Hay, A.B.
1908, was the American portion of the library of Luis Montt, Librarian
of the National Library of Chile. Totaling 4,000 volumes, this collection was considered the most complete and distinguished on Chilean
history and politics outside Chile. It also contained hundreds of other
books on Spanish America, especially Peru and Argentina. Negotiations for its purchase took place when Coolidge and Hay were United
States delegates to the Pan American Scientific Congress in Santiago
in 1908. As one of Harvard's delegates, Coolidge also attended the
tercentenary celebration of the founding of the University of Oviedo,
Spain, with W. Bayard Cutting, Jr.; and Coolidge and Cutting used
the opportunity to send back to Cambridge fifty volumes of Spanish
history, particularly related to the Peninsular Campaign.

For the fifteen years prior to his elevation to the directorship,
there was no greater friend of the Harvard Library in the academic
community than Coolidge, and he gradually became a sympathetic
colleague upon whom the Librarian, W. C. Lane, depended very
heavily.

Where did Coolidge's deep and abiding concern for the Library
originate? In his reminiscences of Archibald Coolidge's boyhood,
Harold Coolidge recalled his older brother's early liking for "political
day-dreaming." A chief hobby was "talking soldiers" — "a game in
which Archy divided up his imaginary world into five countries, each
named after one of the five boys, and then pursued the political, diplomatic, and military history of each country always to the ultimate advantages of 'Archdom' . . . In the course of this game an imaginary

continent was created with a well-drawn map, five capitals with properly connecting railways, frontiers, mountain ranges, and an indefinite hinterland full of wild tribes . . . " [27]

In addition Harold Coolidge remembered his older brother as "always reading. He was never without a book in his hand or in his pocket from the times when as a small boy he walked in the Public Garden in Boston with Bonnechose's *Histoire de France* . . . till his last hours fifty years later, and the book was always worth reading . . . With this taste for reading he was from the first blessed with an extraordinary memory." From such influential beginnings the trend of Coolidge's career to an absorbing interest in history, in international relations, and in the role of libraries in furthering scholarship seems readily understandable.

Roger B. Merriman attributed Coolidge's ultimate feeling for the Library to the almost accidental by-product of his giving History 1. At ten o'clock in the morning, after the ordeal of the lecture was over, Coolidge formed the habit of straying across to Gore Hall for "rest and recreation" in "looking over the new books which had come in during the preceding days." "It was in this manner," Mr. Merriman said, "that he became acquainted with the University's collections — with their specialities whose preëminence he was resolved still further to enhance, with their gaps which he was equally determined should be filled. What began as an incident to his other work, soon developed into an absorbing passion." [28]

Despite all his activities as enthusiastic collector and friend of the Library, Archibald Coolidge had no formal position with the Library until 1908. Then, as a newly elected full Professor of History, he was appointed to the Library Council. This body, composed of the President of the University, the Librarian, and six members of the Faculty (normally senior professors), was a consultative group, designed to establish overall library policy and set the formal rules by which the Library operated. In his fortieth and final year as President, Eliot was the senior member and the others (in addition to Coolidge) were Lane, the Librarian; William Morris Davis, Sturgis-Hooper Professor of Geology; Charles Gross, Gurney Professor of History and Political Science; Morris Hicky Morgan, Professor of Classical Philology;

[27] Coolidge and Lord, *op. cit.*, pp.3–4.
[28] R. B. Merriman, "Archibald Cary Coolidge," *Harvard Graduates' Magazine*, XXXVI (June 1928), 553.

George Lyman Kittredge, Professor of English; and George Foot Moore, Frothingham Professor of the History of Religion.

As constituted under President Eliot, the Library Council was an advisory body, representative of the Faculty of Arts and Sciences only, the main function of which was to insure the Librarian faculty support and counsel in matters such as library hours and conditions of use and in acquisitions policy. One of the most important aspects of the acquisitions function was to "divide up annually the available funds for the purchase of books for the central collection." Since the funds were derived from annual gifts, gift income, and bequests, it was not always possible to do this in proportion to current need and fair play.

When Lowell came into office, there were so many questions to be answered concerning the future of the Library that it was obviously a time for reappraisal. What prompted President Lowell to turn to Coolidge for help with this critical University problem is not entirely evident from the record; but Coolidge was clearly the Library's leading advocate and benefactor among members of the Faculty, and there is enough scattered evidence to suggest what may have been in Lowell's mind when he began fully to assume his presidential responsibilities in the fall of 1909.

By this time William Coolidge Lane, Librarian of Harvard College, had held his post for twelve years and had served the Harvard library system since his graduation in 1881 — all told a total of twenty-eight years with the exception of a five-year term of duty as Librarian of the Boston Athenaeum. He was fifty years old, "a gentle and generous soul" and a man of neat and scholarly habits who had carried out faithfully and skilfully under great handicaps the administration of a much overcrowded, shamefully under-financed, and historically disorganized institution. A man of antiquarian bent, combined with the good librarian's sense of system, Lane could cope with the circumstances of management but in twelve years had not been able to find the means of meeting and solving a crisis of library growth and need unprecedented in the University's history. This is not to say that he did not try, nor that he did not annually, or even more often, emphasize to the community the need for urgency and speed in solving the twin problems of space and order. But he was a man of modest cast, turned inward rather than outward, and with none of the worldly connections which were so badly required to augment the library's resources and support.

Nor did he command within the Faculty of Arts and Sciences or the wider circle of the other faculties the standing of a distinguished and forceful professor who could rally the scholarly community to deal with a nearly impossible situation. As Lowell pointed out in his comments concerning the Library in his first annual report, "The work has been so great that the force employed, far from getting ahead, has not been able quite to keep up with it."

President Lowell decided to create a kind of dual leadership for the Library in which Lane would continue to be the chief staff officer, but a leading faculty member would serve as the active chairman of the committee on which the Librarian was a member. It is not surprising, considering Coolidge's long involvement and special interest in the Library and its problems and his wide acquaintance among the sector of the Harvard community likely to contain its patrons that Lowell should have decided on Archibald Cary Coolidge as the man for the job. Apparently the invitation was issued orally, for no initial definition of the position or of the "new system" exists on paper, save in Coolidge's letter of acceptance addressed to "dear Lawrence" on 5 November 1909:

After thinking over the matter pretty carefully I have decided that I am willing to accept the chairmanship of the Library Council if you wish to offer it to me under the new system. I should like the understanding to be that my college work should be cut down to one ordinary course and one seminary course per year and that I be relieved of all executive and committee work and thesis reading, except where my own special knowledge of the subject makes it desirable that I should take part. Secondly, though, as you wish, I will assume the authority and responsibility, I should like a much more active Library Council than at present and made up of as strong men as possible. I should like to keep George Moore, Kittredge and Morgan of the present Council, and to have Haskins (in place of Gross) both as very valuable in himself and as Dean of the men who go to the shelves more than any other, Lyman (in place of Davis) and Dixon (in place of me).[29] I suppose the existing statute on the composition of the Council will have to be changed. Whether you and Lane should remain on it is a matter to be settled as part of your general policy. I have no strong feeling one way or the other. What I do very much want is a Secretary of the Council who should be a Corporation appointment. I have not worked out all the details yet as to whom I could get, how much time I should require and how the salary could be arranged, but I do feel that I want some one who should not be a regular member of the staff, but my own confidential man of all work, and I am willing to contribute whatever may seem my proper share to

[29] Charles Homer Haskins, later Gurney Professor of History, had been appointed Dean of the Graduate School of Arts and Sciences in 1908. Theodore Lyman, A.B.

his pay. If the principle can be accepted now, the details can be worked out later.

I can begin doing something at once, but can not go on at full steam until I have shed a number of my present occupations. If you decide to appoint some one else instead of me I shall not be without consolation, but I realize how great the opportunity is.

The salutation to the letter and its familiar tone indicate a basis of friendship between the two men, for a more formal address would have been "Mr. Lowell," or plain "Lowell" which was the usual form between familiars and colleagues. Archibald Coolidge knew President Lowell well, had common family connections (he was a third cousin), spoke his language and the language of those who ran Harvard. The managers of the University were a Boston circle. With a Lowell as President went an Adams as Treasurer and, as the Fellows of the Corporation, Higginson, Walcott, Lowell, Cabot, and Perkins.

There was no memorandum of understanding drawn up between the President and the new chairman. Beyond the indication that Lowell talked to Lane about the change, he cannot have spelled it out very clearly, for on 8 December Coolidge begged Lowell, "When you write your letter to Lane, defining the situation at the Library I hope you will say expressly that my duty is to be one of direct and active administration and intervention and not merely of passing on the matters he refers to me. I am afraid he is still not clear on the subject."

When finally dispatched on 9 December 1909, President Lowell's letter to Lane reported the necessary changes in the University statutes relating to the Library administration which had been approved by the Governing Boards, and the President added a word of personal interpretation although as it developed this proved insufficient to prevent later misunderstanding between Lane and Coolidge:

At its meeting yesterday the Overseers approved the following changes in the Statutes of the University which had already been adopted by the Corporation:

"Voted to amend the Statute of the University pertaining to the Library as follows:

"The 18th Statute by substituting for the third paragraph the following:

'Subject to the direction of the Chairman of the Council of the Library,

---

1897 (the son of the President Eliot's friend and first cousin), was then Assistant Professor of Physics; Roland Burrage Dixon, a Harvard classmate of Lyman, was Assistant Professor of Anthropology.

the Librarian has the care and custody of the Library, superintending its internal administration, enforcing the rules, and conducting the correspondence. The Chairman of the Council shall make annually a report to the Library Committee of the Overseers and to the President.'

"The 19th Statute by substituting for the first paragraph the following:

   'Council of the Library. The general control and oversight of the Library is committed to the Council of the Library, consisting of a Chairman and six other persons appointed annually by the Corporation with the consent of the Overseers; any vacancy occurring in the Council to be filled in the same manner for the unexpired portion of the term.' "

You will see that they carry out the plan for re-organizing the administration of the Library of which I spoke to you. They place the ultimate direction of the Library in the hands of the Chairman of the Council, who is responsible therefor to the Governing Boards. He, with the advice and consent of the Council, must determine the policy to be pursued, and it will be your duty to follow his directions in all matters relating to the administration of the Library.

Coolidge assumed his new post about 1 February without benefit of a formal Corporation appointment as chairman of the Library Council. Coolidge wrote Lowell on 13 January, "We are now roughly at the end of the first half-year, and I shall begin regularly on my library work in February. I therefore wish to resign my chairmanship of the Department [of History] as soon as it is convenient to you to appoint my successor."

The next months were not particularly remarkable for immediate progress, but it is evident that for Coolidge it was a time of thought and planning. With Coolidge's active cooperation and perhaps even instigation, the President commissioned a management study by Gunn, Richards & Co. of Boston and New York to survey the organization of the Library, to analyze the distribution of responsibility and to seek conclusions which might point the way to a solution of the Library's crisis. Thirty years of temporizing and patching had left the Library still running but hopelessly behind despite every improvement. "Although," as Coolidge said, "it would still be possible to go on a little longer as we have been doing and getting into ever greater difficulties, it would hardly be too much to say that the present system has broken down and that the time has come to face the question as a whole."

Facing the Question as a Whole

ESPITE careful bargaining with President Lowell concerning teaching time, it is doubtful that Archibald Cary Coolidge foresaw the extent of the responsibility he was assuming when he agreed in November 1909 to take the chairmanship of the Library Council. Yet the more he studied the Library's problems from the standpoint of his new office, the more he could truly say "that the time has come to face the question as a whole." [30]

As Coolidge began to take greater responsibility for the overall planning and to act as the Library's representative in dealings with those most likely to be of a long-range influence and help, William Coolidge Lane, the Librarian, could not but feel cut out of much of the decision-making in which he had at least been a participant in the past. Not meaning to ignore Lane, Coolidge, with all the good will in the world, could not help but rankle the Librarian by some of his actions. And people who counted began to realize that Lane was now quite definitely in the second spot. [31]

There was for example the annual meeting of the Overseers' Committee to Visit the Harvard College Library which Francis R. Appleton, the Chairman, [32] wished to convene on 12 April 1910, the evening before the April meeting of the Board of Overseers, in order to accommodate J. P. Morgan, an Overseer member of the Committee. "Should

[30] A. C. Coolidge, Abstract of Statement Made by the Chairman of the Library Council, January 26 [1910]. (Coolidge Papers, Harvard University Archives.)

[31] William Hopkins Tillinghast and Alfred Claghorn Potter were the Assistant Librarians at the beginning of the Coolidge administration; see p. 35.

[32] Francis Randall Appleton (1854–1929) was a graduate of Harvard College (1875) and of the Columbia Law School (1877). He practised law in New York until 1883, when he became a partner in the mercantile firm of Robbins and Appleton. For two terms he served as an Overseer of Harvard (1903–1909 and 1918–1924) and was Chairman of the Library Visiting Committee during most of Coolidge's directorship, retiring in 1924, when his term as Overseer expired.

we not ask the Librarian also? He has always attended committee meetings," Appleton queried Edgar H. Wells,[33] new Secretary of the Library Council — Coolidge's "own confidential man of all work." [34] "If it is to be a whole meeting of the Library Committee," Wells responded in Coolidge's behalf, then Coolidge and he would "cordially endorse an invitation to Mr. Lane." However, Coolidge and Wells would not feel free to talk in front of the whole Committee. If the company were to be just Appleton, Morgan and two or three others, Mr. Lane should not be included. The smaller group would give Coolidge the chance to "explain to you the nature of the present situation." Wells added, "You must not think that our relations with Mr. Lane are not entirely pleasant, for they are." [35]

Outwardly pleasant though his connection with the vigorous new chairman was, little incidents during the first half-year of their formal association seared deeply into the pride of the quiet and gentlemanly Lane. With a six-month trial of the new relationship behind him, Lane decided the time had come to clarify his position once and for all. "Coolidge & I have done our best," Lane wrote to the President in his clear, strong hand from Mount Desert, Maine, "to pull . . . as a tandem team, and I think we have succeeded reasonably well. But now . . . it has seemed [to me] wise to write out the statement which I enclose." He told the President that he had "shown the statement to Coolidge but took no counsel with him in regard to writing it." He

[33] Edward Huidekoper Wells, A.B. 1897, was one of the most useful of Harvard servants during his ten-year association with the faculty and administration. Instructor in English 1902–1906, he was Assistant Dean of the College 1905–1907, Secretary for Appointments 1906–1910, Editor of the Quinquennial Catalogue 1907–1910, Acting Dean of the College 1910–1911, Acting Regent 1910–1911, and Acting Secretary of the Faculty 1911–1912. From 1907 to 1910 Wells served as Editor of the *Harvard Bulletin* and from 1910 to 1913 as Secretary of the Harvard Alumni Association. From 1903 to 1913 he held the title of Curator of Modern English Literature in the Harvard College Library. But his most important role from the Library's standpoint was as Secretary of the Library Council and Coolidge's right-hand man in a wide variety of matters, particularly connected with donors, fund-raising, and the acquisition of scarce, scholarly books. He left the Library in 1913 but continued to keep a close and affectionate interest in the Library's fate and in the success of the Director. A member of the Visiting Committee from 1913 to 1922, Wells became a moving force in the organization of the Friends of the Harvard College Library in the 1920s when he was a leading rare-book specialist in New York.

[34] A. C. Coolidge to A. L. Lowell, 5 November 1909.

[35] F. R. Appleton to E. H. Wells, 24 March 1910; E. H. Wells to F. R. Appleton, 26 March 1910.

would "try to speak with perfect frankness, but to avoid any personal element as much as possible." The new University statute governing the Library required the Librarian to administer the Library "subject to the direction of the Chairman of the Council." Lane reminded the President that the two chief officers of the Library had been given "verbal instructions . . . to work out their own system of relations under this clause and to adjust for themselves their proper spheres of responsibility and authority." Both officers, he said, "have tried to work in harmony and keep the true interests of the Library constantly in view. For my own part I have felt that I ought to give the newly installed Chairman of the Council a free hand to carry out new policies which he might propose. I have stated plainly any objections that occurred to me . . . I have done my best to carry out fairly whatever has been determined upon, even when in my own judgment the plan should have been modified or postponed." Lane then brought up a point of real issue — that, despite the Librarian's objections, Coolidge had transferred a staff member from one department to another "at a time and under conditions which, in my opinion, seriously diminished the efficiency of the staff as a whole." Lane argued to Lowell that a Librarian should be responsible for staff selection and direction — and declared that Coolidge had "at the beginning of our relations" agreed. There has been, however, he said, a "certain uneasiness and friction and a tendency to appeal from one person to another," a situation almost unknown before. But, far worse, he asserted, is the undermining of the Librarian's authority when he is forced to make changes he does not approve. Lane went on:

The Librarian should be glad to have the Chairman's advice and suggestions; he also ought to find frequent occasions when it will be for his advantage to appeal to the Chairman for advice and even for decision, if he feels himself in doubt; in matters of general policy he is constantly, by the terms of the present statute, subject to the direction of the Chairman; but in matters of detail affecting internal administration, I am clearly of the opinion that the Librarian's responsibility should be complete, in order to obtain efficient administration.

In one other matter of principle it seems to me that a mistake has been made. I have felt myself debarred from bringing it up in the course of the year, but at this time it may be not improper to speak of it.

Under the present statute, the Librarian is no longer a member of the Library Council. When the change was proposed I attached little importance to this, for under the old régime I had taken it for granted that my own place on the Council was primarily for the sake of preparing business and giving information, and I had seldom or never voted. Under the new organization, the Council corresponds closely to the Board of Trustees of a public library, and I was glad to learn that it was to hold more frequent meetings and was to take a larger share in determining the policy of the Library. I knew that almost without exception in the case of public libraries, the Librarian, even when not a member, is present at meetings of the Board of Trustees, and I supposed that our Library Council would naturally adopt the same plan. I was greatly surprised when meeting after meeting of the Council was called and I was not summoned, but I said nothing because I was unwilling to take any step that would seem to force myself into meetings where I was not wanted . . .

Lane argued that the Librarian was important at meetings as an information source and as an intelligent auditor who would later be required to carry out Committee decisions. He conceded that the Chairman had "carefully questioned" the Librarian in advance about the subjects to be discussed, but this was no substitute, he maintained, for the opportunity to hear or contribute to the discussion of policies he would have to carry out.

The result of the present arrangement is, as it seems to me, to make the Chairman of the Council essentially Librarian, yet without the responsibility of carrying out the measures determined upon by the Council, and to degrade the Librarian to a position similar to that of an Assistant Librarian, yet to place upon him the task of carrying out policies in regard to which he has had neither a proper chance to present the facts nor a share in the discussion of those facts . . .

One unfortunate result of the present ambiguous situation has been that I have not felt at liberty to speak of any library matter with any member of the Council, and that no member of the Council (with one exception) has ever spoken to the Librarian in regard to Library affairs in the course of the last six months. It seems to me that this is not the relation which should exist between the principal executive officer of the Library and those members of the Faculty who are responsible for determining the course of the Library's development. In short a plan has been adopted by which the office of Chairman of a Board of Trustees and the office of Librarian are confused . . .[36]

The speed with which President Lowell responded to Lane's fundamental points, in a letter of 7 July, seems to indicate that he and Coolidge had a clear idea of the Chairman's new role, even though the Librarian did not. Lowell was nothing if not formal and direct, despite his expressions of gratitude and good will:

Dear Mr. Lane: —

I have received your letter, and I think I understand your point of view

[36] W. C. Lane to A. L. Lowell, 1 July and 6 July 1910.

perfectly. I recognize that your position has been an uncomfortable one, especially during the past year, and I feel that you deserve gratitude for helping things to run as smoothly as they have.

I will try to answer your two points clearly and briefly. First, as to your relation to the Chairman of the Council and to the library staff. It is clear that there must be one executive head to a library, and that executive head under the new arrangement is the Chairman of the Council. He has very properly worked in the main with the staff through you, but he is responsible to the President and Fellows for the administration of the library, and is regarded by them as the executive head. A similar situation is, I understand, that in the library of the University of Berlin where there is a librarian, but Harnack is placed above him as Director. In this case the title of Chairman of the Library Council seemed preferable to that of Director.

This answers also, I think, your second point about the librarian's being on the Library Council. It is clear that the chief executive officer of the library ought to be a member of the Council, and that no other administrative officer in the library ought to be there. The Chairman of the Council being, therefore, the chief executive officer of the library, and the librarian, so far as his authority in the library is concerned, being as you put it in a position similar to that of an assistant librarian, then the Chairman ought properly to be a member of the Council, and the librarian ought not.

This becomes the more clear when you reflect that the librarian is no longer responsible directly to the President and Fellows, but solely to the Chairman of the Council.

> Hoping that you are having a pleasant summer, I am,
> Very truly yours,
> A. Lawrence Lowell [37]

Lowell's correspondence with Lane cannot have made the Librarian any happier. To ease Lane's distress, which must have been evident to Coolidge, the latter suggested to the President that his own title be changed to that of Director, not only to clarify Lane's position but also to indicate the University-wide nature of Coolidge's interest.

I believe that it would be better for me to have another title, preferably that of Director of the University Library, rather than my present one. There are several reasons for this. I think that it might make the position of the Librarian here less difficult if I seemed to have a place of more general authority instead of one merely superimposed upon him. Secondly, and more important, I feel quite sure that it would make the work easier for me in dealing with the various departmental libraries. As you know, there is great need of coöperation between the different libraries here, and there are several possibilities of making savings of one kind or another. Each of these libraries, however, is very jealous

[37] A. L. Lowell to W. C. Lane, 7 July 1910.

of its own rights; to deal with them will require much care and some little diplomacy. As it is now, I can see that, although I have always met with a perfectly friendly reception in the preliminary reconnoitering I have done, still I appear as an emissary of Gore Hall rather than as a neutral person interested in the welfare of all the departments of the University Library. I believe that it would facilitate matters if I had a title implying a general interest on my part. Of course, my idea is not to attempt acts of authority but rather that I should be in a better position to persuade the different departmental libraries that I was acting in their interests and not as a mere outside busybody.[38]

Following this request Coolidge spoke to Lane about the titular change. "He took matters very well," Coolidge reported to the President, "except that he felt strongly on the question of having my title in the plural form, which he thought would not hit him while the singular would. I told him I had no personal feelings either way." [39] Coolidge, however, had tested the title on Ezra Ripley Thayer, Dean of the Law School, and found that Thayer — ever alert to symbolic threats to the Law Faculty's splendid isolation — favored the singular, while the definition of the Library in the University Catalogue also seemed to give precedent for the singular. Lane "was not convinced" by these arguments, Coolidge recorded. Mr. Lowell settled the matter in the singular.[40]

Once the all-important matter of rank and responsibility had been settled with the President, Lane subsided and, like a good soldier, loyally accepted the second place. There were many instances in which this must have galled the Librarian. For example, before 1910 Lane's annual reports (" reprinted with additions from the annual Report of the President") were always numbered as they were in Justin Winsor's day and headed, as in 1909, "Twelfth Report of William Coolidge Lane, Librarian of Harvard University." In 1910, however,

---

[38] A. C. Coolidge to A. L. Lowell, 23 November 1910.

[39] Undated note, A. C. Coolidge to A. L. Lowell, headed "Thursday."

[40] Some two years later, when writing confidentially to James Rignall Wheeler, Professor of Greek Archaeology and Art and former Dean of the Faculty of Fine Arts, Columbia University, Lowell shed somewhat more light on his conception of the administrative relationship between the Director and the Librarian. The Director, he said, "has full authority and responsibility for the whole conduct of the Library. The Librarian is really in the position of an Assistant Librarian; the Director, in that of Librarian-in-Chief." Lowell continued, "It was some time before our Librarian obtained a perfectly clear conception of his position, but since he has done so I think everything has worked very smoothly, but I ought to add that the Director is a man of singular tact." (A. L. Lowell to James Rignall Wheeler, 8 January 1913.)

the reprint was titled "Report of Archibald Cary Coolidge, Chairman of the Library Council of Harvard University, including the Thirteenth Report of William Coolidge Lane, Librarian." The following year the same form was used with Coolidge styled "Director of the University Library." The form of title page continued until Lane's Twentieth Report of 1917. Then, for 1917–18, both reports were cut to the bone to save paper and money in wartime. Thereafter, Lane's report became less prominent, a kind of appendix to the printed record.

Such subordination Lane had to swallow as well as he could. Lane was a fair-minded man, Coolidge a generous and thoughtful commanding officer. The two of them made an extraordinary working pair, and the achievement of the Library in their subsequent eighteen years of collaboration is a tribute both to Coolidge's generalship and to Lane's large-hearted attitude. There is all too slight a record of their intercommunication when Coolidge was in Cambridge, for their business was carried out informally and person to person. That was Coolidge's way. Whenever Coolidge was on leave, however, Lane was meticulous in keeping the Director informed of the progress of events on the home front. Coolidge's letters back to Lane show his thoughtful and affectionate regard for the older man. While they had their differences, as co-workers are bound to have, they respected each other, and the community soon came to know what an exceptionally complementary team was in charge of the Library.

The Assistant Librarians

Coolidge inherited a highly experienced library staff, the senior members of which were all college graduates, most of them Harvard men, who were willing to work for the University at considerable financial sacrifice both because it gave them unusual prestige in the library world and because they were devoted to Harvard and Cambridge.

Lane, the Librarian, a graduate of 1881, spent some forty-three years of his professional life at Harvard — all of it, in fact, save the period 1893–1897 when he served as Librarian of the Boston Athenaeum. He was an able, well-read man with a flair for detail and planning. A large share of the credit for the successful design of the Widener building is due to his thoughtful and constant concern for the smallest detail of the library operation. Yet he was for five years

Assistant Librarian at only $1,600 per year plus $400 for his house, and as Librarian from 1901 to 1910 his salary remained constant at $4,400 plus $600 for his house. Coolidge managed to add another $1,000 to Lane's salary, but this was the last raise Lane received from Harvard, and he continued at $6,000 until his retirement in 1928.

Coolidge took a salary of only $4,000 throughout his whole directorship but this was because his position was considered half-time. The Assistant Librarians were paid $2,500 and $3,500 at the beginning of Coolidge's term and $4,500 and $5,000 at its close. Such a narrow range in economic advancement made it difficult for Coolidge to recruit and hold able staff members, and implied a very high degree of dedication on the part of those who stayed with the University.

At the time Coolidge became Chairman and Director, the veteran William H. Tillinghast, A.B. 1877, was Assistant Librarian, in charge of cataloguing and shelf classification. Tillinghast had served the Library since 1882 and had also edited the Quinquennial Catalogues of Harvard University in 1885, 1890, 1895, and 1910. To succeed him in 1913 Coolidge appointed T. Franklin Currier, A.B. 1894, Assistant Librarian in charge of classification and cataloguing. Currier served through the Coolidge years and was responsible for organizing and carrying out the reform of the catalogue, which was completed in large part before the Widener building opened and was refined and perfected in the years thereafter. A widely respected specialist in his field, Currier was the author of a bibliography of John Greenleaf Whittier and was also something of an expert on Oliver Wendell Holmes. He became Associate Librarian in 1937 and retired in 1940.

Alfred Claghorn Potter, who succeeded Lane as Librarian in 1928 after Coolidge's death, was connected with the Harvard Library for nearly 48 years, all told. He went to work for the Library in the autumn of 1889, after his graduation from Harvard College, and in 1904 he was appointed Assistant Librarian in charge of acquisitions ("ordering," it was then called). As such he was especially close to Coolidge, who enjoyed his "wise and skilful service," his quiet humor and good sense. Potter directed the book-purchasing of the University for nearly half a century, longer than any other before or since. He retired in 1936. He was the author of a bibliography of Beaumont and Fletcher, and of the important brief account of Harvard's library history, *The Library of Harvard University: Descriptive and Historical Notes* (1st, 2nd, 3rd, and 4th editions, 1903, 1911, 1915, and 1934).

Walter Benjamin Briggs (A.M. Hon. Brown University, 1913) returned to Harvard in 1915, having been persuaded by Coolidge, to become Assistant Librarian in charge of the reference and circulation departments, and he served throughout Coolidge's directorship. In June
1915 Coolidge had unsuccessfully tried to woo Harry M. Lydenberg,
A.B. 1897, then the Chief Reference Librarian and later the Director of
the New York Public Library, but since Harvard could not match
Lydenberg's salary and since Lydenberg felt strong ties of loyalty to
New York, Coolidge then turned to Briggs.

Briggs, who became Associate Librarian in 1936 and retired in 1939,
entered the Harvard Library as a page in 1886 and served as Superintendent of the Reading Room from 1896 to 1904, when he went to the
Brooklyn Public Library as Reference Librarian; in 1909 he moved
to Hartford as Chief Librarian of Trinity College. During the interim
year, 1936–37, between Mr. Potter's retirement as Librarian and the
arrival of Keyes D. Metcalf, who came with a dual appointment as
Director of the University Library and Librarian of Harvard College,
Briggs filled the post of Acting Librarian. Described as one who "lived
for men and books," he died on 31 October 1943.

The New York bookseller and bibliographer, Luther S. Livingston,
was originally picked to be the first librarian of the Harry Elkins
Widener Collection and the officer in charge of the Widener Memorial
Rooms in the new library. Livingston, however, died on 24 December
1914. With Mrs. Widener's assent, Coolidge invited George Parker
Winship, A.B. 1893, librarian of the John Carter Brown Library in
Providence, to succeed Livingston. Winship took up his duties on 1
May 1915, and Livingston's widow, Flora V. Livingston, became his
assistant. Winship served in this capacity until 1926; then, as a result
of friction with Mrs. Rice (the former Mrs. Widener) and his hyperactive restlessness at being confined to a rather narrow range of concerns, Winship was appointed Assistant Librarian with special responsibility for the Treasure Room and the rare-book collections. Mrs.
Livingston succeeded Winship in 1926, and continued as Curator
of the Harry Elkins Widener Collection for the next twenty years.
Among her many talents, she was a specialist in the work of Rudyard
Kipling.

With the exception of the year 1926–27, when Coolidge was busy
raising funds to underwrite Winship's printing course, Winship also
held the title of Lecturer on the History of Printing from 1915 until

1932. He was author of eight books and editor of more than two dozen. He served as editor of *Harvard Library Notes* from 1920 to 1931 and one of his most important researches into Harvard history was his volume, *The First Cambridge Press*, published in 1938, two years after his retirement from Harvard.

Cataloguing and Classification

During the first months of his chairmanship, Coolidge produced for the Library Council the summary statement on "the situation of the Library," which outlined the major problems in clear and simple terms and served as a guide for action.[41] Since almost all other issues were subordinate to it, Coolidge quite naturally emphasized to the Council the critical importance of new space as a first requirement. At the same time he refused to be deterred in his efforts to acquire "all the books we can." About half of his report dealt with the very important question of catalogue reform.

Of all the problems facing the Library that of the book classification and cataloguing was by far the most intricate and discouraging. To put the situation briefly, what most interfered with the utility of the Library — other than the appalling lack of space — was the existence of several different systems, themselves imperfect and incomplete, for locating books. For an understanding of the scope of these imperfections, it is necessary to go back in time to 1841, the year of John Langdon Sibley's appointment as Assistant Librarian, when Gore Hall's fresh neo-Gothic splendor was able to house comfortably the 41,000 volumes of Harvard's Library. Thirty-six years later, when Sibley, the self-styled "sturdy beggar," retired,[42] Gore contained 164,000 volumes and perhaps as many pamphlets.

Through much of Sibley's era the way to look up books was to refer to a printed catalogue (the latest edition of which had been prepared in 1830)[43] and an inconvenient appendix of subsequent accessions,

[41] Coolidge, *op. cit. supra*, note 30.

[42] Alfred Claghorn Potter, *The Library of Harvard University: Descriptive and Historical Notes*, 4th ed. (Cambridge, Harvard University Press, 1934), p. 30.

[43] *A Catalogue of the Library of Harvard University in Cambridge, Massachusetts* . . . Cambridge, E. W. Metcalf and Company, Printers to the University, 1830. Contents — Vol. I: Preface by Benjamin Peirce, Librarian, March 1830 (pp. v–xvii), and author index, A–L; Vol. II: M–Z; Vol. III: Systematic Index. The copy in the Harvard University Archives contains pencil and inked notations and interleavings indicating recataloguing.

much of it hand-written. There was only a very general classification
of the collection, and (to make things still less handy) certain collections were kept as individual units in alcoves. In those days the popular
idea of a great library was a lofty central reading room surrounded by
book-lined alcoves and bordered by galleries.

The growth of the Library demanded something better.[44] In 1861,
thanks to the efforts of Ezra Abbot, later Bussey Professor of New
Testament Criticism and Interpretation, and Charles A. Cutter, later
Librarian of the Boston Athenaeum, the first card catalogue by author
and subject was begun.[45] It was not until 1877, following the introduction of a six-tiered bookstack, that Justin Winsor, Sibley's successor,
was able to start a classification scheme for the whole Library based
on the books' "practical usefulness to the several departments of instruction." Winsor and his staff originally adopted the fixed-shelf
method of classification, a scheme suitable for a small library and eco-
nomical of space. Within a few years the new acquisitions outpaced
the space available, and it became clear that this method would never
do for a library of Harvard's kind, where an extraordinary growth of
one or another of the individual groups and associated groupings of
books might necessitate moving large blocs of volumes bodily to new
locations to provide room for future additions. Consequently the policy
of "relative location" was adopted, and classification moved ahead in
fits and starts on that principle.

To complicate the situation further, Harvard had been using a small
catalogue card, of the sort still to be seen in the Boston Athenaeum, a
card measuring 5 by 2 inches. When the Library of Congress card
became a standard, Harvard was faced with the alternative of continuing on its own with cards that could not be interfiled with those of

[44] In 1841 the total income for book purchasing and binding, W. C. Lane states
in his history, was only $250 per annum, but increased to $11,000 by 1877, some measure of the increased support for the Library. See William Coolidge Lane, "The
Harvard College Library, 1877–1928," in *The Development of Harvard University
since the Inauguration of President Eliot 1868–1929*, ed. Samuel Eliot Morison (Cambridge, Harvard University Press, 1930), pp. 608–631.

[45] It should be pointed out that in the days of Thaddeus William Harris (Librarian
from 1831 to 1856) cards were first used in the official (or inner) catalogue of the
Library to record new acquisitions; these measured $9\frac{1}{2} \times 2\frac{1}{2}$ inches. The Abbot cards
measured 5×2 inches (see illustrations). A long tribute to Abbot's role in the improvement of library cataloguing appears in C. W. Eliot's *President's Report for
1900–01*, pp. 32–33.

other libraries, or conforming to the new card size and eventually replacing 1,300,000 written or printed cards.

Harvard's librarians therefore were like caged squirrels on a playwheel. They put great and unremitting effort into their cataloguing and classification problems, yet they stood still, or even lost ground. Thanks to Coolidge's contributions of money over nearly a decade and to his driving interest in building the history collections and those in related subjects, progress did take place — such as in classifying some of the important sections of western history, French, German, British, and United States. Even so, as Coolidge expressed the dilemma:

Whereas in 1882 we had something over 90,000 volumes still to classify, in 1909, after twenty-seven years of effort, we still had 96,000 . . . We might as well throw up the sponge altogether as go on at this rate, but this is not all. The books with the so-called "fixed shelf" location . . . now amount, in spite of considerable reductions, to some 120,000 and increase at the rate of 4,000 a year. Should we try to arrange first those that are not classified at all but increase slowly, or those that have an unsatisfactory classification but increase fast? . . . Finally, in order to make new classifications, we inevitably need room and room is one of the things we lack most.[46]

There were great gaps in the recording of Harvard's books in the two principal card catalogues. Coolidge pointed out that the 30,000 volumes in the published catalogue of 1830 were in the public catalogue, but not in the official one (now called the Union Catalogue). There were 55,000 titles in the official catalogue but not in the public one, including the greater part of the recent collections, such as the new influx from the Riant Library. Other large groups of new books were not yet in any card catalogue.

What to do? Coolidge encouraged discussion. He reiterated the problem in his first official report to the President (1909–10), devoting a major portion of his statement to these four points:

1. We have now some seventy-five thousand volumes or pamphlets whose titles are not in the public catalogue and which therefore, as far as most of our public is concerned, might as well not be in our possession.

2. We have on our shelves over two hundred thousand volumes either unclassified or in classifications so defective that it has long been an accepted principle that some day totally new ones must be made. Our accessions to these two groups number some five thousand a year. Thus, in spite of the many subjects that have been classified by the Library in the last quarter of a century, we have more volumes still to rearrange than we had when the operation began.

---

[46] Coolidge, *op. cit. supra* (note 30), p. 4.

And it is very needful to continue. To the steadily increasing number of advanced students and of scholars from outside who have access to our shelves, well classified arrangements of the books to be found there are of untold service.

3. By general consent, our subject catalogue requires radical reforms. It has grown up in the course of fifty years, and much that is now in it could well be left out; much not now there could profitably be inserted. Some fifty thousand cards must have their shelf marks changed, and the whole system on which the catalogue is based is capable of improvement. But even such a comparatively small improvement as the new group made last summer necessitated the rearrangement of about one hundred and thirty-five thousand cards. The recasting of the whole subject catalogue would be a formidable task, demanding a large expenditure of time and money. We must content ourselves with such gradual ameliorations as we can make under our present circumstances, and we hope soon to report progress, thanks to the increased appropriations for administrative purposes which the Corporation has recently granted.

4. All our questions concerning cataloguing are affected by our problem of card changing. For reasons too long and complicated to be explained in detail here, it is becoming increasingly evident that the Harvard Library should adopt for its catalogue, as soon as possible, the card of standard size now used by the Library of Congress and by the great majority of other libraries of the United States as well as in Great Britain, Germany, and elsewhere. This is not only a matter of convenience, as compared with using our own smaller size of card; it also brings so many advantages in the way of coöperation and the acquisition of printed cards from publishers and other libraries that the Yale, Columbia, Princeton, Brown, and the Andover Theological Libraries are all either making the change at the present time or look forward to doing so shortly, in spite of the trouble and expense involved. Every day that we delay means so much more to be done over again. It is our hope, therefore, to be able to begin work very soon on this the most pressing of our immediate tasks.

Above all these questions looms that of the necessity of a new library building.

The Gunn, Richards management survey of the Library, completed in the winter of 1910, contained similar comments which it seems likely that Coolidge inspired:

. . . It is perfectly evident that there is a great loss of funds, time and service due to the incomplete cataloguing resulting from one-fifth of the library being out of service except by special inquiry, and a part not even then. It is natural to expect that much of the uncatalogued part of the library does not consist of books in constant demand, but it does contain many. The annual increase of purchases and gifts is certain to continue, and there is no possibility of catching up the back work unless additions are made to the present library staff . . .

The addition of new books to the old classification is greater each year than the reclassification, resulting in a net loss and increased inconvenience. This prevents the greatest usefulness of the library, and increases the cost of administration unnecessarily . . .

A force should be put upon completing the cataloguing of all books now partially catalogued, bringing the official, authors' and subject catalogue up to date and complete so far as the books on the shelves are concerned, — this not to interfere with prompt cataloguing of all new books ordered for immediate use . . .

The sections in the library now catalogued by a fixed shelf classification, but being added to each year, should be promptly reclassified . . . in as small sections as possible, so as to interfere with the general use of the library as little as possible . . .

An extraordinary force should be put on the work, beginning not later than June 1st, 1910. This work should be rushed throughout the summer, and continued with a smaller force during the college year.[47]

Coolidge used the conclusions of Gunn, Richards as a lever to extract more money from the Corporation. "After much fasting and prayer,"[48] he asked the Fellows for $41,000 for general expenses for 1910–11, regardless of fund income for book purchases, any salary increases, and the "university charge" for management of the accounts — a total of about $4,400 more than in the first year of his responsibility. In most respects, Coolidge declared in his eight-page, typewritten letter, the Library was being run economically, and most of the waste was attributable to "the inevitable loss that comes from the disadvantages under which we carry on our present work." He appealed to the Fellows' Harvard loyalty by pointing out that Yale with a situation "confessedly not as serious as ours" had just granted the Yale Library $10,000 extra a year for three years, so that his own humble prayer for $4,400 looked modest indeed. To clinch the argument, Coolidge pointed out how much he himself had had to contribute to the Library to get some of the needed changes under way:

In connection with my request . . . it is perhaps not out of place to mention that, realizing that there are many calls on the funds of the University, I have been glad for some time to assist the Library by gifts of money for additional service as well as for books. Especially in the last few months, in order to get something done, I have put through various changes and, in particular, have had our fifteen thousand volumes on Church History collected and arranged, and have had reclassified this summer the whole of our English History collection. As a result, I have had to contribute in the last six months to the running expenses of the Library some $1,700. I may also mention that my secretary,

[47] Gunn, Richards & Co., "Preliminary Report on Library Organization, 1 February 1910."

[48] A. C. Coolidge to A. L. Lowell, holograph note dated "Friday" [23 September 1910].

almost all of whose time is taken up in connection with Library work, is paid by myself (and for the present, at least, will continue to be), and, as she came from another department of the University, at a considerably higher rate than if she were one of the Library Staff. Although I do not in the least begrudge the money I have spent in these ways, the arrangement does not appear to me a satisfactory or permanent one. I must have some addition, however small, to the allowance of the Library for general expenses, if I am to do anything but follow along helplessly, getting ever a little further behind.[49]

Beginning with the summer of 1910, and for the next five years, the tedious work of catching up and keeping up went on. In September 1911, with the permission of the donor, the Corporation granted Coolidge's request to use the balance of the William Amory Gardner gift — $12,558 — for catalogue work. The first reform was to put cards for recently accessioned books directly into the public catalogue, the second was to improve the subject catalogue without making fundamental changes, and the third was to order new catalogue cases to hold 1,500,000 cards of the standard size. The mere preliminary boring of holes for the cards took nearly three months, but with extra help, much of it fairly unskilled, the Library was able to install in 1910–11 a complete set of Library of Congress and John Crerar Library cards with which to begin to reconstruct the new Harvard catalogues.

"As fast as our straitened circumstances permit," the pressing task of classification and reclassification was proceeding, Coolidge reported to Lowell in 1912.[50] That year 323,000 new cards were prepared and inserted into the new trays, 18,038 volumes were arranged in new groups, and the Library began printing for sale its own cards for titles not in the Library of Congress or Crerar collections. This latter operation (which Coolidge largely financed and continued to finance until his death) it was hoped would recoup some of the high costs of reclassification.

Wisely the Library decided from the outset to intermingle its own small cards with the Library of Congress cards and then gradually to replace the smaller ones. ("Smaller" refers to the vertical dimension — 7.5 cm. for the Library of Congress cards as compared with 2 inches for Harvard cards. The latter, however, were 5 inches wide, and it was necessary to cut a fraction of an inch from the right-hand margin

---

[49] A. C. Coolidge to President and Fellows of Harvard College, 16 September 1910.

[50] *Report of Archibald Cary Coolidge, Director of the University Library,* 1912. p. 4.

Walter Lichtenstein, Coolidge's "very competent book-buyer" and "very loyal Harvard man."

Abbott Lawrence Lowell's election as President of Harvard in 1909 began a
new era in the history of the Library. (Mr. Lowell is standing
in front of the fireplace in his office, University 5.)

Coolidge's partner, the "conscientious and faithful" William Coolidge Lane,
for thirty years Librarian of Harvard.

Thomas Franklin Currier, the Library's expert on classification
and cataloguing, later Associate Librarian.

of each in order to file it in a tray designed for the 12.5 cm. Library of Congress cards.) By November 1912 the fourteen-month task of comparing Harvard's catalogue with the Library of Congress file had been completed. In less than twelve months' time 287,606 printed or typed cards had been added to the public catalogue. From this point on, as new cards were received from the Congressional Library, it was possible to check Harvard's own catalogue to see what old cards could be replaced by the Library of Congress cards. This was slow work, but nearly 3,000 were thus eliminated in the next eight months.

The next task was to prepare cards for books whose titles appeared only in the official catalogue and therefore, as Coolidge said, were "as unknown to the public as if the Library did not possess them." [51] It had been estimated that there were about 85,000 of these, plus 25,000 others not listed anywhere. In the first eight months of this reparatory work 43,000 cards were added to the public catalogue.

The prospect of a new library building — the first sod for Widener was turned on 11 February 1913 — meant that the Library could plan for two catalogues: a public one near the delivery desk on the second floor, and a "union catalogue" on the first floor level which would incorporate the old official catalogue as well as cards of location for all other books in the University and cards for books in collections elsewhere (these cards obtained by purchase or exchange). To make each of these "as complete as may be," required "a vast amount of copying and filing and other handling of cards," Coolidge said in his report for 1913–14. "The present time has also been the obvious one of catching up with arrears, for finishing jobs that have been begun, sometimes years ago, but that have had to lag, for making improvements in the catalogues, for planning for the future and for carrying out certain reforms, in a word, for getting into as good condition as possible in order to begin life in the new building with a really efficient system of administration." [52]

In the autumn of 1913 the death of the scholarly William Hopkins Tillinghast, Assistant Librarian, who had been on the staff for thirty-one years, made it fortuitously possible for Coolidge to effect an administrative change which greatly helped speed the work of classifi-

[51] *Report of Archibald Cary Coolidge, Director of the University Library*, 1913, p. 4.
[52] *Report of Archibald Cary Coolidge, Director of the University Library*, 1914, p. 4.

cation. This was to elevate T. Franklin Currier, A.B. 1894, probably the ablest of the "assistants" in the Library, to the position of Assistant Librarian and to unite under him all the shelf classification and cataloguing. Previously the tasks of title transcription, shelf classification, and subject classification had been carried out as three separate processes. This worked well when the Library was small and when there was close personal interchange among the staff, but as the Library grew it became a wasteful effort, for each book had to be taken up as a new problem by three different sets of workers.

As work on the catalogues continued, W. C. Lane made the discovery that for about 30% of the titles the catalogues could use printed cards — 25% from the Library of Congress, 4% from the Royal Library, Berlin, and 1% from the John Crerar Library. The final stage of the momentous task was to merge the old classified catalogue into a united dictionary of cards arranged alphabetically, using principles adopted by the American and British Library Associations.

In five years the staff prepared and filed over a million new cards in the public catalogue alone — more than half of them typewritten. A grand total of more than two million cards were filed, in addition to the alphabetization and consolidation needed to combine the Library of Congress "depository" with those of the old official catalogue. At last the catalogues of the Harvard Library, with its almost two million books and pamphlets, could be said to be up to date. Of course it required years thereafter to perfect the new system, and even today some of the smaller cards remain in the union catalogue, but the long process of reformation was essentially complete.

Coolidge was not an expert on cataloguing and did not pretend to be, but he became enough of a specialist to participate in the process and to make the decisions necessary so that the Library could adopt the most effective means of insuring its utmost future usefulness to the community and the public. An undated letter to Lane written on shipboard in January 1913 at the start of a winter vacation in the Caribbean (he had had little if any vacation in the summer just past because of the press of business connected with Mrs. Widener's decision to give Harvard the new Memorial Library) reveals how extensively he involved himself in planning and deciding courses of action for the Library during the five years of catalogue reform. He wrote:

Dear Lane:

   I am sorry that I had to leave in such a hurry that we could not talk plans out a little more satisfactorily. Most of the ground, however, I think we had gone over before. Of course, I recognize the value of your long experience and capacity in all library matters, and I think have often yielded to them as I expect often to again. At the same time when I have worked out a scheme after a good deal of thought and remain unconvinced after argument I have got to stick to it—to do otherwise would be to shirk my responsibility.

If we had a clear field of action and were not hampered at every turn by difficulties of time, money, cramped quarters, daily demands by the public, etc. etc. and especially by several uncertainties as to the future we could carry out at one job a complete, satisfactory comparison and revision of our two catalogues. This would be the best and cheapest way. But as the circumstances stand I have decided to go ahead whittling down a bit here and a bit there, getting a number of things done that must be done in any case and the sooner the better, and reserving for a while the question of just how the main part of the work is to be handled. This is messier than the other way, it means more chance of confusion and probability of duplication of labor, which means waste of money, nevertheless I believe it is the best thing we can do as matters stand, and such being my lights I shall follow them. Perhaps I need the lesson of burning my fingers a little to make me more cautious.

My programme, as I told you is as follows. It comprises three sets of operations independent of one another, though lending each other help when it is necessary.

I. Classifications

a. As soon as U.S. is at last finished Miss [name left blank] who is working on it can aid Robinson and begin to do Classical Philology. This ought to be within two or three weeks.

b. When we can, we must elaborate in detail the scheme for the reclassifying of all the books with fixed shelf locations whose numbers are to be changed. I should like to get such things as the changes in Folk Lore and Language (and the renumbering of authors like Pope) out of the way by the middle of June and to begin the main job then at full steam.

c. I should like to set another gang at classifying Government. Here also we can do preliminary work in the spring and the main part in the summer, for we want to have everything finished by the autumn.

In general we must have our changing of numbers on the cards follow much more closely the work on the books than has usually been the case.

II. Miss Stiebel's force.

a. The work of making and putting into the public catalogue typewritten cards corresponding to the old "no [sic] short cards" is more than half done and should be completed by the first of May.

b. Set someone to work at once to copying the general reference cards. For this I have consented to the purchase of a new typewriting machine and the addition of another temporary member to the staff. If need be she can have someone to help her on the filing and refiling. I hope work has already begun on this.

c. Compare the new official and the old official catalogue, taking out from the old one all cards that are in the new. As the sole object of this is to reduce the bulk of the old official catalogue, the job may be done very roughly and expeditiously. If we miss several cards it is no matter. Cards taken out may be stored away.

d. Go through the old official catalogue taking out all long white cards, sorting them into those in permanent classifications and those in temporary (including fixed shelf locations).

e. Compare all the long cards in permanent classifications with the corresponding ones in the public catalogue; have copies typewritten on cards of standard size and file the copies, putting the low cards into the union catalogue. Changes of heading can be made at the time of filing or whenever is most convenient.

f. When this summer's work of renumbering is finished order the extra cards for all books now represented in the public catalogue by an L.C. [Library of Congress] or Crerar card (when there is a change on a recent addition represented by one of our standard typewritten cards the change must also be made on the card in the new official catalogue) and then file our new official catalogue in the union one.

III. Let some one this summer go through our public catalogue taking out all department cards, all cards of the old theological alcoves (this I hope would get out many analyticals) and all cards marked "pamphlet." These last would go to Knowles.

Of course the above plan is susceptible to modifications in detail, but if all goes well under it we shall have by next autumn a public catalogue beginning to be in respectable shape, with a great many more standard sized and many fewer low cards than at present. We shall have got rid of one official catalogue and we shall have done a big work of reclassification which will lighten our task for the future in many respects. I think the advantage to Knowles of having his pamphlet cards together when he tackles the colossal job of getting our pamphlet files into better shape will more than outweigh the disadvantage of not having them in the author files for a year or so.

I am not yet clear what the next step should be when the above undertakings are completed — perhaps the copying of the rest of the long white cards and the mere cutting and filing in union cat. of the rest of the old official ones, perhaps a comparison of the old official and the public catalogues, perhaps a copying of all the low cards in the public catalogue, perhaps some combination of these methods or perhaps none of them for a while. This may depend on all sorts of considerations such as how big the various jobs then appear to us, whether we expect to move into the new building in the summer of 1914, whether we are to have new catalogue cases for centimetre cards only, etc. etc. By that time we ought to know more than we do now.

As for the work of filing cards (with or without retouching) in the union catalogue I shudder at the amount of it that must be done. Fortunately we are in no great hurry there. We can wait many months if necessary, or do bits at odd times, and there is the advantage that work of this sort can be done as well in term time as in vacation for it does not interfere with the public.

Of course I find myself wondering how far along things will be when I get back. With luck the comparison of the two official catalogues may be done and a start made on getting out the long white cards, the copying of the general reference cards ought to be well under way, — and old Gore Hall a thing of the past. I am wondering whether you will have any difficulty in finding its baptismal papers under the cornerstone and how you have fared in your efforts to rescue a specimen of the old stack. If your report comes out in time to reach me in Bermuda please send me a copy there. I am enjoying my vacation so far. I trust you will get a good one next summer. The summer after there will not be much repose for either of us.

> Very sincerely yours
> Archibald Cary Coolidge

On 8 April 1914 Coolidge wrote to Currier, the Library's cataloguing expert, "The only thing of importance is not criticism of the past, but what can be done for the future under extremely limited means. While admitting that the general reform of the subject catalogue would be much better than handling such questions piecemeal, it is hard to see how we can undertake any general reform without funds which are nowhere in sight at the present time. In any case there can be no objection to lopping off single abuses whose existence or non-existence do not affect the general question."

What with his personal distress over the coming of the European war and his efforts to complete the Widener building, Coolidge's mind was in turmoil. He wrote Walter Lichtenstein on 31 October 1914:

My thoughts change rapidly from the latest military events to the problem of how to get standard size cards into the catalogue and smaller ones out of it before we make our great move into new quarters. In general I have a feeling that the library is in a mess and in a state of transition and will continue so for the next six months.

Six months later he still felt overwhelmed by the card problem and wrote Lane on 15 April [1915], "I feel as if I almost have an indigestion on the subject of the sizes of cards and I am glad to get away from them for a week . . ."

And again to Currier on 20 September 1916 on the subject of simplifying the subject catalogue Coolidge remarked, "I am convinced that the lumbering up of the catalogue is one of the greatest dangers with which it is menaced, for when cards are once in, it is difficult to get them out again and subjects may easily become unwieldy for . . . anyone but the specialist."

It is not surprising to find, tucked away in Currier's report on the catalogue and shelf department for 1916–17, mention of the fact that "the revision of the country headings in the subject catalogue has gone steadily forward under Dr. Coolidge's supervision, occupying the greater part of the time of two members of the staff."

In his charming reminiscences of Coolidge, of his "enthusiasm, push, personal help, and cheery words of encouragement," Currier recalled how his breath was nearly taken away one June day in 1914 when the Director suddenly appeared and asked:

"What will you do, Mr. Currier, if all the money you need is put at your disposal this summer to solve the subject catalogue problem?" Fortunately, Yale University Library had already been experimenting on a similar problem, and emboldened by the success there, I managed to gasp, "I'd make a 'dictionary catalogue.'" The whole staff went to it, and for better or worse, the catalogue was transformed and guide cards printed, and the opening of college in the fall found it installed in the new cases.

With the dictionary catalogue once established in rough cast, Dr. Coolidge's interest and personal labor blazed the path for smoothing out rough places and improvements. His address before the conference of the American Library Association at Magnolia shows how his plans for subject headings attempted to find a happy mean between the unthinkable expense of exhaustive completeness and the practicable answering of legitimate demands.[53]

Another staff member remembered how he shared in the process of editing subject headings:

The Director not only outlined the changes, but patiently considered the merits of individual titles, asking me to explain technicalities of the cataloguing, as we read the cards together. He never could distinguish analyticals from series titles, or fathom the difference between red ink and black in the corporate entries. It was work which taxed the patience of a most enthusiastic reformer of catalogues and a willing assistant. But the tedium of card reading, cards large and small, typed, printed and manuscript, was always enlivened for the assistant by the Director's good humor, his rhythmical chanted instructions as we divided the cards into their piles "out," "keep," "cancel" — his entertaining comment on authors, his sudden indignation over "foolish cards" . . .

One day . . . he said to me quite seriously and kindly, "I think we really have made some improvement, but we shall never get any credit for it." [54]

Wherever he went, Coolidge communicated some of his vigor, eager interest, and wide knowledge. Said one cataloguer:

[53] Thomas Franklin Currier, "A Sheaf of Memories from the Cataloguers," *Harvard Library Notes*, No. 20 (April 1928), pp. 166–167.
[54] *Ibid.*, p. 167.

Several of us who worked over subject headings with him felt that we received a liberal education, so concise were his comments on the books in question, showing often both a knowledge of the book, and an acquaintance with the writer. We complained that in an hour's work on his part he could make a week's work for us, but his guiding hand at work for that hour built up a logical and useful bibliography, leaving to us the carrying out of helpful suggestions and references, and the "scrapping" of the "dead wood" as he termed it, which it was his great delight to get out of the catalogue.

His pleasure and appreciation were great when some such collection as the Escoto was sorted, or you stopped to help him weed out a few duplicates from the Alsace-Lorraine books, or rushed through a lot of Madagascar titles. And one got so one no longer dreaded having him ask, as he was very apt to do, "What are you doing now," scanning all the while very closely the books open on your desk, for as you went on to give him an itemized list of your activities, his invariable response was, "Good, good," and he would vanish through the Order Department door or down the room to another interview, still murmuring, "Good, good." [55]

Coolidge, the non-specialist, preached the gospel of scholarly common sense in all aspects of what is now taken as "library science." In cataloguing he consistently urged the simple and convenient approach. Speaking before the Catalog Section of the American Library Association at the national meeting in Swampscott, Massachusetts, on 21 June 1921, Coolidge declared:

I believe that however complicated a great catalog fundamentally is and must be, one of its objects should be to present an outward appearance of simplicity. It can hardly hope to attract the public but it should repel as little as possible. The terms used should be simple and as free as may be from library jargon. We must keep in mind how easy it is to create terminology with which we quickly get so familiar that it seems commonplace, but which looks meaningless or absurd to those not in the profession . . .

The object of cataloging is to make knowledge available to the public, and, as in the case of writing books, the best results can be attained only by clearness of thought, skillful arrangement and wise restriction. Like an unreadable book, an unworkable catalog fails in its object. The fact that its chief faults may have been due to over ambition may soften our criticism but does not affect the result. On the other hand, a good library catalog is a thing to be proud of. It renders a very real service to the public and takes an honorable place among the agencies that contribute to the progress of our civilization.[56]

[55] *Ibid.*, p. 169.

[56] Readers interested in pursuing the history of Harvard's efforts at catalogue reform are referred to Coolidge's address, "The Objects of Cataloging," *Library Journal*, XLVI:16 (15 September 1921), 735–739, and to two articles by T. Franklin Currier, "Selective Cataloging at the Harvard Library," *Library Journal*, XLIX:14

Space for the Library

While improvement in the method of finding books and getting them to students and scholars was a daily pressing concern in the first year of Coolidge's responsibility, there was no single goal more critical than solving the question of space and storage. With the help of the President and the Visiting Committee, Coolidge engineered the appointment (by the Corporation) of an architectural committee to study the space needs of the Library to ascertain if there were stages of development which might temporarily alleviate the situation and promise at the same time some long-range relief. The committee, composed of Charles Allerton Coolidge, Guy Lowell, and Desiré Despradelle,[57] rendered their report on 28 January 1911 in draft form — "only one more pious wish," Coolidge called it — and this draft became the final version and the ultimate framework on which the later architectural plan of the Widener Memorial Library was based.[58] The committee's conclusions may be summarized as follows:

(1) A site in the neighborhood of Gore Hall would be appropriate for a new library, but Gore Hall must eventually be torn down.

(2) As an alternative to the construction of a completely new building, one

(August 1924), 673–677, and "Cataloguing and Classification at Harvard, 1878–1938," *Harvard Library Notes*, No. 29 (March 1939), pp. 232–242.

[57] Charles Allerton Coolidge, A.B. 1881, received his architectural training at M.I.T. and in the offices of Ware & Van Brunt and of H. H. Richardson. In 1886 the firm of Shepley, Rutan and Coolidge succeeded to Richardson's professional practice. Coolidge's firm, under successive partners, designed many of Harvard's notable buildings, including the undergraduate Houses given by Edward S. Harkness. Throughout most of his life Coolidge served as architectural and planning consultant to the University,

Guy Lowell, A.B. 1892, was an architectural graduate of M.I.T. and of the École des Beaux Arts (Paris). A first cousin of President Lowell, he designed the New Lecture Hall (now Lowell Lecture Hall) which Mr. and Mrs. Lowell presented anonymously to the University in 1902 and also 17 Quincy Street (the old President's House, given by the Lowells in 1912 and occupied by the presidential families until 1971).

Desiré Despradelle, a French architectural engineer and graduate of the École des Beaux Arts (Paris), was serving as a Lecturer in the Harvard Graduate School of Applied Science during the academic year 1910–11.

[58] Guy Lowell to A. C. Coolidge, 28 January 1911, together with "draft of the report . . . made up from the material we all handed in" addressed to the President and Fellows of Harvard College. This "draft" is the same report sent to President Lowell by Coolidge on 25 June 1912 preparatory to Lowell's discussion with Mrs. Widener.

stack after another should be added to Gore so that Gore Hall could be continued in use until the funds were found, after which new administrative offices would replace Gore.

(3) The initial stack addition would contain professorial study alcoves and seminar rooms as well as space for book storage.

(4) As the Library increased in size and money came in, stacks would be added to form three sides of a quadrangle with a court in the center. The delivery room would be eventually located in the center of the court with access to the three wings of the stack — the central structure to be low, so as not to interfere with light in the stacks.

(5) Eventually Gore Hall would be removed and the main facade of the new building erected facing the Yard, forming the third side of a quadrangle, with University on the left and Sever on the right. Until this was accomplished, as little money as possible should be spent on Gore Hall.

(6) Included in the plan was space for one large and three small reading rooms, special rooms for special collections, map room, exhibition rooms, and administrative offices. The main reading room was to be screened from the street noises by the stack. Entrances were to be from the Yard and the southern side.

The Committee estimated that the completed building would contain shelving for 2,370,000 volumes and would cost approximately $1,953,000 to erect. If the University were to accept the plan and move ahead with the first step, the western section of stacks and study space could provide housing for 834,000 volumes at a cost of approximately $433,440. Since neither Coolidge nor Lowell could see $2,000,000 in the offing, and since other building needs were in the foreground, Coolidge's modest minimum objective was to achieve the first step by finding donors of the first $500,000.

As their chief argument for razing Gore, the architectural committee cited Coolidge's statement to them concerning the inadequacy of the famous library building:

The present building is *unsafe*, and has been declared so by insurance experts; the electric wiring has all been added since the construction, and is and must remain a serious danger.

It is *unsuitable for its object*. The old stack, or earlier half of the Library, was modelled after an English chapel. The whole construction is ill suited to the working of a modern library, and no amount of tinkering can make it really good.

The building is *hopelessly overcrowded* in almost all respects, and every week makes the situation worse. The quarters of the staff are inadequate; every time any additional work has to be undertaken it is a serious problem to decide where an extra person or table can be put. The general reading room for the students is too small, it leaks when there is a heavy rain, it is often intolerably hot in summer, the ventilation is bad and must remain so with the present roof, and the room is frequently overcrowded. There are no rooms where any of the special reference libraries can be accommodated, desirable as this would be in some cases. There is only one seminary room, although several would be very useful, and many professors are put to inconvenience in holding advanced courses where it is necessary to show a large number of books to the students. For professors, for outside scholars, and for our own advanced students access to the stack and means of working near the shelves are of the utmost importance. Our present conditions in this respect are deplorable. We have not half the tables that we ought to have, and as time goes on we shall have to reduce rather than increase the number.

Finally, as to *the books themselves*. They have been shifted so often in order to gain space that at present practically every part of the Library is equally overcrowded with shelves filled to their utmost capacity; books are put in double rows and are not infrequently left lying on top of one another, or actually on the floor, until some way can be found of squeezing them into place; and the moving of books is always a matter of inconvenience and expense. We have now almost fifty thousand volumes stored outside of the building, mostly in cellars, and yet every day we have need of some of these works and are obliged to send for them. Meanwhile the Library is continuing to grow, and we trust will continue to grow, at a rapid rate. Last year over twenty thousand volumes and a large number of pamphlets were added to it, and it is hoped that the rate will increase rather than diminish in the near future. But the only way room can be made to take books into the building is by taking others out, not perhaps of quite equal value but still integral and necessary portions of the Library.[59]

With the need so pressing and the preliminary planning done, Coolidge kept the problem of the Library continually before the Harvard public, making certain too that President Lowell himself did not let it slip downward in any list of priorities.

There is nothing now for me to add on the subject of our supreme need, a new building. Each year we waste more and more money, and we are put to and put others to more and more inconvenience by storing fresh thousands of volumes in some stray cellar and by continually shifting thousands in Gore Hall in order to obtain a little more space where most needed. It is now getting common to see in our book stacks volumes lying on tables or on the floors of the passageways for weeks at a time owing to the fact that it means hours and sometimes days of work in book moving before the necessary room can be created in a given spot . . . In the meanwhile the danger of a fire . . . is a fact we can do nothing to meet.[60]

[59] Guy Lowell Committee Report, p. 2.

[60] *Report of Archibald Cary Coolidge, Director of the University Library*, 1911, p. 4.

It was particularly important for Coolidge to keep pushing both the President and the Visiting Committee because Lowell was in the middle of planning and seeking funds for the first of the new freshman dormitories (the present Gore, Standish and Smith Halls) as well as worrying about badly needed laboratory space for the sciences.

Coolidge's predicament in the matter of financing new space for books was epitomized in his response to a query from Warren Barton Blake, A.B. 1905, in New York:

> I am afraid there is not much that I can tell you about the prospect for a new Harvard Library building. Things at present are in a state of suspended animation. We are doing a little planning and pondering so as not to be entirely unprepared if the lightening [*sic*] were to strike us but, between ourselves, not only is there nothing immediately in sight but we do not want to agitate the question until the money has been raised for the Freshman dormitories. We are thus living, however badly, from hand to mouth.[61]

By January 1912 the search for donors began in some earnest. Lowell had an exchange of letters with J. P. Morgan, Jr., regarding the possibility of arousing Andrew Carnegie's interest.[62] Since Morgan was a friend of Coolidge and an enthusiastic Overseer member of the Library Visiting Committee, it was a rather natural inquiry for Coolidge to urge Lowell to make. Morgan in turn sought out Joseph H. Choate,[63] who discouraged the idea, feeling that "Harvard is too dignified to have a Carnegie Library." [64] The dignified Mr. Lowell retorted that he would not "object to having our library called the Carnegie Library if he [Mr. Carnegie] would give us the whole of it." The idea cooled, however, until Bishop Lawrence, President Lowell's "Cousin William," made a strong case for consulting J. P. Morgan, Sr. This seemed at least possible and Lowell was grateful, commenting:

> When I cease to be President of Harvard College I shall join one of the mendi-

[61] A. C. Coolidge to W. B. Blake, 26 November 1911. Warren Barton Blake (1883–1918) took his A.M. at Harvard in 1907 after graduation *cum laude* from the College. Following study at the Sorbonne, he became a free-lance journalist, wrote for *Scribner's*, *The Atlantic*, *Lippincott's*, *The Chicago Dial*, *The Nation*, and *The Independent*. In the last four years of his life he was a regular contributor to *Collier's Weekly*. During the World War he was chief of the editorial and historical division of the American Red Cross in Paris.

[62] A. L. Lowell to J. P. Morgan, Jr., 31 January 1912.

[63] Joseph Hodges Choate (1832–1917), the distinguished lawyer and diplomat who was a graduate of Harvard College (1852) and of the Law School (1854), was then close to Andrew Carnegie.

[64] J. P. Morgan, Jr., to A. L. Lowell, 13 February 1912.

cant orders, so as to have less begging to do; and if mendicancy is a virtue, I have a right now to feel virtuous.[65]

On 3 April Lowell asked the younger Morgan,

Do you know anyone who could speak to your father about the Library? If he happened to take a real interest in it, he could do any part of it or the whole thing; although he has done so much for us that we have no right to ask him. Still there is truth in the saying that "one good turn deserves another"; only the second is generally done by the same person as the first.[66]

Lowell also inquired as to what the younger Morgan thought about the possibility of interesting "G. F. Baker, the father" or "the Winthrops." On 5 April J. P. Morgan, Jr., reported that his father was abroad and that he thought that the next summer when the senior Morgan would be in "Bar Harbor and north-east [*sic*]" would be the best time for Bishop Lawrence's approach. "I think," said the son, "perhaps it would be a good plan to tell him that possibly Mr. Baker would like to join. He likes to do things with that gentleman, but I believe it must all wait till later on . . . My impression is that Grenville [Winthrop] will not do anything." [67] Such was the state of the presidential fishing expedition, when out of tragedy came the completely unexpected possibility of a solution to Harvard's predicament.

In the late winter of 1912 Walter Lichtenstein was again in Europe on a buying expedition for Coolidge and the Harvard Library. His letters and postcards reporting prices and progress arrived regularly every few days, together with news and comment about his travel experiences and happenings on the home front. On 29 April, two weeks after the sinking, he told Coolidge, "I had mail on the *Titanic*, but not for Cambridge," and added, "I trust that you lost no friends on the vessel."

It was almost a prescient remark. Among the 1,517 victims of the North Atlantic tragedy was Harry Elkins Widener of the Harvard Class of 1907. Coolidge had known him as an undergraduate, even then an ardent book-collector. Now, in death, he was to prove him-

---

[65] A. L. Lowell to William Lawrence, 1 March 1912.

[66] A. L. Lowell to J. P. Morgan, Jr., 3 April 1912. J. P. Morgan, Sr., had given three of the new Medical School buildings to the University in 1906 in honor of his father, Junius Spencer Morgan.

[67] J. P. Morgan, Jr., to A. L. Lowell, 5 April 1912. Grenville L. Winthrop, A.B. 1886, later gave his collection of art objects and furniture to the Fogg Museum, together with a fund to care for them.

self perhaps the greatest friend of the Harvard Library in its long history.

Although only 27 at the time of his death, Harry Widener already had a high reputation in the book world as a collector with an exceptional knowledge of bibliography. Of course, he was also a young man of independent means, one of the heirs apparent to the combined fortunes, estimated as high as $75,000,000, amassed by Peter A. B. Widener (1834–1915) and William L. Elkins (1832–1903) in street railways, real estate development, and other activities in Philadelphia and elsewhere.[68]

Harry Widener had gone abroad with his parents in March 1912 and had spent a happy time in London at Sotheby's and Quaritch's perusing and acquiring new items for his collection. There is a story (related by A. Edward Newton in *The Amenities of Book Collecting*) that on this trip Harry successfully bid at the Huth sale for the 1598 edition of Bacon's *Essaies* and, instead of having it shipped, said to Quaritch, "I think I'll take this little Bacon with me in my pocket, and if I am shipwrecked, it will go with me." When the *Titanic* struck the iceberg on its maiden voyage to New York, Mrs. Widener managed to get away safely in one of the lifeboats, but Harry Widener and his father, George Dunton Widener (only surviving son of P. A. B. Widener), went down with the ship.

It took only a few weeks for Harvard to hear of Harry Widener's will. Coolidge wrote to Lichtenstein on 24 May:

The great event and excitement for me of the past week has been the Widener library. Young Widener, who was in the class of 1907 and whom I knew in college, went down with his father on the Titanic. A week ago the news came that his collection had been left by will to Harvard, as soon as we should have a proper place in which to put it. Two days ago the newspapers came out with the statement that his grandfather was going to give us "a wing" to house the collection. I enclose the clipping from the New York Sun. So far we have not had any confirmation of this story from the Widener family, but there has been no denial, and I see no reason to doubt the substantial accuracy of the report. It is uncertain what the phrase "a wing" means. If it is an addition to this old building, my enthusiasm for the gift is dampened, but I have good reason to know that a copy of our proposed new plans with estimates as to the cost of each section has been in the hands of some members of the

---

[68] See Charles K. Bolton's account of "Harry Elkins Widener" in *Dictionary of American Biography*; also Hobart S. Perry on "Peter A. B. Widener" and John H. Frederick on "William L. Elkins."

Widener family for about a fortnight, and I have little doubt that "a wing" refers to the new plan. At any rate I expect to go down to Philadelphia within a few days, and once there I shall see what the situation is, and if there is anything for me to try to do. You can imagine that I am in a condition of no small excitement over it all and inclined to be jubilant, but afraid of a fearful disappointment.

Somewhat more detail was forthcoming after the trip to Philadelphia. Coolidge wrote on 31 May to his friend and contemporary, J. P. Morgan, Jr.:

I have just been down to Philadelphia where I have seen Mrs. George Widener. The state of the case is that Harry Widener left his collection to his mother, with the request that it be given to Harvard when it could be provided with proper accommodation. She and her father-in-law [P. A. B. Widener] are prepared to do something pretty substantial towards furnishing this accommodation. They had seen the plan recommended by your committee and at first thought of giving one wing of it . . . ; then they had a change of heart feeling that what they wanted was a memorial which should keep Widener's name and they feared that a mere wing of a large building would not have much individuality. In point of fact, what they would have to give would be not the wing, but the front, for only there could one provide well the sort of a memorial room that they desire. Mrs. W. asked me if the Corporation would accept a separate small building with funds to keep it up, etc. I said I could not answer for the higher powers, but threw what cold water I could on the plan. At present the W.'s are thinking the matter over. It seems to me not impossible that they may give the whole building, but two million is a good bit, and I do not wonder that even old Mr. W. should hesitate. However he decides, I feel pretty hopeful that we shall get something satisfactory out of it.

Morgan, who knew the Wideners, gave Coolidge encouragement:

I should not be surprised if the Wideners did the whole thing. It would be much better than having a small detached library just for Harry Widener's books. If I can put in a word — and I may have an opportunity — I shall of course do so. The $2,000,000 could be spread over such a long time that Mr. W., I think would feel that it was all right, and the necessary additional amount for looking after the new building and increasing the usefulness of the Library, which in our report was stated to be $500,000, could without doubt be acquired through the year or so before the new building was completed.

Even if Harry Widener had simply willed his books to Harvard and said nothing about a building to house them, it would have been cause for gratitude and joy, but the prospect of a wing or a building of some sort set the hopes of Harvard's high command into a flight skyward. Evidently Coolidge in his eagerness may have slightly overplayed his hand, for President Lowell wrote to John Batterson Stetson, Jr.,[69] Mrs. Widener's adviser, on 12 June:

Thank you very much for your letter. I am very sorry that Mrs. Widener has got a little put out with us. I am not surprised, for the reports in the papers naturally were provoking, and perhaps we also were too eager. The fact is that people who are selfish for their institutions are much less conscious that they are selfish than those who are selfish for themselves. However, I will try to profit by your advice. It confirms me that I was right in putting off going down to see her until after Commencement. If she is willing to give $2,500,000, that will build all the library we should need for some years, a fund to maintain it, handsome rooms in it for Harry Widener's books, and income for adding rare books to his collection. For a million more, which you mention, all this could be done, and a library building could be provided large enough for an indefinite period which would bear his name, and be a magnificent memorial to him.

I agree with you that the books are the important thing, not the building, but, at the same time, it must be remembered that the Harvard collection of books, apart from what we hope to get from Harry Widener and from the income of the fund, will be the greatest collection of books in America, and as the public connects inseparably the building and its contents, it is hard to conceive of a more enduring — certainly a more striking — memorial than that of the building to house our collections.

With Commencement past and the certain knowledge that President Lowell would soon make his personal call on Mrs. Widener, Coolidge assembled as much helpful background information as he could to aid the President in discussing Harvard's case. His letter of 22 June outlined the principal needs and financial prospects of the College Library:

Dear Lawrence:—

I am sending you a few rough figures which may be of some use to you in connection with your journey to Philadelphia.

You may remember that at the dinner of the Visiting Committee last year I declared that the Library needed a gift of five million, — two for a building,

[69] John Batterson Stetson, Jr., A.B. 1906, son of the Philadelphia hat manufacturer of the same name, was a neighbor, friend, and contemporary of Harry Widener and also an "avid book collector." He served as U. S. Ambassador to Poland (1925–1930) and for many years was President of the Board of Trustees of John B. Stetson University, founded by his father. Through his generosity and Coolidge's persuasion, the younger Stetson gave the Palha collection of Portuguese books and manuscripts to the Harvard Library and he served as Curator and Honorary Curator of Portuguese Literature in the Library from 1923 until his death in 1952. He was a translator of Pero de Magalhaes' *Histories of Brazil* (1920).

two for maintenance, and one for book purchases. The two for a building correspond to what we are asking for in our official architects' plan. The income of the other two, i.e. $40,000 for books and $80,000 for administration, as it happens roughly corresponds to what we have been spending during this last year. Five million, therefore, merely represents a new building plus our present rate of administration.

Of course our expenditures for this last fiscal year have been exceptional, but they only represent a normal, which would be far from extravagant under new conditions. The University is particularly fortunate in the fact that the purchase of books for the Library costs the general funds practically nothing, that is to say, that the money comes with but slight exception from restricted funds, which can only be used for that purpose. I do not think any important college in the United States is as well off in this respect. These restricted funds, however, are far from being sufficient, as they amount to only about $20,000 a year. The other $20,000 of this year's expenses comes from gifts of various sorts, a welcome, but precarious source. Even with an assured income of $40,-000 a year we could not of course afford to buy without special provision rare editions of the kind in the Widener Library.

Expenses for administration during this last year will come to about $80,000, — roughly $24,000 for salaries, and $56,000 for wages and general expenses. The $24,000 for salaries are not satisfactorily distributed, but the total does not represent any more than we are likely to need in the future. Of the $56,000 spent on wages and administration, only about $40,000 come from the regular budget of the University. $16,000 are extra, and therefore exceptional, but although I shall ask the Corporation for practically the same regular budget as this last year, $40,000 is certainly not enough to keep the College Library running in proper shape, and $56,000 would not be a high estimate for our necessary expenses in a much larger building, which will undoubtedly cost a good deal more for lighting, heating, additional service, etc. Indeed even in our present cramped quarters, I could easily go ahead and spend as much as I have this year for an indefinite future without feeling that I am wasting money or indulging in luxuries, and even with this sum it would be a long time before I could catch up with all arrears. For general purposes therefore I think we can look on $80,000 a year as representing a normal cost of administration in the near future. Of this, some $23,000 a year (or the income of $600,000) comes from restricted funds, which have to be spent on the Library. The rest or about $57,000 would be a burden on the general resources of the University. The income of the Sheldon fund would alleviate this burden a little, but would not remove it. (Of course every little counts.) To relieve the University of all administrative expenses for the College Library at least for the present, we should require a gift of $1,400,000 devoted to this exclusive purpose.

I may say in conclusion that I do not think my figures are in any way unduly fanciful or extravagant. They are indeed modest compared with those of several other libraries, and I could undertake with ease to spend profitably a very much larger amount. Also, I feel sure that the severest critic would not claim

A "long card" from the catalogue established about 1847
(reduced from original size: 9½ by 2½ inches).

A "small card" from the catalogue begun in 1861
(trimmed slightly on right-hand margin to fit
trays designed for Library of Congress cards).

Gore Hall: the original building of 1841.

Gore Hall in 1912, showing additions of 1877 and 1907.

Gore Hall Reading Room in 1885
(ten years later, three levels of stack were installed in the lower level).

Gore Hall stacks about 1912.

that the wages paid in the Library here are high. The expenditure for salaries at the Boston Public Library for last year, (including the branch libraries, but not counting $7000 in the Printing Department) was $208,623.13.

Very sincerely yours,

Archibald Cary Coolidge [70]

Then Coolidge added a postscript and memorandum to cover the possible chance that "the W's remain firm and refuse to give either a new building or a portion of one, but offer a building for special collections." The memorandum pictures a kind of Houghton Library, far from ideal in today's terms, but still a reasonably useful supplement to Gore Hall. Coolidge hastened to warn Lowell that the contingency plan was "what seems to me would be most desirable, without taking into account the question of expense for building or maintenance, as it is evident that we cannot run such a library from our present funds."

Three days later more background information and another letter went to President Lowell from the hopeful Director:

Dear Lawrence:—

I enclose in a separate envelope a certain amount of library literature, which can serve you as reading matter on the train. The three things about our Library have already been seen by Mrs. Widener, but I doubt if she has paid much attention to any but the Report. She has also seen an article on our Treasure Room. The picture and account of the new Harper Memorial Library in Chicago may possibly be of some service. As for the figures of our running expenses — I think my note to you of the other day covers them sufficiently.

Sincerely yours,

Archibald Cary Coolidge [71]

Fortunately Mr. Lowell's visit with Mrs. Widener — in Newport, rather than Philadelphia — went well. The President reported to John B. Stetson on 3 July:

I went to see Mrs. Widener at Newport last week and she says that she will send her architect to Cambridge before long. I think she understands the situation with extraordinary clearness; still to have her architect on the spot will also tend to make the possibilities more clear.[72]

But events moved tantalizingly slowly. As late as 9 July Coolidge was still uncertain about Mrs. Widener's intentions. "There is nothing

[70] A. C. Coolidge to A. L. Lowell, 22 June 1912.
[71] A. C. Coolidge to A. L. Lowell, 25 June 1912.
[72] A. L. Lowell to J. B. Stetson, Jr., 3 July 1912.

to report . . . " he told Lichtenstein. "We still have hopes in that direction, but as yet they have not materialized." [73] Then came a note from Stetson to President Lowell marked "Private and Confidential" which sent expectations sky-high. "I thank you for your letter of July 3rd," Stetson wrote. "At the same time I had the same news from my end, with the additional report that Mrs. Widener has about made up her mind to furnish the whole library building at a cost of $2,000,000.00. Personally I am tremendously pleased at the outcome, and as an alumnus of Harvard, I am most grateful for her generous impulses." [74]

Coolidge's high excitement was only dampened by his realization of the need for prompt action. He confided triumphantly to Lichtenstein on 16 July:

> In all probability we are going to get a library, and by that I mean our whole plan or something very near it, from Mrs. Widener. Nothing has been promised definitely yet, so that we must keep everything very quiet, as any premature leaking out might cause the lady to change her mind, but we have seen her architect and work on the plans will probably begin at once. You can imagine what a twitter I am in.

Mrs. Widener's architect turned out to be Horace Trumbauer (1868–1938), favorite architect of Harry Widener's grandfathers, P. A. B. Widener and William L. Elkins. Trumbauer built both the Elkins and Widener mansions in Elkins Park and Ashbourne, Pennsylvania. His firm was known for their designs of numerous private residences for the very rich and for such major projects as the campus of Duke University, the Philadelphia Museum of Art, the Benjamin Franklin and Ritz Carlton Hotels in Philadelphia, the Widener Building in Philadelphia, and the Philadelphia Free Library. "Trumbauer understood," Wayne Andrews has written, "as did few other architects of his generation that only a magnificent setting could hope to satisfy an American with a magnificent income . . . He had no rivals when it came to tempting clients to spend immodest sums." [75] As an Elkins who had married a Widener, thus uniting two fortunes long closely associated, Mrs. Widener was familiar with and very confident of Trumbauer's merit.

[73] A. C. Coolidge to Walter Lichtenstein, 9 July 1912.
[74] J. B. Stetson, Jr. to A. L. Lowell, 11 July 1912.
[75] See Wayne Andrews' account of "Horace Trumbauer" in *Dictionary of American Biography*.

After Trumbauer's initial visit, two of his draftsmen came to Cambridge for "about a week" in late July and worked on a "first plan" for Mrs. Widener. Until Trumbauer's return with the hoped for good news that "everything has been approved and the work will begin promptly," Coolidge was "kept in a good deal of flutter." [76]

In the meantime Coolidge, Lane, and the rest of the staff were busy laying plans for the very complicated evacuation of Gore Hall and the move to temporary quarters. To his two staunch fellow Council members, Professors Chester Noyes Greenough and George Foot Moore, then absent from Cambridge, Coolidge sent glad tidings:

I have some very good news to tell you. It is not quite certain, but pretty nearly so, that we are going to have a new library and the whole of one. It will follow in the main the plan proposed by the architects' committee. Work may be begun this autumn. Next summer we shall probably move into what is then completed as temporary quarters, and two years hence everything ought to be done. An amusing thing is that after having waited in vain for ages, our good fortune has not only come all of a sudden, but is going ahead with such speed that we are expected to have plans ready at the earliest possible moment. We have been working hard at it for some days now and expect the architect from Philadelphia on Wednesday morning. He has been chosen by the donor, Mrs. George Widener. If you have any ideas that you want to suggest as to our future accommodations, I should be very glad to have them as soon as possible. [77]

With "no absolute definite promise in black and white" from Mrs. Widener and no word from Trumbauer, who "was due some days ago," Coolidge confessed to J. P. Morgan, Jr., on 6 August that: "I have been sitting here on pins and needles waiting . . . Still I do not feel alarmed at the delay and continue in a very happy and jubilant condition. I had wanted to be able to write you that all doubt was passed . . . "

But obviously Coolidge was not literally "sitting" in Cambridge. In preparation for the imminent move, the Director sent out letters to all corners of the University asking for emergency storage space. The President and the Director had a face-to-face conference on 13 August to discuss how best to evacuate Gore Hall and set up a temporary Library in various locations within or close to the Yard. Two days later Coolidge had further thoughts to communicate to the President:

[76] A. C. Coolidge to Walter Lichtenstein, 26 July 1912.
[77] A. C. Coolidge to G. F. Moore and C. N. Greenough, 22 July 1912.

I beg to report progress since we parted Friday afternoon. The idea of using the Stadium is in abeyance. Two more promising possibilities are the hiring of the Randolph Tennis and Racket courts and putting up a stack in them, and second the building of a corrugated iron structure back of Massachusetts Hall. The most promising idea of all is to move the whole east stack bodily (we can take care of the west one) straight up the hill in the direction of your house. It will make your view a trifle monotonous for a while, but will help to keep off from you the noise and dust of two years building operations below. The would be mover (one Cavanagh) guesses that he can do the job in two months but intimates he can work a great deal faster for a sufficient bonus. I am going to ask him for an ordinary estimate and one for doing the job in four weeks beginning a week from tomorrow. I expect to close the Library to the public during those weeks.

Will you kindly do two things? First write to Ezra Thayer [Dean of the Law School], telling him we are at his mercy and asking him to lend us all the shelf space he possibly can either in the old or the new building of the L.S. Second will you write to Mrs. Widener and get her to have her lawyer meet you on Saturday. My idea is to have estimates in by Thursday, the Corporation meets Friday, you will go to Newport and wind up everything Saturday, and the work begin on the following Monday. We shall start on the clearing out of the west stack tomorrow.

Now as to finance, if you can put it to Mrs. W. that at every inconvenience to ourselves we can undertake to have one half the building emptied and the other half actually out of the way by the first of October or sooner at such and such a cost, she would be almost forced at least to pay the bonus for extra speed and perhaps the whole thing. The extra speed makes a great deal of difference to us as it means having the building open when the term begins. For the rest of our countless extra library expenses for the next two years I think the Corporation could use — not the capital but the accumulated interest (ca. $50,000) of the Sheldon bequest. It has already made use of that source last year when it made the Treasure room safe. Of course it will be a great blessing if Mrs. W. will help out, but the Sheldon interest money is there if the worst comes to the worst.

Yours very sincerely

Archibald Cary Coolidge.

P.S. I should like to have seen Channing's [78] smile when he heard that he would probably have to write the next volume of his great work under the Stadium.[79]

Meanwhile Mr. Lowell was doing his own inquiring. Dean LeBaron Russell Briggs, Chairman of the Faculty Committee on Athletics, ascertained that there would be no objection to using parts of the space

[78] Edward Channing, McLean Professor of Ancient and Modern History, was author of a multivolume *History of the United States.*

[79] A. C. Coolidge to A. L. Lowell, 15 August 1912.

under the Stadium for a stack but, more reasonably, he queried, "Is it conceivable that you could get on by sacrificing the whole of Massachusetts and establishing a reading room in Harvard?" Henry L. Higginson, Fellow of the Corporation and donor of the Union, suggested that the Union might be a suitable and easy solution.

The search for storage space went on at high speed. Typical was Coolidge's begging letter to Paul Henry Hanus concerning the educational collections:

It is more than probable that we shall have to vacate our present library quarters almost at once, and store our hundreds of thousands of volumes in any nook, corner, temporary building, or storage warehouse that we can find.

I write to ask about the nine thousand volumes of educational reports, etc., and the six thousand volumes on education that are here.

Is there any possible way in which they can be housed in Lawrence Hall for the next two years? We should of course have to pay all expenses of the temporary stack. I am afraid it will put you to great inconvenience, but it is even more for your interest than ours, as I cannot say what remote corner we may otherwise have to put the books in. This seems like putting a pistol at your head, but I hope you realize that I am in a pretty desperate situation.[80]

The responses were friendly and understanding, like that from Hanus on 21 August:

I don't know how it would be possible to store the 15,000 volumes in Lawrence Hall, but you could judge for yourself what available space we have if you would be good enough to take a look at our library rooms. We would naturally do all that we could to help store these volumes during the time when they must be removed from the general library. I am, however, reluctant to have more books stored in Lawrence Hall than we already have there. I am constantly haunted by the fear of fire, as it is. The building would burn like tinder if it took fire. Nevertheless, if you think Lawrence Hall is the only available place where we could put the books and there is room for them there, we would crowd ourselves to the utmost to take the books in.

Coolidge realized that not all his colleagues were going to be equally cooperative. He was not so much worried about some of the more independent of the libraries, like the Law School, but rather how individuals and departments would react to speedy changes. He confided his thoughts to the President on 20 August:

[80] A. C. Coolidge to P. H. Hanus, 20 August 1912. Professor Hanus (1855–1941) had been since 1891 the head of the Department (division) of Education. From 1901 to 1921 he held the title of Professor of the History and Art of Teaching.

In connection with our conversation this morning, I wish to submit for your consideration a number of disconnected ideas that are in my head.

First, as to the time when work here may be expected to begin: Of course I know how complicated those things are, and that people never either start or finish when they expect to; but we must remember that Trumbauer has a very large and well-organized office; that they have undoubtedly been doing all sorts of preliminary work in the last month, so that their contractors will have been spoken to, preliminary drawings made, etc. etc. Above all, he is acting under great pressure from Mrs. Widener, — the pressure which of all others will affect him most. From the first he told us that he wanted to break ground in September. You remember that Friday he said he would like to begin in a fortnight, and that he ought to have his cellar done by January. I am convinced that he intends to go ahead with most unusual speed, and will succeed in doing so.

Now, as to this end of the line: A day now is worth three to us later on. It is the deadest time of the year; there is but small demand on the books in the Library, and we can go ahead with a minimum of inconvenience. It is to be remembered that on a rainy day, even if they are covered, it is risky to move books, for there is danger to them. Now, supposing we have to take all of the books out of the Library, and supposing we can take down, move and set up 10,000 volumes a day when we get well going — which is pretty optimistic — at that rate, making allowance for Sundays, bad weather, etc., the job will demand three months; and the moving of the books is, of course, only a part (even if the largest part) of what we have to do. When once college begins we shall be putting people to a fearful amount of inconvenience; so you can see how anxious I am to go ahead without wasting an hour. As for expense, I doubt whether under the best of circumstances $25,000 will more than cover the whole thing.

In view of the fact that everyone is out of Cambridge, I am afraid I shall have to ask for almost arbitrary powers in such things as where the books shall be stored in given cases. Of course this does not apply to institutions like the Law School; but I cannot stop to argue out with each particular department, or even chairman of department, whether so and so many shelves may be put up in his room. I had to take at first a pretty sharp tone of authority with my own staff about putting things through. Of course I do not want to be autocratic wherever I can possibly avoid it, and am anxious to save everybody's feelings, but the thing has got to go as a great machine which cannot be delayed in its parts by argument.

For his part President Lowell displayed his most authoritative charm in carrying out Coolidge's request that he help him with Dean Thayer of the Law School:

I hope you are having a pleasant and restful summer. It would be more so with me were it not for the many new buildings to be built — for which I am devoutly thankful. One of them, as you know, is to be a new University Library, given by Mrs. George D. Widener as a memorial to her son, Harry Widener. By the way, in this connection we are begging for as much temporary storage in the Law School as possible while this library is being built; for Mrs. Widener wants to build it all at once both for economy and speed, and therefore Gore Hall will have to come down immediately. Professor Coolidge is in touch with your library for that purpose.[81]

In the interim the Corporation had met on Friday, 23 August, to hear of Mrs. Widener's offer of the new Library, formally to accept her gift, and to authorize the President to sign an agreement with her regarding the project. That same day Lowell wrote the following letter to the donor:

Dear Mrs Widener: —

I presented your offer of a Library, with the plans, to the Corporation, and I wish that they had heard nothing of it before so that I might have seen their surprise and delight. They accepted it, of course, with the deepest gratitude, and empowered Mr Charles Francis Adams 2nd, the Treasurer, and myself to execute such an instrument in regard to its construction and preservation as you spoke of the other day. I shall be glad to come to Newport for that purpose at any time that it is convenient to you, except that the week after next I expect to be away at Mount Desert for a few days.

We have given no information as yet to the press, and we want to do so only in the way that you would prefer. Perhaps you can tell me about this when we meet, unless you want to send me word beforehand.

By the way, if you have occasion to telephone me, my number is 57 Cotuit, Southern Telephone Company.

In accordance with your request we are preparing to move out with the utmost possible despatch. In fact, as I look from my window I see the books already coming out of the old Library.

Yours very sincerely,
A. Lawrence Lowell

Mrs. Widener replied in an undated holograph note from Newport on the mourning stationery she had had engraved for use at Lynnewood Hall, her Ashbourne place:

I don't believe it will be necessary for you to come to Newport again — With regard to the deed of gift, of which we spoke when you were last here — I can talk it over with my lawyer when I get home & send a copy to you, if it is approved then you can sign it & send it back to me — Will you let me know if this is entirely satisfactory to you —

In regard to the Press — please use your own judgment — the only thing I

[81] A. L. Lowell to Ezra Ripley Thayer, 27 August 1912.

would want emphasized is, that the library is a memorial to my dear son & to be known as the "Harry Elkins Widener Memorial Library" & given by me & not his Grandfather as has been so often stated [82] — I expect to be in Cambridge about the 15th of September, when I shall hope to see you — believe me —

Very sincerely
Eleanor Elkins Widener

Lowell assured Mrs. Widener on 28 August that her suggestion about the instrument would be "perfectly satisfactory." However, the matter dragged for months and was not finally consummated until January, long after the central collection had been dispersed to the four corners of the Yard. The final decision as to the temporary location was announced as tactfully as possible in a broadside to the community when it reassembled for the opening of the University year in September:

IN order to make way for the erection of the Harry Elkins Widener Memorial Library it has become necessary to remove the College Library from Gore Hall at as early a date as possible. The regular service of the Library will be continued with as little interruption as may be, but under difficulties of administration which will doubtless make it necessary to ask the indulgence and forbearance of officers and students alike. For the present the arrangements will be as follows: —

The general Reading Room is transferred to Upper Massachusetts, where substantially the same reference books and reserved books will be found as have heretofore been shelved in the Reading Room in Gore Hall. In Lower Massachusetts will be found the reserved books in American History (heretofore in the smaller Gore Hall Reading Room), the whole collection of British Parliamentary documents, and the whole series of United States documents. These two rooms will be open every week-day during term-time, holidays included (except Thanksgiving Day and Christmas Day), from 8.45 A.M. until 10 P.M.; on Sundays, from 1 P.M. to 10 P.M.

Reserve books may be taken out at 9 P.M., to be returned before 9 o'clock the next morning.

On Saturdays reserved books not specially restricted may be taken out at 5 P.M., to be returned Monday morning before 9. Restricted books (those behind the attendant's desk) may be taken out at 9 P.M., to be returned before 2 o'clock on Sunday.

[82] That the donor felt particularly strongly about the part the Elkins money played in her memorial gift is borne out by a letter from her second husband, Alexander Hamilton Rice, who wrote to President Lowell on 10 December 1927: "Will you do your best to see that in all official reports, etc., the Library is referred to as the Harry Elkins Widener Memorial Library? — 'Widener'! Not one cent of Widener money, one second of Widener thought, nor one ounce of Widener energy were expended on either the conception or the construction of the Library."

The reading room for History and Economics in Harvard Hall will be open as usual on week-days (except holidays) from 8.30 A.M. to 5 P.M., but on Saturday the room closes at 1 o'clock. Books may be taken out for overnight use as usual.

The Delivery Room and the Card Catalogue remain for the present in Gore Hall, but will presently be removed to Randall Hall. Books are already in process of transfer to other buildings, — Emerson Hall, Robinson Hall, the Fogg Art Museum, the Divinity School Library, the Peabody Museum, the Museum of Comparative Zoölogy, and the Andover-Harvard Library, — but the greater part of the Library's collections will eventually find a place in Randall Hall.

Because of the scattering of our books, it will be impossible to serve borrowers as promptly as heretofore, but a regular automobile messenger service will be maintained, and books not at present shelved in Gore Hall (and later, books not shelved in Randall Hall) will be sent for on application at the Delivery Desk. Such books asked for at the Delivery Desk before 11 o'clock can usually be delivered at 1.30; those asked for between 11 and 2.30, at 5 o'clock; those asked for after 2.30, at 10.30 the next day.

The public announcement about the general plans for the Library produced a flurry of correspondence, some of it critical. R. Clipston Sturgis, A.B. 1881, an architect about four years President Lowell's junior, wrote to him on 17 September to ask why the Library of Harvard University should be entrusted "to a man like Mr. Trumbauer" whose "work is not distinguished if it is not individual." He has "no standing in the profession, is not even a member of the Institute, to say nothing of a Fellow . . . " The President dispatched him quickly with a "dear Clip":

Tho reason that Mr. Trumbauer was employed as the architect of the new Library is that the donor so decided. I shall be very glad to talk with you about it more fully at any time.

To another architectural critic who had tackled Charles A. Coolidge, A.B. 1881, a member of the architectural committee on the new library, Lowell suggested a soft answer. The President thought that the response should come from Coolidge — "I think perhaps I had better not be writing anything that might look like criticism on the building." Lowell indicated that Coolidge might say something to the effect that:

Mrs. Widener does not give the University the money to build the Library, but has offered to build a library satisfactory in external appearance to herself. She accepted the plan of the former committee of architects so far as the size of the building and its interior arrangements were concerned except the Memorial Hall and place for the collection of her son's books; but the exterior was her own choice, and she has decided architectural opinions. Her gift is most generous and munificent, and I hardly think anyone would suggest risk- ing the danger of losing it because he might think the form of architecture open to criticism.[83]

Albert Bushnell Hart, Eaton Professor of the Science of Govern ment, wanted to know if it would not be possible to build Gore Hall — "a beloved landmark" — into the new building. He thought it a tragedy to lose it completely; there would no longer be a reason for the picture on the seal of the City of Cambridge. His was one of many letters deploring the loss of a building which went back almost seventy years into Harvard's past. While the forces of destruction were ada- mant, the Overseers' Visiting Committee was asked to consider what should be kept of Gore. Among the mementos, the Committee de- cided that the pinnacles on the roof would be worthy souvenirs — "not beautiful but . . . very characteristic of the building . . . We . . . recommend that four . . . shall be reserved when the building is pulled down." [84] Coolidge told Lowell of the recommendation, ad- ding, "Of course if you wish and direct that the rest should be pre- served, that is not our affair." [85] Although Mr. Lowell's response to this barb was not recorded, F. W. Hunnewell, the Comptroller, told Coolidge that he had spoken to the President and "from the way he talked I imagine that the fewer that are kept the better pleased he will be." [86]

[83] A. L. Lowell to Charles A. Coolidge, 3 October 1912.

[84] F. R. Appleton to A. C. Coolidge, 8 January 1913.

[85] A. C. Coolidge to A. L. Lowell, 8 January 1913.

[86] F. W. Hunnewell to A. C. Coolidge, 9 January 1913. Two of the finials from Gore Hall now stand just outside the Massachusetts Avenue door of Widener Li- brary.

The Passing of Gore and the Building
of Widener: A Documentary Tale

B Y MID-AUGUST 1912 Archibald Cary Coolidge and his associates of the Harvard Library were confident enough to start
the process of emptying Gore Hall. Horace Trumbauer, Mrs.
Widener's architect, conveyed his client's desire to move as swiftly as
possible. Thus while the plans for the new building were going forward, Coolidge, Lane, and the others began planning the staged evacuation. As Coolidge recorded, "Thanks to persistently good weather
and to other favorable circumstances the task of clearing out books,
furniture, etc. was accomplished between the latter part of August and
the end of December." [87]

The autumn months were filled with conferences and correspondence among Lowell, Coolidge, Lane, and Trumbauer, even occasionally between Lowell and Mrs. Widener. But the President's attention
was particularly focused on perfecting the formal arrangement between
the University and the donor.

The Governing Boards approved the revised plans for the Library
in November — a somewhat smaller library building than the 1911
architectural planning committee had originally proposed, but Mrs.
Widener's generosity was so great that President Lowell was more
than willing to go her way, to tolerate her architect despite the independent course he happily pursued, even eventually to see that Trumbauer received from Harvard an honorary degree.[88]

[87] *Report of Archibald Cary Coolidge, Director of the University Library*,
1913, p. 3.
[88] Not only was Commencement Day 1915 a day of joy for Harvard with the
opening of the new library, it was an especially notable day for the donor. A great
library building named for her son became reality, and both her favorite architect
and her future husband received honorary degrees. In a none too inspired citation,
President Lowell hailed "Horace Trumbauer, architect of Harry Elkins Widener

The final version of Mrs. Widener's agreement and trust arrangements with the University did not reach Lowell for ratification until
January 1913. "Until Mrs. Widener's agreement arrived," Lowell told
Trumbauer, "I did not want to tear down Gore Hall." [89] From then
it took one month, until mid-February, to demolish Gore and surround
the site with a high board fence.

While the Harvard community patiently endured the difficulty of
using a library with its catalogue and stacks in one place, its reading
rooms in another, and its book storage at scattered points, the big
excavation in the Yard grew ever bigger. The first spadefuls of earth
were turned on 11 February 1913 by Harry Widener's brother,
George D. Widener (in the absence of his mother, who had a bad
cold), and a symbolic group composed of Lowell, Lane, Kittredge
of the Library Committee, Potter the Assistant Librarian, Dean Briggs
of the College, and the architect himself. (Coolidge was on vacation
in the Caribbean.) By June 1913 all was ready for a cornerstone laying.
Mrs. Widener applied the trowel 16 June before the Alpha Chapter
(Massachusetts) of Phi Beta Kappa, and Coolidge briefly spoke.

During the summer and the next fall and winter the building gradually took shape, filling the Yard with its bulk. In the late spring of
1915 the building was completed. The dedication took place on
Commencement Day, 24 June 1915, with Senator Henry Cabot Lodge
the chief speaker. Coolidge ceremoniously carried into the building
John Harvard's copy of John Downame's *Christian Warfare*, the
only volume remaining from the founder's library. A few hours later
came the first trucks with their loads of books from Randall Hall.
The catalogue followed on Saturday, 7 August; and the next Monday,
9 August 1915, the Harvard Library, as Coolidge said, "began life in
its new home."

It was a new home ample and comfortable in its public rooms but
still lacking furnishings and other amenities behind the scenes.

29 August [1912]: W. C. Lane to A. C. Coolidge

We ought to get a number of good photographs of the present building and

---

Memorial Library. They who enter its doors will ever admire the design and the
adaptation to the use of the company of scholars." Mrs. Widener's husband-to-be,
Alexander Hamilton Rice, A.B. 1898, M.D. 1904, was rather cryptically lauded as
an "explorer of tropical America, who heard the wild call of nature and revealed
her hiding place." Dr. Rice and Mrs. Widener were married on 6 October.
[89] A. Lawrence Lowell to Horace Trumbauer, 10 January 1913.

of the portions of the Yard to be affected before any destructive work is done. Pray don't let any trees come down, for instance, this week.

17 August to 7 December 1912:
From W. C. Lane's Annual Report

On August 17th, it was announced that Gore Hall must be demolished immediately in order to make way for the new building, and that everything — books, reading-room, catalogues, and staff — must be moved without delay. To do this seemed at first an utter impossibility, yet what has to be done can be done, and plans were soon forthcoming for doing it. On August 20th, a beginning was made by shifting books in the Divinity School Library building (fortunately no longer occupied by the Divinity Library) so as to make room for more books from Gore Hall, and other places of storage were sought for and prepared in haste.

Before September 23d, when the term was to open, a Reading Room at least must be ready for use elsewhere. Massachusetts Hall was available for this and had already once before been used for the same purpose — when Gore Hall was remodelled in 1895 . . .

Several plans for the accommodation of the books and staff were discussed — the moving of the East stack as a whole further east, the erection of a temporary building close to Massachusetts Hall, and even the building up of a bookstack under the seats of the Stadium. The suggestion . . . that Randall Hall [90] should be used, proved to be the right one, and here about two-thirds of the books from Gore Hall have been placed. For the other third, space was found in other college buildings and in the new and commodious library of the Andover Theological Seminary, where the Trustees generously provided shelf room for some 90,000 volumes in addition to the groups which had already

[90] Randall Hall, which until 1964 stood at the end of Divinity Avenue near Kirkland Street on the present site of William James Hall, was built in 1898–99 at a cost of $100,000. Of this sum, $70,000 derived from a gift made to the College by the trustees of a "charitable corporation" constituted under the will of John Witt Randall, A.B. 1834, and his sister, Belinda Lull Randall. Originally the building was intended as a dining hall to provide less expensive fare than that offered at Memorial Hall. President Eliot maintained (*President's Report* for 1898–99) that "a frugal student, who has good judgment in the selection of his diet" could eat at Randall for "not more than $2.50 a week," taking advantage of the "combination meals" which cost 14 cents for breakfast or luncheon and 16 cents for dinner. In the long run, however, Randall was not a great success as a dining hall, and the inconvenience caused by its transformation into a library stack was not so great as one might think. Other sites, including the new freshman halls, helped take Randall's place and by the time Widener was finished Randall was no longer needed as a dining hall. It became in 1916 the headquarters of the Harvard University Press and Printing Office. The Press gradually moved out of the building after 1932, but the Printing Office remained in Randall until its transfer in 1964 to its new quarters beyond the Stadium. Then Randall was demolished, but a tablet in William James commemorates the Randalls and the former hall.

been placed there the year before. Emerson Hall, Robinson Hall, the Fogg Art Museum [later Hunt Hall], Lawrence Hall (occupied by the Department of Education) and the Museums each were able to receive the collections most appropriate to the uses of the building . . .

The main body of Randall Hall is one large room, 90 x 66 feet and about 35 feet high, with tall windows on the two long sides, north and south . . . We found that we could build a stack four stories in height . . . capable of holding some 400,000 volumes . . . One of the difficult problems of the game was for the carpenters to clear out the shelves and rip up the floor of the old stack, pressing close upon the heels of the men who were moving books, and then to work this material into the new stack in time for the books to be shelved. It was almost as if we were forced to hold the books in our arms while floor and shelves were being torn out of one place and built into the other. The fact that we had made a beginning by using the other depositories first and so gave the carpenters a start before we began at Randall, alone made it possible.

For moving the books, open wooden boxes were used, about four and a half feet long and fifteen inches wide, with strong handles at each end. A crew of men in Gore Hall, working under the direction of one of the young men familiar with the shelves, placed the books in these boxes in precisely the same order in which they stood on the shelves and numbered the boxes in succession. They were then passed through a window and slid down a chute outside that ended in a platform at just the height of the automobile truck which carried them to Randall. Each load consisted of twenty-four boxes . . . At Randall another crew of men took the boxes from the truck and carried them in by number to the shelves, where the books were put up in the same order in which they stood before . . . From thirty to forty thousand volumes were moved each week, the count running up to fifty and fifty-five thousand volumes, respectively, for two weeks. Other libraries have moved into new buildings much more rapidly than this, but considering that the construction of the stack was going on at the same time with the moving, and that the new stack could be built only as fast as the old one was dismantled, the record seems a good one . . . The first books were moved to Randall Hall on October 10, and the work was practically completed December 7, about 350,000 volumes having been put in place.

As soon as the books began to disappear from Gore Hall, where the delivery desk still remained open, an electric runabout was put into commission and made the rounds of all the depositories three times a day, bringing back books for which requests had been left at Gore Hall, and taking back to their places books which had been returned there by borrowers. In this way, throughout the moving, no books were inaccessible, except those which were actually in transit, and we could maintain what, under the circumstances, was considered a reasonably prompt service . . . On Saturday, December 7, the book moving having been finished so far as the stack in Randall Hall was concerned, the delivery counter and other furniture were taken over to Randall, and the impedimenta of the catalogue department were transported at the same time. On Sunday most of the men of the staff assembled either at Gore Hall or Randall Hall, and with everyone's help the 3382 trays of the public catalogue and of the Library of Congress file were safely moved from one building to the other. It was no small task . . . but the next morning the library opened in Randall Hall ready for service as usual. The other portions of the staff moved over at intervals of a day or two, and suffered no serious interruption in their work.

23 September 1912: A. C. Coolidge to A. C. Potter

College begins today, that is to say, the undergraduates come up to register and swarm around the Yard. The Reading Room in Upper Massachusetts is entirely ready and will be open tonight. In Lower Massachusetts the last volumes were got in this morning, but the electric light is not yet completely installed so that the room will have to remain closed in the evening for a day or two. Book moving is proceeding steadily, if not extraordinarily fast. So far we have been lucky in our weather. Lane has not yet received any indication that his presence is wanted in Philadelphia [to see Horace Trumbauer and his firm], which I tell him is in keeping with their previous conduct as regards myself. He is worrying over a new idea of having the Delivery Room in the basement and the places two flights up reserved for Treasure Rooms. So far my attitude is not sympathetic. Our electric vehicle to carry books arrived this morning, but we have not yet had the necessary carpentering done to it . . .

16 October 1912: A. C. Coolidge to A. C. Potter

My suggestion that we may close the Library during Christmas week and get the staff and catalogue out at that time still looks to me the most probable thing. Book moving has proceeded steadily, thanks to the almost uninterruptedly fine weather we have had. It has been rather a complicated job owing to the difficulty in keeping the carpenters going far enough ahead of us, especially as they have needed the floors and shelves here in order to make progress themselves. Of course we have not proceeded quite as fast as we had hoped but the result on the whole is satisfactory. We have moved all of the West stack, except Economics, newspapers, and some of the History sections in the basement and we have made a beginning on the sixth floor of the East stack. We go back to it this afternoon, and henceforward shall proceed regularly floor after floor from the top down . . . Trumbauer turns up again tomorrow. I wonder what he has up his sleeve this time.

6 November 1912: Memorandum from A. C. Coolidge to A. L. Lowell

In the discussions so far the difficulties have been to settle satisfactorily three main points, — first, the number of studies and cubicles; second, the amount of stack space; third, the quarters for the staff and the various special rooms. If the architect is able to provide for the minimum requirements on which we are insisting, we can accept his plan as eminently satisfactory and feel nothing but gratitude. What we wish for is:

First, 80 studies and 350 cubicles.

Second, stack space (as technically counted) for 2,500,000 volumes, and this without counting what may be put along the walls of certain rooms or the space necessary for a newspaper collection, and without sacrificing space in the basement necessary for many miscellaneous purposes.

Third, the plans last presented, with such modifications as were approved by Mr. Lane in his visit to Philadelphia, may be accepted as adequate to the needs of the staff and the administration of the library, and to the department and other special rooms, but no further encroachments on this space should be made, for it is not abundant now.

13 November 1912: A. C. Coolidge to A. Lawrence Lowell

. . . Of course the thing as a whole is very splendid, even after every subtraction has been made, so that we are filled with gratitude and enthusiasm whatever disappointment we may feel in detail when we compare the present plans with the earlier ones. Of the three points that I spoke of in my memorandum I think we can regard the question of administrative quarters and everything of that sort as satisfactorily settled, provided they are not further tampered with. The two other matters are rather serious. First as to stack accomodation [*sic*]. The plan accepted by the Overseers as a Report from our Committee of Architects, which has been our starting point since that time, provided for a building with shelving for 2,370,000 volumes, and this exclusive of all basement space which was to be reserved for miscellaneous storage and also exclusive of any shelves that might be put up about the walls. This figure was reached after considerable discussion and was accepted as being ample, but not extravagant. The total reached by Mr. Trumbauer, 2,114,784, includes a first tier in the basement holding 244,300 volumes, and I think some 50,000 volumes to be put on shelves that he has put in the storage rooms. Omitting these two items, we get roughly stack space for 420,000 less than the plan approved by the Overseers. Secondly, as we count the studies and cubicles on the plan we find 79 studies which is only one less than your minimum, but only 192 cubicles, which is very much less than what we asked for, in fact so much less that I feel as if we must have made some mistake in counting, although I do not see where it comes in. The number of cubicles could be increased according to the present plans, but only at the expense of the stack. We may estimate each cubicle as representing stack room for 575 volumes, so that another one hundred or more taken at their expense would mean further serious reduction.

The easiest way to enlarge the building without greatly disturbing the plans would be as you have urged to lengthen it. It is for the architect to judge whether this would seriously interfere with the proportions and appearance of the side. The elevations and internal arrangements would remain practically untouched, so that the work of changing the plans would be comparatively slight. If the building were lengthened by twelve and a half feet, that is to say, by one bay, we calculate that we should gain additional space for eight studies, twenty-four cubicles, and about one hundred and forty-seven thousand volumes

Harry E. Widener.

Harry Elkins Widener who (as reads the plaque placed by his classmates in the entrance hall of the Widener Memorial Library) "loved the books which he had collected and the college to which he bequeathed them— 'He laboured not for himself but only for all those who seek learning.'"

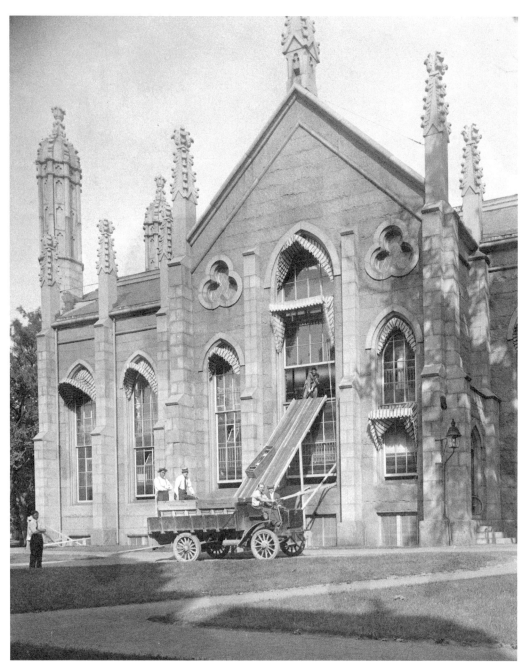

Early October: Sliding the books down the chute to the loading platform.
The books moved at the rate of 40,000 to 50,000 volumes a week from
Gore (above) to Randall.

British documents stored temporarily
in Massachusetts Hall.

Frank Carney, unsung hero of the move
out of Gore and into Widener.

Gore Hall in process of demolition, revealing "the first example of a
modern library bookstack," which had been installed in 1877.

Photographs by W. A. Boughton

Excavation for the Widener Library, looking toward Emerson Hall and
President Lowell's house.

(147,000), which would be an appreciable consideration. Twenty-five feet would give us twice as much.

We regret that it was not found possible to make any connection between the central portion and the sides across the light court, even on the ground floor.

14 November 1912: A. Lawrence Lowell to Eleanor Elkins Widener

Mr. Trumbauer has sent the latest plans to us, and they have been examined by Mr. Coolidge and Mr. Lane of the Library, as well as by me; and, while I need not tell you again how grateful we are for this superb Library and for your generosity in giving it, I think it would hardly be fair if I did not report what I said the other day, that we are somewhat disappointed at the amount of reduction in size over the earlier plan. The tentative plan of the Board of Overseers of the University two or three years ago, with which you are familiar, contemplated a building for 2,370,000 volumes, exclusive of the space in the basement, and also exclusive of shelving in the reading rooms. According to Mr. Trumbauer's letter to me the stack space in the present plans is for 2,114,784 volumes, including roughly 300,000 in the basement and reading room shelves; so that the stack space is less by 550,000 volumes than the plan approved by the Overseers. Mr. Trumbauer's earlier plan provided for about 3,000,000 volumes, or quite as much, if not more, than the plan submitted to the Overseers.

Moreover, the study rooms and cubicles for professors, students, and visiting scholars, which are one of the distinctive and most admirable features of this Library, have been reduced in this last plan. The number of studies is nearly as large as before, but several of them are not in close contact with the stacks, and the number of cubicles has been reduced from 350 to 192, as we count them. Perhaps 350 was unnecessarily large, but 192 would seem inadequate.

The reduction in the height and width of the facade of the building is a distinctive advantage, but the reduction in length would not appear to be necessary. Mr. Trumbauer is anxious to keep the south front of the Library well back from the street, but that would not seem to be important in view of the fact that the Library is separated from the street by a fence, and of the fact that the principal and monumental front is on the other side. An increase of the length of the building by a couple of bays would decidedly increase the stacks, cubicles and studies. Such a change need not affect the interior court at all, or the exterior except in lengthening the centre part of the side; nor would it involve much delay, because it would not alter the arrangement of the rest of the building.

Of course, it would add to the cost, and that is a thing of which I feel that I cannot speak. Your generosity has been so great that we should lack good sense and good feeling if we asked you to increase the expense of the building beyond what you felt inclined to do; but, on the other hand, I know that you would not forgive me if I did not tell you of our apprehension that these plans, although magnificent for the present, would fulfill less completely the needs of the future than those that Mr. Trumbauer submitted to us before.

I would not write this letter did I not know that with your knowledge of affairs you would understand entirely what I mean and why I write it.

25 November 1912:
A. Lawrence Lowell to the Fellows of Harvard College
PLAN APPROVED BY OVERSEERS

Cost: $2,000,000. (No costly features.)
Contents: 2,400,000 volumes.
Area: 300 × 210 ft.
  ”   1st Plan of Arc.   282 × 206 ”
  ”   2nd Plan of Arc. 272 × 206 ”
  ”   3d Plan of Arc.   253 × 194 ”
          Contents (3d plan) 2,114,784 vols.

The President submitted the new plans for the Widener Memorial Library on a somewhat reduced scale, and it was voted [by the Corporation] to accept them on the same terms as the sketches formerly submitted.
(Regular Vote)   OF RECORD
                                                      Nov 25 1912

26 December 1912: Ellis Ames Ballard [91] to A. Lawrence Lowell

Mr. Adams [92] sent me some days since a copy of the report of the Treasurer of Harvard University, and also specific answers to the questions I asked with regard to the amount of the general endowment fund and the income therefrom. With this information at hand Mrs. Widener has decided to draw the deed of trust so that this fund shall be kept separate and apart from the general endowment of the University until it reaches, by accretions and re-investments, the principal sum of $200,000, when Harvard may add it to its general endowment fund . . .

I have also redrawn, at Mrs. Widener's direction, the clause relating to the appointment of the curator, and have provided that the curator shall be nominated by Mrs. Widener and his salary fixed by her, but shall receive his appointment from Harvard. . . .

[91] Ellis Ames Ballard (1861–1938), Philadelphia attorney and graduate of the University of Pennsylvania (A.B. 1881, LL.B. 1883) served for many years as general counsel of the Philadelphia Rapid Transit Company in the creation of which the Elkins and Widener families had played a financial role. He was a collector of books and prints. He was the senior partner of the firm of Ballard, Spahr, Andrews & Ingersoll. The letter quoted refers to endowment and other arrangements for the Memorial Room and the collection described in the Widener-Harvard agreement.

[92] Charles Francis Adams (1866–1954), A.B. 1888, LL.B. 1892, LL.D. 1929, served as Treasurer of Harvard College from 1898 to 1929 when President Hoover appointed him Secretary of the Navy. He was President of the Alumni Association in 1933 and, after retirement from the Cabinet in 1933, served as Chairman of the Board of the State Street Trust Company.

I have added a clause that the rules and regulations respecting the collection shall prohibit any of the books being taken from the two rooms specially set apart as a memorial — except of course for repair, etc. . . .

I am having the papers carefully copied for execution and will send you two copies, duly executed, in the course of a few days.

31 December 1912: The Widener-Harvard Agreement

AGREEMENT entered into this (thirty-first) day of (December), One thousand nine hundred and (twelve) (1912), between ELEANORE [93] ELKINS WIDENER, of the Township of Cheltenham, County of Montgomery, State of Pennsylvania, hereinafter called the DONOR, of the first part, and THE PRESIDENT AND FELLOWS OF HARVARD COLLEGE, a corporation, hereinafter called HARVARD, of the second part.

WHEREAS, Harry Elkins Widener, a graduate of Harvard of the Class of 1907, was lost upon the sinking of the steamship "Titanic", and by his last will and testament bequeathed to his mother, the Donor hereunder, his library of rare books, and in his will expressed his desire that the said books should ultimately be given to Harvard University whenever proper permanent arrangements could be made for the care of them; and

WHEREAS, the Donor in carrying out the wishes of her son desires also to establish for him a perpetual memorial at Cambridge by erecting a library building which shall not only house the special collection of her son but also the general library of Harvard.

Now THEREFORE, in order to carry out the purposes hereinbefore outlined, and in consideration of the covenants entered into on the part of Harvard, the said Donor, Eleanore Elkins Widener, hereby covenants and agrees as follows: —

FIRST: That she will at her own cost and expense cause to be erected and completed upon the site hereinafter mentioned (being part of the grounds owned by Harvard and set apart by Harvard for this purpose), a library building in substantial accordance with plans and specifications which have been prepared by Horace Trumbauer, architect and submitted to and approved by Harvard. These plans and specifications are made a part hereof and are numbered "Work" No. 2176; "Sheets" Nos. 1 to 30, inclusive, and are identified by the signatures of the Donor and of the President of Harvard. The Donor reserves the right from time to time as the building progresses to make minor changes in the same, and Harvard has appointed its President as its agent and representative to approve of such changes.

SECOND: Harvard sets apart for the location of the said building the present site of Gore Hall and gives to the Donor the right, at her own expense, to demolish the same and to make use of any salvage in the erection of the new

---

[93] This document and the family genealogy spell Mrs. Widener's name with a terminal "e"; however, she appears to have dropped the "e" for her personal use and consistently signs herself to President Lowell without the "e." In his various Class Reports her second husband, A. Hamilton Rice, also consistently lists his wife's name as "Eleanor."

building. Harvard also gives authority to the Donor to do grading and land-scape work on the grounds in the immediate vicinity of the new library building to complete and set off the same, all of which work is to be done at the sole cost and expense of the Donor.

THIRD: The said building shall be known as the "Harry Elkins Widener Memorial Library". The Memorial Hall and the room immediately in the rear thereof, as shown on said plans, are set apart exclusively as a memorial room and a library for the collection of rare books of Harry Elkins Widener, and this collection, together with such books as may be added to it by members of the family of the Donor, shall at all times be kept separate and apart from the general library of Harvard, and no part of said general library shall at any time occupy those portions of the library building specially set apart hereunder.

FOURTH: The Donor further covenants and agrees upon the completion of the said library to give to Harvard the collection of rare books bequeathed to her by her son as aforesaid. These books are to be cared for in the portions of the building specially set apart as aforesaid, and there is to be at all times a special curator or librarian in charge of the same.

FIFTH: In order to provide for the expense of the said curator, for keeping the said books in good condition, and for maintaining that portion of the library building specially set apart for these books as aforesaid, the Donor has set apart certain securities of a value of approximately One hundred and fifty thousand dollars ($150,000), which are the subject of a declaration of trust executed immediately following the execution of this instrument. While reserving to herself as Trustee of the said fund during her lifetime the custody and control of the said investments, she, the Donor, agrees that she will appropriate the entire net income therefrom to the expenses aforesaid, to wit, the salary of the curator or librarian, maintenance of the books and of those portions of the building above specified. If the said fund is not sufficient for those purposes the Donor will make up the deficit. If there is a balance left over she reserves the right to expend it in the purchase of additional books to be added to the said collection or to capitalize the surplus income and add it to the principal of the fund. Upon the death of the Donor Harvard shall be substituted as Trustee of the said fund, the principal of which shall thereupon be paid over unto it without any further action by will or otherwise on the part of the Donor. Whereupon Harvard shall assume the expense of paying the curator, maintaining the said books and the said portions of the said building, but Harvard is not, out of the said fund or otherwise, ever to add anything to the said Harry Elkins Widener collection. Harvard accepts the said fund as sufficient for the said purposes. In any year that there is any surplus of income it shall be added to the principal of the fund until said fund reaches the sum of Two hundred thousand dollars ($200,000). Thereafter any surplus income may be applied by Harvard toward the maintenance and operation of the library building generally.

SIXTH: The Donor reserves the right to nominate the custodian or curator in charge of said Memorial Hall and memorial library and to fix his salary, the formal appointment to be made by Harvard. Upon the death of the Donor the right to nominate shall devolve upon her oldest living child for the time being. Upon the death of the Donor's last surviving child the right to select and appoint the custodian and fix his salary shall vest absolutely in Harvard.

Harvard herewith accepts the gift of the said library building and of the said collection of books, and of the said endowment fund, subject to all the terms and conditions set forth in this paper and in the declaration of trust herein referred to, and does agree that it will maintain the said library building in good condition so that it may remain a perpetual memorial for the said Harry Elkins Widener; and it particularly agrees that it will not permit any structures of any kind to be erected in the courts around which the said building is constructed, but that the same shall be kept open for light and air; and that it will not make or permit to be made any changes, additions or alterations to the exterior of the said building or to the portions of the building hereinbefore specially set apart, to wit: — Memorial Hall and the library room in the rear thereof, or in the entrance halls on first floor and main stairway to second floor. The rules and regulations governing the custody and use of the books comprising the collection of Harry Elkins Widener shall at all times provide that the said books shall not be taken or removed from the two rooms specially set apart in said library building for the custody thereof and as a memorial as aforesaid, excepting only when necessary for the repair or restoration of any volume, and that at least once in each year an inventory of the said books shall be taken in order to ascertain that none are lost or missing.

IN WITNESS WHEREOF the parties have caused this instrument to be duly executed and delivered the day and year first above written.

Signed, sealed and delivered   Eleanor Elkins Widener
    in the presence of: THE PRESIDENT & FELLOWS OF
Ellis Ames Ballard   HARVARD COLLEGE
F. W. Hunnewell 2d [94]   By A. Lawrence Lowell
                                         President

January 1913: A. C. Coolidge to A. Lawrence Lowell [95]

There has not been at any time an interruption in the use of the books. All have continued to be accessible, except a few rare ones which have been sent to a safe deposit vault. The 350,000 volumes in Randall can be taken out as quickly as of old. Those stored elsewhere are reached three times a day by a small specially fitted electric automobile, which brings them to Randall to be given out at the regular delivery desk and takes them back when they have been returned. The interval between the time of application for a volume not in Randall Hall and its delivery from the desk there is at worst only a few hours.

[94] Francis Welles Hunnewell, A.B. 1902, A.M. 1905, A.M. (hon.) 1933, was Controller of the University, 1912–1920, and served as Secretary of the Corporation from 1913 to 1918 and from 1919 to 1934.

[95] Sixteenth *Report* (1913) of William Coolidge Lane, Librarian, p. 3.

31 January 1913: W. C. Lane to A. C. Coolidge

Your steamer letter came this morning and I am glad to have so full a statement of your plans. I have not had time to read them carefully a second time
yet, because just then the telephone from the President's office rang and I was
summoned over to see the plans, and that took most of the morning. There is
no change except those suggested but the cutting down of the South stack is
more than necessary I believe and rather serious.

3 February 1913: A. Lawrence Lowell to Ellis Ames Ballard

I enclose one copy each of the Indenture and Deed of Trust both signed by
me. I am also sending one copy of the general and framing plans for the library.
I have to suggest to Mr. Trumbauer, who, I believe, comes on this week, some
minor alterations in the plans which do not affect the memorial rooms or the
approaches thereto . . . They are none of them very serious.

14 February 1913: A. C. Potter to A. C. Coolidge

Since you left (and perhaps because you have left) the Library has been
unusually quiet and peaceful . . . Gore Hall is now nothing but a pile of stones
and rubbish mercifully concealed by the high fence which surrounds the site
of the new building. Among the papers I am sending you by this mail you will
find a copy of the Crimson describing the rather foolish ceremony of turning
the first sod. Mrs. Widener herself got as far as Boston, but was detained there
by a cold, so she did not come out to do the digging, but let George [Harry's
brother] do it. As it has been very cold for the last few days the ground had
been softened by a bonfire kept burning over it for forty-eight hours and over
the spot softened a tent was erected to keep off the snow storm that we had
to mark the day by. Your friend Trumbauer was very much in evidence during
the performance jollying the newspapermen and posing for their cameras.

The final plans as given to the contractors arrived last week. There are very
few changes made in them, the most important one being in the length of the
shelves in the stacks . . .

29 May 1913: A. C. Coolidge to A. C. Potter

If you have had cold and rainy weather in Paris, all you need to do is to
multiply it a few times in order to know the sort of climate we have been
having here during the month of May. It is the coldest month of May that I
remember in this part of the world, but personally I enjoy it.

There is not very much to report about the Library. Things are going on
steadily, but nothing startling has happened. We shall soon begin the grand
work of changing numbers on the cards in the fixed shelf locations . . . I wish
I felt more complete confidence in either the rapidity or the accuracy of the
boys, who will have to apply our rather complicated system. I can only hope
and pray that all will be done by next autumn and the Library have settled
down to a more ordinary pace by the time I start for Europe. It is now settled

that I am going to Berlin . . .[96] We are to have the ceremony of laying the corner-stone of the new building in a little over a fortnight. The Phi Beta Kappa are to be present to serve as audience and I have got to make a speech, which bores me beyond words. Work on the hole in the ground is proceeding at last pretty vigorously . . .

29 May 1913: A. Lawrence Lowell to A. C. Coolidge

Mr. Lane has suggested a ceremony which, with my emendations, is as follows:

LAYING OF CORNER STONE OF
HARRY ELKINS WIDENER MEMORIAL LIBRARY
MONDAY, JUNE 18, 1913
at 11.00 A.M.

————

President Lowell presides
Opening Remarks by the Director of the University Library
Laying of Corner Stone by Mrs. Widener
Address by Mr. Justice Swayze, President Harvard
Chapter of Phi Beta Kappa [97]
Singing by Chorus or Choir

————

How does this strike you? It seems to me that it is probably rather better not to submit it to Mrs. Widener, unless she has requested us to do so. It might frighten her.

16 June 1913: A. C. Coolidge —
Remarks at the Laying of the Cornerstone of the new Library

Mr. President, Mrs. Widener, Ladies and Gentlemen, and Brothers of the Phi Beta Kappa. This is a notable day in the annals of Harvard. We are assembled to witness the laying of the corner stone of a building that will not only surpass in its splendid proportions any other that has been erected for us in the two hundred and seventy-seven years of the life of Harvard University, but it will also fill a long felt and grievous want, for it will furnish a place where our students can make the best use of every volume helpful to their education; a home for the treasures of learning and literature that have accumulated here

[96] From mid-October 1913 until the end of February 1914 Coolidge was lecturing at the University of Berlin. He gave two courses, one on the history of United States foreign policy (twice a week), the other on fundamental problems of international politics (once a week).

[97] Francis Joseph Swayze, A.B. 1879, LL.D. 1916, Justice of the Supreme Court of New Jersey and the state's "foremost jurist," twice served as President of the Harvard chapter of Phi Beta Kappa, and was a Harvard Overseer from 1909 to 1915 and from 1917 to 1923. He was President of the Harvard Alumni Association, 1915–1916.

in the course of generations, making those treasures accessible under ideal conditions to scholars and investigators and book lovers in future days. Thus our most crying need is the one that has been most generously met.

But our deep gratitude on this occasion is sobered by the recollection that our good fortune has come to us under the shadow of an appalling calamity. The great monument to be erected here will commemorate a son of Harvard, who while still in his earliest manhood met a hero's end in one of the most touching tragedies of modern times. Life had seemed to hold out to him the fairest promise. Secure in the affection of family and friends, — for he had won the respect, admiration and attachment of those who knew him, free from the harsh necessity of toiling for his daily bread, he could pursue the scholarly interests that were dear to him and gratify the refinement of his taste. A lover and seeker of the rarest books, and familiar with them in their minutest details, he had gathered together in a brief space of time a collection of choice volumes that has but few equals in the whole world. This collection that was so infinitely precious to him is coming by his desire to the University from which he had graduated not five years before. It will remain as a memorial of his love for his College in the centre of the superb edifice which will henceforth bear his name and which will link it imperishably with that of Harvard. With these thoughts in our mind we now thankfully but gravely greet the moment of the laying of the corner stone of the Harry Elkins Widener Library.[98]

20 June 1913: A. C. Coolidge to A. C. Potter

I think the dedication ceremonies went off satisfactorily. Commencement celebrations and so on are just over, leaving me to settle down to this summer's work of which I have a plenty. I shall not be able to devote much time to the Library, but doubtless enough to interfere with the other things I ought to do . . .

13 August 1913: A. C. Coolidge to Walter Lichtenstein

There is not much to report on the Library now. The new building is going on very rapidly at the present time. Something like fifty thousand bricks are being put into it every day. Otherwise this is the dead season. I alternate between Cambridge and New Hampshire.

15 August 1913: A. Lawrence Lowell to Eleanor Elkins Widener

On my return from Europe I am delighted to see the progress that has been made on your library. It is literally growing out of the ground, and it does look great in proportions, suggesting the vast services it will render to scholarship in the future.

You were here, I am told, the other day, and I hope you were satisfied with

---

[98] A rough draft of Coolidge's proposed remarks is in the Library files in the University Archives. This version, in part rather strikingly changed, was published in the *Harvard Graduates' Magazine* XXII:85 (September 1913), 212.

the way it is getting on. They have just begun with the stonework on the northwest corner, and as soon as they get this started along the front, the visible progress will show fast, and the impression of the whole building will become evident.

13 November 1913: W. C. Lane to A. C. Coolidge

I sent you a "Crimson" two or three days ago with a notice of the strike in progress on the Library building. I am glad to learn this afternoon that the strike is declared off and that work begins again tomorrow morning. About four days have been lost — an unfortunate loss just now — but they have been making very good progress . . . The work on the stack has not been interrupted and the uprights have reached the top story almost all the way along . . . I was notified last week that the illuminating engineer would appear on Wednesday of this week but so far . . . nothing has been heard of him. I have been working busily on laying out the equipment of the several rooms and their needs as to lighting . . . Until I tried to fit in tables and desks I did not realize how much the building had been cut down from the original plans on which our first estimates were made. It is really very difficult to get in what is needed. For example, — the Main Reading Room was 44 x 136 feet, now it is 40 x 124. The Catalogue Room was 40 x 52, now it turns out to be 35 x 42, and it is as much as ever that I can get in as many catalogue cases as we ought to start with . . .

28 November 1913: W. C. Lane to A. C. Coolidge

Mrs. Widener and her friends and Mr. Trumbauer were out here on Saturday morning. She has a fixed idea that the Library will contain about three million volumes and Trumbauer, I notice, does not discourage it. Figures seem to play no part in it.

7 December 1913: David Heald [99] to A. C. Coolidge

Here is the latest news of the new Library . . . Ordinarily I drop in two or three times a week on my way to work in the morning & look around casually to see what is going on, but yesterday I made a systematic exploration, from the bottom to the top. And going to the top now is a very different story from what it was when we used to visit the building last summer. You go up ladder after ladder, and you walk on floors much less secure than those we had in Gore last year; the iron girders are usually in place, and an occasional plank laid carelessly across them serves for a floor. You look down through the gaps between the planks and pray that you're sure-footed — for its [sic] a very long way to the bottom. On the whole though I suspect that you're safer on top

[99] David Heald (1882–1945), who graduated from Harvard College in 1904, served the Harvard Library for sixteen years and was Superintendent of the Ordering Department from 1912 to 1919. He then resigned to enter the travel business in Boston and was associated with Raymond & Whitcomb Company until his retirement in 1939.

than down below — down below you stand a fair chance of having half-a-brick hit you on the head; one missed me yesterday by less than a foot.

The front of the building, meaning the north wall and the east and west walls as far back as the north line of the light courts, is now practically done as far as the outside walls go. The north east corner & the eastern half of the north side has reached its height and a couple of days should bring the rest to the same point. A couple of the roof trusses in the north-east corner are in place. The east wall is done to and including the limestone cornice, the south wall about as far, and the west wall to, but *not* including, the cornice. If the weather holds good the roof of the front part ought to be well along by New Years; the roofing of the stack is less pressing.

The skeleton of the stack is done to the top; some of the stairways have also been put in . . .

12 December 1913: W. C. Lane to A. C. Coolidge

At the building they tell me that the brickwork to the top of the 3d story will be finished on the E. side on Dec 16 (six months from the cornerstone) and practically done all round. Iron trusses for the roof are already going up on N.E. corner and the roof will be on by Jan 15 if weather is favorable and the building heated in February. They all seem to be in good humor.

15 December 1913: David Heald to A. C. Coolidge

Now that we have got the hang of things we are not far behind you in efficiency in the management of the weather. It is still unseasonably warm and work on the Library goes on without interruption. The place is as active as a bee hive — bricklayers on exterior & interior walls, stone cutters at work on the capitals of the front columns, concrete layers putting in floors, iron & steel workers placing beams & trusses for the roof . . . and ventilating pipe fitters on the lower floors — and I dare say several more trades scattered about . . .

20 December 1913: W. C. Lane to A. C. Coolidge

The third story is practically complete on three sides of the building. The compressed air machine is installed now so that the carving of the capitals goes on rapidly and the roof is well started.

4 January 1914: David Heald to A. C. Coolidge

The Library has reached a point where the growth from day to day is not obvious at a glance. The floors — concrete — are in the front part up to & including the reading room storey. The roof is not yet on but the framework is all in place. On all sides except the back the walls have reached the top; the limestone coping that finishes them off even is in place. I like the sides rather better than the front, but the steps will no doubt alter the appearance of that part a good deal.

In Randall things go on. You will see from my figures that orders have picked up a good deal over last year . . . There have been no considerable gifts that I think of, either of books or money . . .

9 January 1914: W. C. Lane to A. C. Coolidge

Work continues to go on rapidly. We have had some freezing weather but nothing severe yet. It makes me a little uneasy, however, when I ask Mr. Eliot, the foreman, about laying bricks in freezing weather to have him say "Oh, we cover them up at night and take our chances on it" . . . There is no one on the ground to represent the architect. The iron trusses for the roof are complete over the Reading Room and the east side, and will soon be put up, I have no doubt, on the other sides. The roof supports over the Widener Rooms are also nearly complete, as I noticed yesterday. Stag, of the Snead Company [installers of the stacks], was here yesterday . . . They are somewhat disturbed over the progress of the rest of the building because the builder is hurrying to complete the roof instead of laying the floor of the third story, and they cannot make any further progress on the stack until the floor . . . is laid. When that is done they can clean down the work and begin to put on the shelf supports, but they cannot begin to paint them and they cannot put down any marble until the plastering of the ceiling and walls is finished . . .

Did I write you that I had discovered that the elevator between the administrative rooms and the stack which is shown on the plans as opening on the Shelf Department, Catalogue and Delivery Room floors, as well as at the different floors of the stack, had been cut off from both the Delivery Room and the Archeological Room level by a heavy iron beam across where the door would come? . . . Also I discovered that for the book-lift at this point no opening had been left in the floors . . . Now that the Catalogue Department floor is in I see where we can get additional window and floor space . . . and I am trying to present the matter in a reasonable light to Trumbauer . . . It will give us room for at least four more desks . . . besides a little other leeway . . .

12 January 1914: A. C. Potter to A. C. Coolidge

I am afraid I shall have to give up the Colonial Club as a lunch place, for every time I go there I am besieged with demands to know just when you are to return. Lest you may feel too much flattered by this anxiety on the part of the college world to see you again, let me hasten to tell you that the main reason for its eagerness is because the whole faculty is getting uneasy about their studies in the new building. And the assignment of these rooms is a question that should be taken up if possible immediately after your return . . . One other thing is giving me some uneasiness and that is the question of furniture. Nothing more has apparently been heard from Mrs. W. on the subject than that she will provide fixtures, such as built-in bookcases and delivery desks. My own feeling is that she will also give the reading-room tables and chairs, but not much more. . . .

22 January 1914: A. C. Potter to A. C. Coolidge

Between half and three-quarters of the roof is on the new building, but several inches of snow yesterday is delaying things a little. Trumbauer has not been on for several weeks, nor has he deigned to reply to several important letters that Lane has sent him.

26 January 1914: W. C. Lane to A. C. Coolidge

Work on the building has been held up seriously the last fortnight by extremely cold weather, the roof unfortunately having been only partly finished before the cold came on — 9° below by the thermometer at first and only occasionally above freezing since that time.

7 February 1914: W. C. Lane to A. L. Lowell

You may like to have a memorandum of changes made or proposed in the plans of the Library, both those which we have asked for and those which Mr. Trumbauer has made without reporting to us, also other matters relating more properly to equipment and so not shown on the plans and specifications. As yet we know nothing definite as to how far Mrs. Widener is willing to go in regard to equipment.

I have blue prints from Mr. Trumbauer showing definite changes on his plans in regard to the points marked *. These he has sent on from time to time for information or approval, and I have given approval or have indicated in what way they needed modification. I think, as I said yesterday, that these points ought to be accepted as already approved, without further action by Mr. Trumbauer, and that we ought not, by treating these points as still lacking your consent, to give him an excuse for disregarding what suggestions and requests I may have occasion to make in the future. The question of the expense of changes already made has hitherto never come up. This, Mr. Trumbauer passed upon as he has done in regard to all other matters, contracts and all. About expense we have known nothing from the beginning, and we have no means of controlling it.

Of course, now that you learn that changes are being made in the specifications in regard to quality of material and the excuse is given that the expense of other changes has made them necessary, you are justified in inquiring about the expense of the other changes. Why not ask Mr. Trumbauer simply to report on the cost of these specific changes if they amount to anything, and to state what other changes he refers to. I suspect that he will bring up the mechanical book-conveyor which really *is* a large item (about $20,000) and which, being technically *equipment*, did not figure in the plans and specifications but which has been insisted upon by us from the beginning as necessary in some form. If the main difficulty is here I should favor sacrificing one part of this device (which seems to me less important) for the sake of keeping the rest which seems to me of vital consequence.

**Memorandum of Changes Made in the Library Plans Since the
Contract between Mrs. Widener and the Corporation was signed.**

I. Changes made by Mr. Trumbauer without notice to us.

The elevators in the main corridor reduced from two to one.

The partitions through the Shelf Department and Catalogue Department rooms have lost their large central openings so that the two parts of these rooms are much more distinct than we expected. This change was only discovered by us after the walls were actually built, and we were told that the position of the sewer underneath made the change necessary for strength.

The shelving in the stack has been reduced by one entire floor and by leaving out about one-sixth of the shelves throughout the rest. On plans only the lowest story of all is shown in skeleton; the other nine stories being shelved in full. Each section is represented as having either six or seven movable shelves; the number has been reduced to five movable shelves and we have only eight stories shelved —

The plan of the two Widener rooms has been entirely changed involving much heavier foundations and thus diminishing the available space on the first floor and ground floor.

The plan of the stairs from the second to the third floor in the northwest corner of the building has been greatly changed, seriously diminishing the size of one Seminary Room and of three studies. This appeared first in the re-drawn plan of the third story. We expressed our regret for the change but could not well do more.

II. Changes proposed by us which have been embodied in the plans or agreed to.

The shelving in the Reading Room has been increased by making the cases between the windows higher and by introducing cases under the windows. I think I have not seen this change actually embodied in any plan.

* The stairs in the stack, both east and west, have been opened into the third floor.

* A shifting of toilet-room accommodations in the ground floor was made, involving one additional seat but probably no other additional expense. The change was made necessary by the enlargement of the foundations at this point.

The locker-room for the ladies is still very inadequate and I have lately proposed another change which involves the cutting of one door through a heavy wall already built, the addition of one short partition and the stopping up of two doors. This latter change I have not yet heard from.

* The re-arrangement of rooms on the third story. A re-drawing of the plan of this floor was expected from the beginning, but certain points have perhaps involved additional expense. viz. Partitions to be partly in glass; A case for the storage of roller maps built into the map-room; doors from one room to another throughout so as to use any two adjoining rooms together if needed; access by stair-way from the Business School Reading Room to the

upper story of the stack a portion of the upper story being cut off from the rest of the stack.

* The stairs and elevator openings between the west stack and the Administration Rooms have been re-arranged. The first suggestion was, I believe, by the architect but it was gladly accepted by us as a distinct improvement.

* A book-lift at the south side of the Administration Rooms connecting Shelf-Department, Catalogue Department, Delivery Room, Art Room and third floor. This seemed to be necessary as we studied further the problem of distributing books.

An additional hand-basin at the level of the Stenographers' Gallery. I am not sure whether this has been accepted or not, but I was asked by Mr. Bechtel to indicate my preference as to its position.

III. Other suggestions or changes not yet acted upon so far as I know.

Prismatic reflectors in the stack, such as are used in the Albany State Library, giving admirable light on the tops of the books from top to bottom. These reflectors are probably rather expensive.

A simplification of the partitions in the Order Department giving more floor space and easier access between Order and Catalogue Departments, and would, I should suppose, save expense rather than increase it.

A change in the partition wall at the south of the Catalogue Department which gives floor space for at least four more desks and protects the Shelf Department below from troublesome draughts coming from the stack which would make the room quite unusable unless a part, at least, of the changes proposed were carried out. A little additional expense is involved here but I should think it must be well under one hundred dollars.

The elevator at the back of the Administration Rooms should open on the third floor as well as on the floors below. Possibly this involves a change in the roof to give sufficient height. I will try and find out about this from the makers of the elevators, who, I learned today, are a Cambridge firm.

IV. Matters of equipment not shown on plans or included in specifications.

From the stack plans in the Snead office we discovered that the light switches in the stack were at one end only. We called Mr. Trumbauer's attention to this and they have been changed so that lights can be turned on or turned off at either side of the stack.

The Color of the Stacks.

Mr. Trumbauer asked us whether we preferred dark green or light gray. We replied in favor of the lighter color, of course, and understood that Mr. Trumbauer preferred this also. I have since learned that this involves additional expense.

Card-holders on the end of the stack rows were included, I am told, in the stack specifications at first as an integral part of the stack structure. They were cut out from the contract but still have to be provided from some source.

The Mechanical Book-Conveyor.

This has been under discussion from the beginning and several different schemes have been worked out. The plan now in Mr. Trumbauer's hands, with its accompanying pneumatic tubes, costing about $20,000, will, I hope, be accepted. Mr. Trumbauer wrote to the Lamson Co. that if they could bring their estimate down to this figure it would be satisfactory.

Catalogue Cases for the Public Catalogue upstairs.

I have sent a statement of our needs and general lay-out of the cases including 4000 trays. My impression is that they intend to put in these cases, but I have no definite statement from them. I have also sent specifications in regard to the equipment of the Periodical Room with about 800 trays for unbound periodicals and two cases for current numbers. These plans follow out and improve upon plans which were sent to us from the architect's office, indicating that they intended to provide at least the cases for current numbers.

Most of the above details of equipment involve considerable expense. The catalogue cases would no doubt cost over $5000. The equipment of the stack with card-holders, book-supports, etc., Mr. Stag tells me this morning, will be about $9000. The mechanical carrier, as already stated, costs $20,000.

Nothing has yet been said or done in regard to the tables or lights in the Reading-Room, and so far as I know, no designs for them have been drawn, though I discussed with Mr. Milnor of Mr. Trumbauer's office the kind of light required. The specifications and plans for light, electric bells, telephones, etc. which I have lately examined and returned to Mr. Trumbauer say nothing in regard to fixtures or lamps; they are concerned solely with wiring.

10 February 1914: W. C. Lane to A. C. Coolidge

Lowell called me over to his office the other day to tell me of a letter from Trumbauer & to read me his own reply. Burke [Walter Safford Burke, Inspector of Buildings and Grounds] had told him that cheaper materials were being substituted for the heating system than what the specifications called for. Lowell wrote to Trumbauer about it & T. replied that the changes demanded by Mr. Lane were so expensive that he had to make up for them in this way — an absurd excuse which the Pres. saw through of course. His answer to T. however did not please me but I could not get him to make any substantial change in it — His object was to force T. to give him a detailed account of the expense & so he fell back on the clause in the Widener-Harvard contract that changes must be approved by the Pres. in writing. None of these had been, hence T. must send him plans & specifications in regard to them. It seemed to me that this put me into a hole & I frankly said so, for he has sent me certain blueprints which I have approved or modified as the case might be & these I insisted ought to be accepted as already approved. He found no fault with me for the action I had taken & disclaimed any idea of embarrassing me, but all he would do was to add a postscript that these changes would be approved as soon as they were presented. This seems to me poor policy & likely to be troublesome in the future. I am willing to be sacrificed if I deserve it if anything is to be gained thereby — but this simply brings us to a situation where T. is likely to snap his fingers at us & feel entitled to disregard our suggestions completely . . .

13 February 1914: David Heald to A. C. Coolidge

The roof is on — as I've written you several times — & there are several gangs at work but the results of their labor are not particularly obvious — nothing like those of the happy days when swarms of bricklayers were on the job & the building grew visibly between morning & night. But I suppose it's all in the days work & is a stage that every building passes through. Perhaps by the time you arrive things will have got into a happier condition; at any rate it will be warmer then — we've just gone through a ten below zero spell of weather — and better weather for steam fitters and such tribes . . . If you strike these parts on Sunday let me know. I'd like very much to be on hand when you first explore the Library.

24 March 1914: A. C. Coolidge to Walter Lichtenstein

For me the tremendous question is the one of finance. How are we going to move into the new building, how are we going to run it when we are in, how can we buy any more books, or catalogue them when we have got them, — all these things seem crowded on me in overwhelming mass. At times I feel rather hopeless and bewildered. At any rate I never was in a position where I could do less to turn daydreams into realities, and I look forward without enthusiasm, it must be confessed, to a time of sailing very close reefed . . . Even my private finances are crippled . . .

15 May 1914: A. C. Coolidge to Walter Lichtenstein

[The new building] certainly is imposing and dominates the part of the yard that it is in. So far the looks are a great success. The exterior including the steps is now completed, and work is going on actively indoors. We have given up all idea of having the dedication this spring. My guess is that the whole building will practically be finished by some time next autumn, or let us say, by the end of this year. As I shall hardly be able to begin my book moving before next October when the term will have started, I shall probably proceed in a pretty leisurely manner instead of hurrying as I did last time. At any rate, I need not decide on this for some months yet.

16 June 1914: A. C. Coolidge to Walter Lichtenstein

One thing that complicates matters is our increasing difficulty from lack of space. Randall Hall is getting crowded to its utmost capacity, and anything opened elsewhere is distant from the catalogue. I am hoping to have one room in the top floor of the new building ready for me in the course of the summer, perhaps in time to put the Lanza cases [100] in it, but as I say, if I open them

[100] The Lanza Collection was a library assembled by Donato Lanza y Lanza, particularly strong in Bolivian pamphlets and newspapers, which Walter Lichtenstein

"Mr. President, Mrs. Widener . . . This is a notable day in the annals of Harvard."
Professor Coolidge speaking at the cornerstone ceremony, 16 June 1913.

Laying the cornerstone of Widener Library.
Above: Mrs. Widener flanked by President Lowell and Professor Coolidge.
Below: The workmen lower the cornerstone into place.

The Widener Library under construction, 4 December 1913.

The cedication of the Harry Elkins Widener Memorial Library, 24 June 1915.

there, I do not see how I am going to compare them with the catalogue, but this is only one of many questions I have got to work out.

As I said in my last letter, the Library is booming as far as accession of books is concerned . . . Yesterday, the Phi Beta Kappa procession walked past the new library, and I thought with some satisfaction that only a year ago they assembled there to consecrate the laying of the corner stone. Progress has certainly been rapid, and the result so far is most excellent, but many long months will pass before we are fully established.

10 August 1914: A. C. Coolidge to Walter Lichtenstein

We are in the middle of midsummer stillness. Work at the new library goes on actively, though with no very apparent rapidity. I should not wonder if a number of the marbles and things of that kind were to have been brought over from Europe. In that case, if they have not arrived already . . . they will upset all calculations. It is indeed hard to talk or think of anything at this moment besides the war.

31 October 1914: A. C. Coolidge to Walter Lichtenstein

Work on the stack part of the new library, which has been held up for months by a strike, began again day before yesterday. Unless there is fresh trouble, the building ought really to be done by Commencement, though most of our book moving will have to be put off until next summer. The war still occupies . . . a great part of people's thoughts and conversation.

25 January 1915: A. C. Coolidge to Robert F. Herrick [101]

My congratulations on your new appointment as Chief Marshal for Commencement. It means a good deal of drudgery, but it is always an honor. I do not know how soon you will take up the preliminary work in connection with your office, but I want to put in a word early about a matter which is of much importance to me, and I think to the University.

Mrs. Widener would like to have the dedication of the new library take place on Commencement day. It seems to me that there is every reason why her wish should be gratified, and that the occasion should have as much eclat as possible. It is the largest gift the College has ever had, and deserves the fullest recognition on our part. The question is how it could be worked in

was able to purchase as Harvard's agent during his South American buying trip in 1913–14 because the Bolivian Government could not at that time afford to spend the funds to keep the collection in Bolivia.

[101] Robert F. Herrick, A.B. 1890, Boston lawyer and Chief Marshal of his College Class, was probably most notable in Harvard history for his long-time support of rowing. He brought to Henley the famous 1914 second crew which won the Grand Challenge Cup. He coached the 1916 varsity and second varsity crews which beat Yale. He was instrumental in obtaining the land and securing funds to build the crew training quarters at Red Top on the Thames near New London. Herrick also served as Overseer from 1915 to 1921.

with other parts of the Commencement program. It has occurred to me that perhaps the procession could start a little earlier than usual (there has always been some waste of time there) and march first, followed by all the graduates, to the steps of the library, and that there short ceremonies could be held; one reason for the shortness being that in the speeches that will take place behind Sever, there will doubtless be a number of references to the library, which would be a good reason to give for not taking too long on the spot itself. Another suggestion that has been made is that the speaking this year should be not behind Sever, but from the library steps. I do not know whether this is practicable, but it seems to me worth considering. I expect to turn over to George P. Winship, the newly appointed Widener Librarian, the running of the whole affair as far as the library end is concerned. When you have thought the matter over and can spare the time, perhaps we three, and I suppose John Warren,[102] might meet together and discuss things.

12 February 1915: A. C. Coolidge to G. L. Kittredge

I find I have no note whatever of what the English Department is likely to want in the way of seminary rooms in the new library besides the Child Memorial Library room and perhaps one of the Shaw rooms for Baker's courses. What between Shaw having accepted and the growth of the Business School, I am getting a little worried whether we have space enough to meet all legitimate demands.[103]

26 March 1915: A. C. Coolidge to the President and Fellows

. . . There seems no reason why the expenses of the Library [for general oversight, cost of books and binding, accessions, classifying and cataloguing] should be much affected by its moving into the new building. What does and will affect them is the steady growth of the institution and in particular of the Funds and Bequests devoted to the special purchase of books, not to speak of

[102] John Warren, A.B. 1896, M.D. 1900, Assistant Professor of Anatomy, was the University Marshal and in this capacity responsible for the official arrangements for Commencement and other important academic occasions of the University. Warren would normally have had charge of the morning exercises, and Herrick only of the afternoon alumni meeting. Winship was the newly appointed Librarian of the Harry Elkins Widener Collection.

[103] George Lyman Kittredge, who became Gurney Professor of English Literature in 1917, was a member of the Library Council and one of the zealots in building Harvard's folklore collection, largely begun by Francis James Child, Boylston Professor (1851–1876) and Professor of English (1876–1896). The "Shaw rooms" were those assigned to the theatre collection, a major portion of which was given in 1915 by Robert Gould Shaw, A.B. 1869, who served as its Curator from 1915 to 1925 and as its Honorary Curator from 1925 until his death in 1931. George Pierce Baker, A.B. 1887, Professor of Dramatic Literature, was naturally interested in a location near the Theatre Collection, while the essentially homeless Business School, still a decade away from achieving its own campus and library building, was eager for book and study space.

gifts of books themselves, sometimes thousands of volumes at a time. This growth we could not stop if we wanted to. All the books that come have to be attended to, and even the looking up, handling and getting rid of great numbers of duplicates is a costly matter . . .

In the new building there will be an inevitable and considerable increase of expense [for circulation, including care of books on the shelves, superintendence of special reading rooms, libraries, maps, etc.]. The distances that the boys who will get the books will have to go will be so much greater than in the past that we shall have to augment the number in order to maintain anything like the not too high standard of efficiency that we had before. It is probable too that the number of books taken out by our students and others will and should greatly increase in our new and improved condition. There will also be an increase in the expense of the superintendence in such places as the Treasure Room and the special libraries. Most of these libraries will be situated on the top floor of the building which is easily accessible to the public and will need watching. A higher standard of availability will be demanded including keeping rooms open at night . . .

In [caretaking] there will inevitably be a great increase and one quite beyond my power to keep down below what is necessary for an ordinary standard of cleanliness and efficiency. It is impossible to make an accurate estimate of what the expense of running the building is likely to be. Only experience can teach us this. I have tried to get at the question in various ways, by estimates as to the amount of work to be done in each particular branch, and by comparison with other large buildings such as the Boston and New York Public Libraries and the Harvard Medical School. The cost of cleaning alone will be many times what it was in Gore Hall. There are a vast number of windows, large halls, great staircases, many rooms, large and small, and some four and a half miles of marble floor in the stacks alone . . .

In this difficult situation, I respectfully . . . request that the Corporation make to the Library for the year 1915–16 exactly the same grant as before, and on the same terms . . . With these sums allotted to me and with what I can save on cataloguing and various extras and present expenses, I will do my best to meet the heavy increased charges . . .

30 March 1915: A. C. Coolidge to G. L. Kittredge

I have been at the library looking again at the sixth floor, for I find that Folklore is down to go there. I do not think it is at all a bad place. In arranging our classifications of books, as we have no longitudinal carriers, we were obliged to put the great groups containing the works most called for by the public — namely, English literature, Economics and American history — as near the delivery desk as possible, and to carry out the rest of our plans more or less in consequence. Folklore is one of our most valuable collections, but one which is comparatively little used by the general public. It was, therefore, natural to have it a long way from the delivery desk. On the other hand it will be easily accessible in the stack, for it will be at the extreme north west end of the floor, which has a door in this place, so that it is very easy to reach from the reading room, as well as from the top story. This was so much the case that at one time I thought of putting the Learned Societies there. Anthropology comes, I think, just under it, and I thought that the vicinity of the Child Memorial Library would also be a convenience. There will be plenty of stalls by the collection itself. I admit that when I went there this afternoon the air seemed to me a little stuffy, but I believe that was due chiefly to the large amount of fresh paint which just now is to be found there and in other parts of the stack.

25 April 1915: W. C. Lane to A. C. Coolidge

I am afraid the *key* man . . . may turn up & him I really want to see for the locks between the stack and the catal. room, Treasure room &c are not of the right type and must be tinkered in some way. They lock the stack against the rooms, but the rooms themselves *cannot* be locked against the stack — i.e. anyone in the stack can at any time enter freely the staff rooms, the Hist. reading room, the Treasure room &c. Was ever anything more stupid? Yet I do not see that the specifications expressed this.

You will be disgusted (as I am) to see the superfluous book-shelves set up in the Catal. Room & *nothing* available for the Bibliog R. Trumbauer definitely agreed to the change on his previous visit, but on Friday (Apr. 16) orders came to put them in according to the contract & the work was finished up instanter. What the hitch was I do not know — very likely irritation on Mrs. W's part at an extra — So there's a good chance lost & extra expense probably thrust upon us. There was no time to protest & protest probably would have been useless.

Mrs. W. & T. were at the Library on Thursday last, but I did not go over there & did not see either of them. I hear that it is proposed to have the dedication immed. after Sanders, but I do not think the President & Dr. Warren [John Warren, A.B. 1896, M.D. 1900, University Marshal] who are at that time occupied with the official reception in Univ. & at the Pres. house realize that you cannot get the crowd together at that time as you can later. It is just in the midst of the gathering in the college rooms & visiting back and forth. This all begins & is in full swing before the Sanders exercises are over, for very few graduates go there any way. The Sanders audience is not the audience we want to catch — it is made up of the graduating class & *their* friends & in moderate number of faculty & overseers but *not* graduates in any number. The procession at two o'clock however gets the great body of graduates, & might get almost all, for everything else is over & everybody would join in for the dedication even if he were not going to the Sever quad.

Burke thinks that rats & mice are rampant in the building & must be vigorously and promptly dealt with as soon as we get possession, and that in advance of that they are a source of danger to our books. I think in the meantime I should keep the basement well supplied with food for them . . .

I have been over the figures again for book-supports & think we can safely pare down this order to $4200 . . . but I think the order should be placed without delay. What more can I say about this than I have said already? Already our work ahead is to be more difficult in that we have not got them *now*. With further delay we shall not be able to have our shelves in good order when the term opens. Think how much this means as effecting [*sic*] the general satisfaction with our condition when work begins. We have a chance still I think to do a good job. Let us not throw it away or let it slip through our fingers. The shelf labels ought to be got at the same time & be finished up this summer.

My total figures after talking with Burke came to about $22000, I believe, but this included $1000 (?) for the map room, and 600 (?) for the standard room. Unless we can find someone to put the whole sum down (which is unlikely) I see no better line to work on than to persuade the Corporation to let us use not more than 25000 of the Sheldon principal & then set about ourselves to limit the amount actually used as much as we can, by getting individual items supplied in other ways as far as we can . . .

Eliot says the opening at the back of the Deliv. R. is actually to be made but they have *painted* and *grained* the walls *dark* Alas, alas.

27 April 1915: A. C. Coolidge to W. C. Lane

I am glad that you are getting a bit of much needed rest, and I wish you could stay at Northborough until Monday, even if there is plenty to do here.

The plan decided upon between the President, Mrs. Widener and Warren is that the Commencement exercises shall begin half an hour earlier, and that after these exercises the audience shall come over to the library, and the opening of the doors take place then. After that there will be a ceremony inside for the unveiling of the picture of Harry Widener with short addresses before the faculty and chief invited guests. The plan may not be ideal, but Mrs. Widener had turned down with some sharpness the previous suggestion, and I gave my approval in advance to anything the others might decide upon . . .

I am having a pretty peck of difficulties on the question of the assignment of room and the end is not yet. Let us trust that the key man will not be here before your return. The various other lapses are quite in keeping with our previous experiences. I have spoken to Carney about the rats and mice.

The main and most important part of my news is that at the meeting of the Corporation yesterday my budget, so the President tells me, was accepted. Until I have got a fuller report and feel sure that there is no string attached to this, I shall not dare breath [*sic*], but it looks as if our first and greatest care were removed. Now as to the question of the extras, I grant that they are much needed, but supposing the Corporation to have given me the full sum I have asked for for running expenses, I am convinced that it would be both useless and unwise to go to them now with any fresh demands whatsoever. It will very possibly be years before I shall feel in a position to ask them for anything, whether from the capital for the Sheldon Fund (which I do not think they would grant) or any other source. We appear to be the only people who are getting, and in generous measure, what we have claimed is necessary for our general efficiency. I am willing to authorize the expenditure of $2,000 for book supports. Somehow or other, we must contrive to find the money for these and also for bulbs for the lights. This represents the limit to which I am prepared to go. All the other things . . . will have to wait perhaps indefinitely. Mrs. Widener has turned down sharply the idea of a Winsor Memorial Map Room.[104] She does not wish for any memorials in the building besides those for her son. All this is not pleasant, but such are the facts, and we have got to accept them.

13 May 1915: A. C. Coolidge to M. A. DeWolfe Howe [105]

I shall try to write an article such as you ask for and have it ready for you by Monday of June 7 [for the special issue of the *Harvard Alumni Bulletin*, 16 June 1915]. As for illustrations, you would better get all permissions from Mrs. Widener. Until Commencement we have no control of the building and only entry by courtesy, so we want to avoid any assumption of control.

I think your idea of suggesting that Mrs. Widener, herself, contribute a few lines to the special number is a good one though I do not believe for a moment that she will consent to do anything of the kind. Nevertheless she may be pleased by the request and may have some suggestions as to the number itself.

24 June 1915:
M. A. DeWolfe Howe recounts the story of Widener's dedication

In order to provide for the ceremony of presenting the Widener Memorial Library to the University, the Commencement program on Thursday, June 24, was begun at an earlier hour this year than usual. The weather was unseasonably cool, and the Yard seemed less filled with graduates than in other years. The presence of women as invited guests at the Library exercises made good the deficiency in numbers . . .

Through the earlier beginning of the exercises in Sanders Theatre, they came to an end at about noon, whereupon the new alumni headed the procession to the Widener Memorial Library. There they massed themselves on each side of the steps, and the President, the governing bodies and members of the faculties of the University, many wearing academic hoods, the new recipients of honorary

[104] Although Mrs. Widener was originally opposed to the inclusion of any memorial rooms other than the Widener Memorial Room, she eventually agreed to the creation of the Justin Winsor map room (see Coolidge's *Annual Report*, 1916). The Farnsworth Room was established during the subsequent academic year.

[105] Mark Antony DeWolfe Howe, A.B. 1887, Litt. D. 1954, edited the *Harvard Alumni Bulletin* from 1913 to 1919 and the *Harvard Graduates' Magazine* from 1917 to 1918. He is, however, better known as an editor of *Youth's Companion* and *The Atlantic Monthly* and as the editor or author of several score works of biography and history, many of them important sources of information on New England life and letters. Among them are biographies of George Bancroft, Charles Eliot Norton, Barrett Wendell (Pulitzer Prize for biography, 1924), and John Jay Chapman. He also edited the five-volume *Memoirs of the Harvard Dead in the War Against Germany* (1923–1924).

degrees and invited guests, approached the doors of the Library. Here Mrs. Widener handed the key of the building to President Lowell, who spoke a few words in acceptance of the great gift to the University. The procession then entered the building, mounted to the outer room of the Widener Memorial, and overflowed to the stairways and corridors. Among the first to enter was Professor A. C. Coolidge, bearing the only remaining volume of John Harvard's bequest of books to the College. Bishop Lawrence opened the ceremony with a brief prayer, followed by Senator Lodge's remarkable address of presentation on behalf of Mrs. Widener. To this President Lowell made a brief response on behalf of the University, and Bishop Lawrence pronounced a benediction. There was not a word too much or too little. On the conclusion of the exercises the building was thrown open to general inspection . . .

Dr. Walcott, president of the Alumni Association, presided over the afternoon exercises in the space enclosed, and covered with canvas, in the rear of Sever Hall. The Alumni Chorus provided the music for the occasion. . . .

Senator Lodge's Address

This noble gift to learning comes to us with the shadow of a great sorrow resting upon it. Unbidden there rises in our minds the thought of Lycidas, with all the glory of youth about him, the victim of

> . . . that fatal and perfidious bark
> Built in the eclipse, and rigged with curses dark,
> That sank so low that sacred head of thine.

But with the march of the years, which have devoured past generations, and to which we too shall succumb, the shadow of grief will pass, while the great memorial will remain. It is a monument to a lover of books, and in what more gracious guise than this can a man's memory go down to a remote posterity? He is the benefactor and the exemplar of a great host, for within that ample phrase all gather who have deep in their hearts the abiding love of books and literature. They meet there upon common ground and with a like loyalty, from the bibliomaniac with his measured leaves, to the *homo unius libri*; from the great collector with the spoils of the world-famous printers and binders spread around him, to the poor student, who appeals most to our hearts, with all the immortalities of genius enclosed in some battered shilling volumes crowded together upon a few shabby shelves. . . .

These are some of the aspects, some of the inevitable suggestions of a library, of a great collection of books. In this place, in this spacious building, they offer one of the best assurances a university can have of strength and fame and numbers, for a great library draws men and women in search of education as a garden of flowers draws the bees. Carlyle indeed went even further when he said "the true university of these days is a collection of books." Such a library as this is not only a pillar of support to learning but it is a university in itself. . . .

It is a great, a noble gift which brings us all this in such ample measure and lays it at the feet of our beloved university. The gratitude of all who love

Harvard, of all who love books, goes out from their hearts unstinted to the giver. . . .

President Lowell's Address

Brethren of the Alumni: I come before you again, after what seems to me a very short twelve months, to render an account of that which has happened in the University within that time.

This last year has been one, like its predecessor, of building. But this year has been a year of the completion of buildings. We have all had the pleasure this morning of going over the Harry Elkins Widener Memorial Library, and certainly that gift is one of the great events in the history of the University. We have felt for many, many years that the condition of the old library was a detriment to scholarship, and I think that if those of you who went over the new library this morning had examined carefully the stacks, you would have found that this library is better adapted to scholars' use than any other library building ever constructed in the world. Not only is there a great reading room, and a good many smaller special reading rooms, for the ordinary students, but there are stalls running through every floor of the stacks for tables and chairs, where men may sit and consult the books, taking them from the shelves themselves as in their own library . . . Then there are about seventy rooms in the stack where professors can work and dictate and receive and instruct their advanced students. There is nothing like that in any great library in the world. And I think when we walked over that library this morning we all felt that it was a rare debt of gratitude that we owed to our benefactress.[106]

24 June 1915: William Lawrence [107] to A. C. Coolidge

I cannot close this day without sending you a word of congratulation. You have received it from many — and you deserve it all. This is one of those instances where *will* seems to have been a determining factor.

You have been so determined that Harvard should have a new Library that it had to come.

Now that it has come and in a way beyond your imagination you must be more than gratified. The detail which you have overseen[?] was felt today in the perfection of the Building and the Ceremony — I am only sorry that you did not have a chance to hold up John Harvard[']s book as a token of succession — With best wishes that all will work out according to your best hopes.

June to October 1915: W. C. Lane on the problems of moving [108]

The new Harry Elkins Widener Memorial Library was dedicated on Commencement Day, June 24th, and the same afternoon the moving in of books

[106] *Harvard Alumni Bulletin*, XVII:38 (30 June 1915), 712–716.

[107] William Lawrence, A.B. 1871, LL.D. 1931, Protestant Episcopal Bishop of Massachusetts, had been elected a member of the Corporation in 1913 and, during eighteen years on that board proved to be one of Harvard's most effective Fellows, particularly in fund-raising.

[108] Excerpts from the Eighteenth Report of William Coolidge Lane, Librarian,

began. Every detail of the process had been carefully planned beforehand, and every group of books had been measured and assigned (on paper) to its place in the new stack. Only a few changes were found necessary as the work progressed. The system of classification of the Harvard Library, whereby the whole is broken up into some 150 groups . . . allows entire freedom in the disposition of the several groups. They may succeed each other in any order that is found convenient, convenience depending in some cases on the natural relations of different subjects, in others on propinquity to delivery desk, to reading room, catalogue staff, and so forth . . . The experience gained in moving out from Gore Hall three years before was most useful. Books from the several outlying buildings were naturally moved first, while those in Randall Hall were taken later, after the staff and its impedimenta with the card catalogue and delivery desk records had been transferred (August 7 and following days).

For transportation we provided in advance 130 open boxes with end handles, 38 inches long (the length of a book-shelf), 15 inches wide, and 10½ inches deep, in which the books were to be packed resting on their front edges and in the order in which they stood on the shelves; and eighteen small truck platforms, 30 by 14 inches, with swivel end wheels, to hold four boxes piled one on top of another, and easily pushed by hand. An auto truck with driver was hired by the day . . . and was kept continuously busy from June 25 to October 7, making from ten to twelve trips a day and carrying on each trip a load of thirty-two boxes. Sixteen men handled the work, — two members of our own staff familiar with the books directed the workers at each end, two men packed the books into the boxes, ten acted as carriers, five at each end, and two rode back and forth on the auto and helped to load and unload the books . . . At the Widener end chutes with rollers were built just inside three of the windows on the ground floor, where three service lifts in the stack could be used to take the boxes to the nearest point on the right floor . . . Each load could be disposed of in the library in just about the time it took the auto truck to go back and bring another load, the empty boxes being ready to be taken away on the return of the truck. The work went on without interruption, and with what speed was necessary, an average of about 46,000 volumes a week being moved. One week we reached a record of 71,492 volumes, and three other weeks saw more than 65,000 volumes transported. In moving out from Gore Hall we handled 530,000 volumes in fifteen weeks; in moving back into the Widener

---

in *Report of Archibald Cary Coolidge, Director of the University Library*, 1915, pp. 28–30. As to Coolidge, "under his watchful eye," Thomas Franklin Currier has recorded, "the gigantic operation moved forward . . . An example of his interest is shown by the way in which he corralled the able-bodied men of the staff and captained them one Sunday morning, when the card catalog was to be shifted to the new building without interfering with its use by the public. He himself headed the human chain that passed the trays along from hand to hand from the old cases out thru the main floor of Randall Hall into the waiting truck" — Thomas Franklin Currier, "Archibald Cary Coolidge," *Library Journal*, LIII:3 (1 February 1928), 133.

Library we took in 645,000 volumes in fourteen weeks and placed them on the shelves allotted to them. By employing an additional truck and doubling the force the work could have been done more rapidly, but would have been more difficult to plan and oversee.

But the moving of the books was only a part of our undertaking. To establish ourselves in working order in the new building required the installation of what seemed an endless number of desks, tables, cases, counters, and other furniture, our problem being to find an appropriate place for every article that we already had in use, and to restrict new equipment to the very fewest items possible.

The main public rooms of the Library are furnished by the generous donor of the building . . . but the work rooms and offices of the staff, the treasure room, and the special library rooms and seminary rooms on the upper floor remained for us to furnish. The result is better than we dared to hope. It is surprising how well our old cases and counters fit into the spaces . . . We have not everything that we want . . . but we have enough to make it possible to begin our year's work unhampered by crowding and by temporary expedients, and with an abundance of elbow-room, air and light, such as we have never known before.

The transfer of the catalogue from one building to the other and from old cases to new was the most difficult part of the whole moving, but was accomplished, almost to our surprise, in a single day. The job was complicated by the fact that we were still in the midst of the reorganization of the subject catalogue, so that not only were large blocks of cards entirely out of the catalogue, but the catalogue itself still consisted of three separate alphabets which had to be merged into one as they were transferred to the new cases . . . All the men and boys of the staff, with some of the ladies and some volunteers from outside, took part. Chain lines passed the trays from the cases in Randall and from hand to hand to the cases in the truck; another chain passed them from the truck through the window in Widener to the case in the lift, and still another from the lift, when it reached the second floor, to the tables and shelves in the reading-room. The two lesser alphabets were moved first (the place and classed catalogues) and the trays were arranged in their proper sequence so as to stand alongside the trays of the main alphabet when that was received. The transfer of the cards, tray by tray, to the new cases began immediately, and before night this portion of the work was complete. The next day the mingling of the three alphabets and the extension of the whole into more open order in a larger number of trays was begun, and this occupied twenty-eight working days.

The trays of the Union catalogue were moved in the same way, but were spread out for some days on the shelves of the catalogue department while the carpenters were moving and setting up the cases which had formerly held the public catalogue and were now to be used for the other . . .

3 September 1915: W. C. Lane to A. C. Coolidge

I am glad you are prolonging your vacation a few days, but we shall be glad to see you back on Tuesday. I have been trying to get together some further notes in regard to the probable expense of moving to supplement what I gave you when you went away, but there have been so many mechanics to look after and so many other calls that I have not yet put them in order . . .

To-night half a dozen of us are coming over to the Library in the evening to see how the reading room lights up. We tried it out only imperfectly, you remember, once last June . . . The book moving goes on satisfactorily, I think. Carney has been able to get in eleven and twelve loads a day recently instead of ten, which means a substantial saving in the end. Carpenters and painters have been busy, and most of the things which affect the well-being of the staff will be in order before they come back. The lower reading room tables have come over and will be taken in hand by the electric light men and the painters as soon as other jobs are out of the way.

We have had wonderfully good weather for work . . .

Friday A.M. The light inspection last eveng was satisfactory, & in most respects we shall be well pleased . . .

September 1915: A. C. Coolidge on "The Harvard College Library" [109]

. . . For the scholar and the investigator, which terms include the professor, the advanced student, the learned visitor, and even the unlearned one pursuing research work, the Widener Library offers unequalled opportunities . . . We aim to make the Library the glory of Harvard, to have it add to the fame and the influence of the University, and to constitute one of the chief attractions to all connected with the institution, whether as teachers or as students, and we also hope that the ever increasing value of its collections and the opportunities for the use of them will draw scholars from near and far and send them back enthusiastic over what they have found and grateful to the name of Harvard.

The dark side to the picture is the staggering cost of running, and running efficiently, as well as in a liberal manner, such a Library as Harvard now possesses. You can live as simply in a palace as in a cottage, but you cannot keep it lighted and cleaned at the same price. Treasures of learning, like other treasures, are expensive things to take proper care of and to make useful to the community. But we need not enter now into the question of ways and means. In its Library, as elsewhere, Harvard has to accept the burden of greatness. It has one of the finest things of its kind in the whole world and one that can and should be of untold value to the University. Whatever difficulties such a possession brings with it, they must and will be overcome. At the present moment the one dominant feeling of every Harvard man in regard to the new Library should be deep gratitude.

17 September 1915: A. C. Coolidge to J. P. Morgan, Jr.

Since I saw you at Commencement time, we have been moving books all summer so the Harvard library is now pretty nearly installed in its present

---

[109] Archibald Cary Coolidge, "The Harvard College Library," *Harvard Graduates' Magazine*, XXIV:93 (September 1915), 30–31.

quarters for the opening of the term which comes week after next. We are now brought face to face with the fact that there are certain essential, or nearly essential things, which we have not got and have no means of getting. Mrs. Widener has done the thing very handsomely, but she was not interested in certain mechanical details of administration, and not unnaturally felt that it was Harvard's business to look after those things itself. We obviously can not go to her under the circumstances. To ask for anything would result in a sharp refusal and perhaps permanent anger. Also I do not see my way to getting anything more from the Corporation. They have agreed to the demands I made upon them for the running of the building for the next year — demands that were large and which were ungrudgingly acceded to. There is the dilemma at present, and I do not know what I am going to do about it.

As a first step, I have had a list made out of some of the things we most urgently need with estimates of what they will probably cost. I may have to make a public appeal on the subject, but there seem to me a number of pretty serious reasons against this, and at any rate I am going to begin by turning to a few people to see if they are willing to help out. I enclose a copy of the list. The things on it are of unequal value and necessity. Perhaps the most pressing of all are the tables and chairs and electric table lamps for the stacks. There is something rather humiliating in having to proclaim to the world that we have 300 stalls in the new library which furnish unequalled opportunity to the scholar and investigator who wishes to come here, but that in order to use these opportunities he must bring his own chair, table and electric lamp. We have a few old tables, but nothing like enough. We also have a certain number of decrepit chairs and the College will lend us more of this kind as a very unsatisfactory make-shift. You have been very generous in the past, which in this greedy world is the sort of thing that stirs up people to turn to you again. I am sorry to have to do so, but I do not see what else I can do in my present situation. Any advice on the subject would be most welcome . . .

25 September 1915: A. C. Coolidge to J. P. Morgan, Jr.

You will hardly need to be told that I am most grateful to you for your very generous gift and the promise of a later one. They and another one that I have received pull me out of a pretty desperate situation. I shall follow your suggestion as to tables, chairs, and lamps, and in general apply the funds I have on hand to the most pressing things. I am a little conscience stricken because I have decided that the estimate on the first item I sent you as to the book supports was too high, but others of the guesses were rather low so that the general total stands. You are so busy these days that I feel that it is kind of you to give me attention at all, but I want to say once more that I am very grateful, not only for the Library but also personally, for your generosity on this and other occasions. By the way, unless instructed to the contrary, as your check is made out to the treasurer I shall assume that the gift is not anonymous.

1 March 1921: A. C. Coolidge to Andrew Keogh, Librarian of Yale University

You are not quite correct in your recollection of what I said about the cost of the Library here. I do not know it and never expect to know. My basis of reasoning is that the original theoretical plan furnished by the committee of architects called for a building that it was estimated would cost about $2,000,000. That plan was cut down twice in size despite my protest, but on the other hand the cellar was made deeper than had been foreseen and we had no thought of gorgeous marble staircases and memorial rooms. During the time of the building we had a long strike and the cost of building materials went up considerably. I have therefore always had the private opinion that the building had cost nearer three million than two and this was what I said to you. As you see, I have little real knowledge.[110]

[110] One official university source gives the total construction cost of Widener as $3,510,000 (*Education, Bricks and Mortar: Harvard Buildings and Their Contribution to the Advancement of Learning*, Cambridge, published at the University, Copyright 1949 by the President and Fellows of Harvard College). At the time the $14,284,276 estate of Mrs. Rice [the former Mrs. Widener] was appraised for tax purposes after her death in 1941, her executors noted that she had given Harvard a total of $1,967,188 in the period from 1916 to 1937. A considerable portion of these gifts must have been for costs incurred during the Library's construction. Therefore it seems likely that Mrs. Rice's total benefaction came to more than $4 million, putting her among the largest donors to the University in the first half of the twentieth century.

Special Collections: "The Strength and Glory of a Great Library"

T
O REFORM a catalogue, to get a new building — these would be aspirations and achievements enough for any library director. For Coolidge, a man of vigorous, unremitting energy and of far-ranging curiosity and common sense, they were but two very important pieces in the total effort to manage books, money, and people, so that Harvard's library could more effectively serve a constantly expanding scholarly world and a community awakening to new horizons.

Utterly dedicated to the importance of building the scholarly collections, Coolidge, as a member of the faculty, had for fifteen years preached the gospel of the Harvard Library and backed it with his personal funds. Now, even more, as Director, Coolidge was in the forefront, seeking donors, scouting sources, giving liberally himself.

Despite the handicaps of inadequate housing and servicing, the search for more books went on. It was a constant struggle to match opportunity and donor. The sharp-eyed Potter and his staff pored over catalogues, consulted with Coolidge. Together they — and in the early years, Edgar Wells or various members of the scholarly community — plotted ways to find the money to pay for the books which Coolidge was convinced the Library should have. What difference if a new building were simply in the mind's eye? What difference if the cataloguing were behind-hand and the storage space wholly inadequate? On sheer practical grounds, the quest for needed books must not lag, Coolidge argued in his first report as Chairman of the Library Council:

> . . . the . . . difficulties, harassing as they are, should never make us lose sight of the necessity of continuing to build up our collections by every possible means. This is not a thing that can be postponed until we are more com-

fortably situated. The price of old and rare books is rapidly rising. Complete sets of the publications of academies and learned societies, of archives, monumenta, and other things of the sort, which the Harvard Library ought to possess in as great numbers as possible, are becoming scarce and will soon be unobtainable . . . There will never be so favorable a time again. The same is true about the building up of collections of old publications, particularly those containing rare pamphlets or early editions. Within a generation, at the present rate, these will fetch prices within the reach only of wealthy private collectors. Every gift that the Harvard Library receives for acquisitions of this sort is as welcome as it is timely.[111]

Augmenting the Special Collections

The whole Lane-Coolidge period was one of spectacular continuous growth of what were then called "special collections." Recognizing that the Corporation's necessarily limited subsidies and the modest income from endowed book funds could not of themselves make the Library great, both Lane and Coolidge continually emphasized to the public the importance and the opportunity which gifts of scarce, important books and pamphlets presented. As Lane wrote in his annual report for 1909–10:

The receipt of repeated gifts for the same purpose and possession of funds the income of which must be used in a restricted field are a welcome source of strength to a library, both because they insure the constant growth of some specialty and because in so doing they lessen the many claims upon the general funds which are the Library's main dependence for purchases in all directions.[112]

Much the same thought found expression in Coolidge's report the following year, his first with the title of Director. Coolidge declared:

It should be remembered that all our collections, with the exception of a very few specially provided for, can be enriched only through the liberality of friends of Harvard. The ordinary resources of the Library suffice at best to meet somewhat inadequately the needs of the various departments for the current scholarly and scientific literature on their subjects. Yet it is the special collections that constitute the strength and glory of a great library, and we must never lose a chance of adding to those we possess, no matter how inadequate may be our present accommodation for them.[113]

[111] *Report of Archibald Cary Coolidge, Chairman of the Library Council of Harvard University*, 1910, p. 5.

[112] *Thirteenth Report of William Coolidge Lane, Librarian*, 1910, p. 9.

[113] *Report of Archibald Cary Coolidge, Director of the University Library*, 1911, p. 3.

It was hard going to find the outside money to make such purchases. There were not many who were willing or able to give so readily and generously as J. P. Morgan, Jr., Coolidge's contemporary and friend, the major donor in the group which made possible the acquisition in 1910 of the Marshall C. Lefferts collection of Alexander Pope's works. This store of treasure — 387 volumes and 128 pamphlets — included all the first editions of Pope's poems, 22 editions of *An Essay on Man*, and 26 of *The Dunciad*. Morgan's part in this acquisition was to be kept anonymous, and even in the matter of a bookplate the Library went to some pains to save money. As Coolidge told Morgan:

> Ordinarily we have to put in a rather ugly printed seal in place of an engraved one unless we are fortunate enough to have been given one specially. It so chanced that we had a book-plate made for another collection, which the donor for some reason or other disapproved of. Accordingly we had the inscription on it changed, and you see the result.[114]

Many valuable books came to the Library without solicitation as gifts or as bequests, but what really pleased Coolidge, Lane, and Potter was to raise small sums for those books which could not otherwise be obtained. A little coterie of supporters gave from ten dollars to a few hundred dollars a year on a regular basis. Mrs. Edward D. Brandegee was a faithful donor of funds for classical incunabula to supplement the Weld Memorial gift of the library of Richard Ashurst Bowie which she had made in 1908. John S. Lawrence, A.B. 1901, when reminded, was always good for ten dollars for biographies of successful men. Professor George Lyman Kittredge annually donated $50 for works on the history of witchcraft. Alexander Cochrane, A.B. 1893, gave repeatedly for Scottish history and literature. James Loeb, A.B. 1888, contributed $100 a year to buy labor periodicals, and Walter W. Naumburg, A.B. 1889, usually had $100 ready for works by or about Shakespeare. The historian James Ford Rhodes gave every year for books on the history of the South. The Dante Society and the Saturday Club made annual donations. There were of course many others, like Harold J. Coolidge, A.B. 1892 (A. C. Coolidge's brother), for works on China, Ellis L. Dresel, A.B. 1887, for German drama, John Hays Gardiner, A.B. 1885, for books on Burma, Edwin S. Mullins, A.B. 1893, for folklore, Horace B. Stanton, A.B. 1900, for Molière, Harold W. Bell, A.B. 1907, for numismatics, Professor Roland B.

---

[114] A. C. Coolidge to J. P. Morgan, Jr., 27 September 1910.

Dixon, A.B. 1897, for Tibet, or J. Lloyd Derby, A.B. 1908, for materials on the Philippines.

The level of giving, however, was relatively low, and it was a special project indeed that could call forth the assistance of a J. P. Morgan, a James A. Stillman or a Robert Bacon. Coolidge had small hesitation in bothering members of the Visiting Committee when he thought the cause was just. For example, in 1912, only eight days before the end of the fiscal year, Coolidge foresaw a "deficit" and turned to Morgan for quick help:

How do you feel about giving me a helping hand at this moment for the running expenses of the Library? The situation is as follows: —

As you know, I have been changing the size of the cards here, which has included a great many extras of all sorts, and have been undertaking a good many other things, without any subsidy from the Corporation, being less fortunate than the Yale Library, who have been getting a special ten thousand dollars a year for the same sort of work for the last half dozen years. I have begged, borrowed, or stolen all that I could to put the matter through. First came your gift of two thousand dollars. Then I laid my claws on some thirteen thousand dollars given by Amory Gardner, and I have fleeced Radcliffe to the extent of five hundred dollars. In spite of this I can see that I am coming out some two to three thousand dollars short at the end of this fiscal year, that is to say, July 1st. This grieves me, but does not surprise me greatly; in fact I have foreseen it for some time, and if need be I am prepared to face the music myself, but I have already given the Library something like five thousand dollars this year for books. This is also the year of my twenty-fifth anniversary, which is you know an expensive amusement, and I have had various other things, so that my pocket is feeling depleted.

You will ask how much longer I am going to keep up this expensive and unbusinesslike gait. My answer is that the work of getting in the Library of Congress cards, on which we have some six extra people employed, ought to be finished by near the end of the summer. We shall not have a large number of miscellaneous expenses and we hope to be able to save several thousand dollars in various directions, so that, although I do not see how I can get my next year's expenses down to the level of the budget given me by the Corporation, I expect to spend a good deal less than I have in the last twelve months, and shall contrive to push through matters somehow. Perhaps within six months the Sheldon fund may be released enough for me to pick up a trifle from it. As things stand, however, I shall be grateful for any help you feel like giving me.

I think I can say with confidence that, though some mistakes have been made in detail, the work of putting through the card changing and a good many other reforms has been accomplished satisfactorily and economically. A few months more will see us out of the woods on our present undertakings, and before we try anything more on a large scale, we shall have to wait on developments in connection with the new Library building, etc.[115]

Morgan responded two days later with a check for $1,000 and sent "a like amount" on 1 August. By 1917 the cost of the tithe exacted by Coolidge reached $2,500. As Coolidge wrote to him (20 June 1917), Morgan's lot was that of "being bled to the tune of twenty-five hundred dollars a year for the Library."

Much of the serious buying and collecting of scholarly books was carried out with Coolidge's financing by either gift or loan, and a very considerable portion of the Library's regular acquisition activity was inspired and often paid for by him. There was scarcely a year in his association with the faculty when he did not spend $2,000 to $5,000 — and sometimes more — on books for Harvard, when he did not finance cataloguing operations, when he did not underwrite some enterprise related to the library. During Coolidge's faculty association the purchasing income for the central library advanced from $19,000 to nearly $70,000 but this sum had to cover all Library purchases. Gift income was much less generous (about $25,000 in the best year, 1927–28), and over the whole period Coolidge's gifts for purchases, particularly in the early years, sometimes amounted to almost half the Library's gift income. Such generosity and ardent interest gave him special force when he appealed to President Lowell to support the recommended appointment of Robert Howard Lord as Instructor in History for 1910–11. With real justification, Coolidge used his contributions to the Library as a partial argument:

Owing to the fact that I have cut down my work in the Department by one half, we are losing that much teaching of history. Unless the deficiency can in some way be made good we must forfeit a part of the teaching in the history of Eastern Europe and of Asia which we have offered for a good many years. This the Department feel would be a serious loss. Not only has the fact that these subjects were taught here helped to bring graduate students to the University but, in the course of the last fifteen years, we have built up extensive collections of books. For the Far East we have perhaps the best working library out of Washington; for Russia and the other Slav countries, the best (not in Slavic languages) in the United States; for the Ottoman Empire and the Near Eastern question, perhaps the best collection in the world. At the present moment three of our recent Ph. D's in history are offering for the Harvard Historical Monographs theses they have written in these fields, and two of the men

[115] A. C. Coolidge to J. P. Morgan, Jr., 22 June 1912.

who come up this year have chosen topics of the same kind. To diminish the attention paid here to Eastern European and Asiatic history would be not only to weaken ourselves in a field which is of great present interest but would mean, to a certain extent, the undoing of much of what we have built up. These are the sentiments, as I understand them, of the whole Department. I need scarcely add that I feel them myself with particular intensity for obvious reasons.[116]

In the face of such powerful support and reasonable argument, Lowell could hardly deny Lord the place, and he served on the faculty for the next seventeen years.

Harvard Agent in Europe

Although Coolidge admitted that Harvard's librarians were "at their wits' ends as to where to house our acquisitions," nevertheless he commissioned Walter Lichtenstein, the Curator of the Hohenzollern Collection, to go abroad again as a purchasing agent for Harvard in the academic year 1911–12. Just at the time of Lichtenstein's departure, E. C. Richardson issued his first version of the "Union List of Collections on European History in American Libraries," [117] and Coolidge directed a quick but necessarily superficial search to discover which of the 2,205 titles on the Richardson list were held by Harvard. Lichtenstein was authorized to locate as many as he could of the missing items — including numerous sets — and to help eliminate duplications in cases where he recognized them. As a result of Lichtenstein's extraordinary memory of what Harvard did and did not have and his unflagging determination to help Coolidge make Harvard the supreme university library in historical and related fields, the trip of Harvard's agent was an unusual success. Not only did he increase the number of Richardson items at Harvard from 1,509 to about 1,900, he was able to help identify many of the remaining 300 as parts of serial publications which Harvard already owned, while a few others were already in Harvard's possession but had been missed in the original check of the list.

"When the job is done," Lichtenstein wrote to Coolidge on 1 May 1912, "there won't be many libraries in the world that take it all in all will equal the Harvard Library as a place to study European history." A week later, Lichtenstein expressed the hope that Coolidge was not

---

[116] A. C. Coolidge to A. L. Lowell, 25 February 1910.

[117] Ernest Cushing Richardson (1860–1939), bibliographer and student of the history of religion, headed the Princeton University Library from 1890 to 1923.

"growing impatient" that invoices were not pouring in more rapidly. "You must remember that I have gleaned the German market pretty thoroughly in years past. What we have not got in German history are to a large extent sets and books, which — to put it moderately — are somewhat scarce. Still, I have been finding much, and . . . not paying high prices."

One of Lichtenstein's greatest coups was the acquisition of the great library of the Marquis de Olivart for the Harvard Law School. Containing nearly 7,000 titles (and about twice as many volumes) the library was so extensive that its catalogue was a standard bibliographical reference work for the field of international law. "Rich in original documents, including some cases of importance of which it contains the single known copy," the collection contained the "complete" works of 16th, 17th, and 18th century writers on jurisprudence and public law, documents and pamphlets relating to the international relations of Central and South American countries and to the Spanish War.[118] But obtaining this great collection on what the Law School Librarian, John Himes Arnold,[119] considered "very favorable terms"[120] seems also to have included some personal responsibility for entertaining the vendor. Coolidge recounted the story to Lichtenstein:

One of your letters had led me to hope that the gracious Marquis Olivart might not visit this country after all. You can imagine my pleasure when I found his card in my office and the news that he was coming again within a day or two. He went down to the meeting of the International Law people in Washington and there had a chance to get hold of Professor Wilson [George Grafton Wilson, Professor of International Law, 1910–1936], who survived the ordeal, but with some difficulty. On his return here I walked him around a little and took him to call on the President. The Law School rose to the situation by inviting Olivart to lunch with them at their Faculty Luncheon, which happened to come that day, and at which the President was present. But they played the mean trick on me of asking me to come around at 2.15 P.M. to take

[118] "Extract from Report of the Dean of the Law School" in *Report of Archibald Cary Coolidge, Director of the University Library*, 1912, p. 29.

[119] John Himes Arnold, A.M. Hon. 1902, served as Librarian of the Law School from 1872 until his retirement in 1913. For Arnold's contributions to the Law School, see Arthur E. Sutherland, *The Law at Harvard* (Cambridge, 1967), pp. 218–219.

[120] Coolidge wrote to Lowell on 5 January 1912 that the total cost of acquiring the Olivart Library was $14,500, including packing and freight, although the Law School Library was prepared to pay as much as $25,000 (plus extras) for it. "The saving we have made has been in large measure due to Lichtenstein's zeal and skill." At the instance of Dean Thayer, Lowell decided to pay Lichtenstein $750 for his work in connection with the purchase.

Olivart away so that they might go on with their business. I did this and
marched him around some more. He showed me his last written agreements
with you and talked of his desire to give lectures here. He also presented us
with a catalogue of the latest additions to his library, explaining that it was a
mistake to think that they were to make up for any insignificant missing volumes. They were really a friendly, gracious gift. I answered politely, but
vaguely. All has gone off well so far. But though I hope our Spanish friend
has about reached home by this time, I have little doubt but that he intends to
favor us again with his presence before very long. He more or less intimated
as much . . .[121]

Lichtenstein was representing several libraries other than Harvard
and was entranced with his responsibility. "I am rather glad," he told
Coolidge in a letter on 22 May, "that the Boston Public Library doesn't
want my services, for I have my hands full as it is. In one week I had 40
letters, 3 cables and 1 postal and that does not include family letters.
You see I am coming pretty close to running a bureau . . ." Lichtenstein suggested, as he had on a number of previous occasions, that the
resultant value of his trips from 1905 to 1912 was a strong argument for
his establishing himself as an American library agent in Europe. Coolidge, however, was unconvinced by Lichtenstein's trial balloons, and
told him, "You have never quite been able to convert me about the
advantages of having a permanent agent in Europe." [122]

From Paris, Lichtenstein went to Italy and Portugal, and Coolidge
expressed pleasure with the results to that point and offered to increase
the purchasing funds:

I think we can manage to allow you about two thousand dollars for Portuguese history, in addition to the five hundred dollars already promised for the
history of Brazil. Of course if you see any very remarkable chance costing
more than that, you can always cable us . . .

Judging by the invoices you have sent or had sent and by the various other
ones in the offing, you are having a most successful time as far as we are concerned. If I were not pretty well hardened, I should be almost alarmed at it;
instead I merely laugh at the alarms of other people. Altogether the record of
the Harvard Library for this year is let us say a progressive one. With an allowance of some forty thousand dollars for wages, etc., I shall have succeeded in
spending about fifty-six thousand. As for the purchase of books, — the largest
amount ever spent before in a single year has been between thirty and thirty-
one thousand. This year it has been forty-seven thousand, and mind you, this
means Harvard College alone, not counting other libraries with such details as

[121] A. C. Coolidge to Walter Lichtenstein, 10 May 1912.
[122] *Ibid.*

the Olivart collection, but where this Rake's progress of mine will end I cannot undertake to say.[123]

Lichtenstein's persuasions to the contrary, Coolidge was not interested in spending money on "Germanistic literature" at that time. His aim was to move ahead with the Richardson list and greatly increase the Library's holdings of Portuguese and Brazilian material. But his acquisitive instincts rose high when Lichtenstein located an important collection of 175 Italian *statuti* and a library on criminology. Lichtenstein reported that "together with what we have had in the Law School and in the Harvard College Library, this collection gives us nearly . . . every edition mentioned by Manzoni in his great bibliography of Italian statuti." [124] Because "the conservative party at the Law School have got the upper hand in the question of buying books on foreign law," Coolidge told Lichtenstein that Roscoe Pound would probably give the *statuti* to the Law School, but, "no matter how wonderful," there was no chance at that time to get consent to purchase the criminology library. Coolidge added:

> Accordingly, I have undertaken to buy the library myself on condition that the Corporation lend me the money, to be repaid to them by June 30th next year. This they have agreed to. I shall then tell the Law School that that library is at their disposition until June 1st at cost price, at the end of which time I shall reserve the liberty to sell it for anything I can get to anyone else. You see the thing is a good deal of a gamble, but I feel pretty confident that if the chance is a remarkable one and the Law School finds itself face to face with the prospect of having that collection go to some rival, somehow or other they will find the means to make the purchase . . . My willingness to run a pretty large appearing risk of this kind brings out pretty clearly what my confidence is in your judgment.[125]

As for the *statuti*, Coolidge found the collection "perfectly splendid" and reported on 26 July that he was "bubbling over with enthusiasm about it."

Portugal and South America

In Portugal, Lichtenstein found "beautiful things for little money," among them "a mass of contemporary pamphlets in Portuguese on

[123] A. C. Coolidge to Walter Lichtenstein, 12 June 1912.
[124] Quoted in the *Fifteenth Report of William Coolidge Lane, Librarian*, 1912, pp. 27–28.
[125] A. C. Coolidge to Walter Lichtenstein, 16 July 1912.

the Seven Years War" which "cost a few cents" and "it didn't take me long to make up my mind about them."[126] All told, Lichtenstein succeeded in spending $7,550 for the Harvard College Library, $1,000 for the Law School, and $350 for the Gray Herbarium out of $15,500 allowed him by Harvard, Columbia, and Chicago.[127] As to his successes with Portuguese and Brazilian material, Lichtenstein wrote to Coolidge on 15 August: "I wonder what *you* will say. *I* think that the lot is un-rivalled and will make the collections outside Portugal look like 30 cts." He was ecstatic about his successes for Harvard and eagerly asked Coolidge if he could not continue in Harvard's service:

> Don't you need an aide-de-camp while your building is going on?!! North-western might give me a leave of absence for such a worthy purpose, and prob-ably by the time your building were finished I would be glad to be back at Northwestern. Think it over. Mr. Potter is away and so I might fill a much felt gap *und wer es glaubt wird selig*.[128]

Coolidge saw the merit of Lichtenstein's suggestion and got him a temporary post with the Library until 1 December 1912. For a few weeks, therefore, their regular correspondence lapsed, except when Coolidge was obtaining a non-resident membership for Lichtenstein in the Colonial Club or receiving critical comments from his "aide-de-camp" concerning the design of the new Library.

Coolidge was extremely pleased with his "very competent book-buyer" — and "very loyal Harvard man."[129] He told Lichtenstein, back at Northwestern, that he hoped the next time Lichtenstein went to Europe for Harvard he would have "five rather than one thousand dollars to dispose of."[130]

For the next few months Lichtenstein was much occupied with try-ing to arrange another cooperative book-buying venture, this time in South America. "Cooperative," for him, meant finding books for Har-vard first and then supplying other libraries. "It is almost a platitude to say that the institution I want to serve is Harvard, and not Yale,"[131] Lichtenstein asserted. The irrepressible Lichtenstein went ahead with

[126] Walter Lichtenstein to A. C. Coolidge, 8 August 1912.
[127] Walter Lichtenstein to A. C. Coolidge, 8 September 1912.
[128] *Ibid*. Potter was on leave of absence for the first half year of 1912–13 and later had to extend this because of his wife's illness.
[129] A. C. Coolidge to A. L. Lowell, 5 January 1912.
[130] A. C. Coolidge to Walter Lichtenstein, 13 March 1913.
[131] Walter Lichtenstein to A. C. Coolidge, 4 April 1913.

his arrangements despite Coolidge's deep concern that the proposal might cause a clash with his old friend, Hiram Bingham, then Assistant Professor of Latin American History at Yale and the prime supporter of Yale's library collections in the field. Largely as a result of his unwillingness to tread on Bingham's territory, Coolidge initially decided to stay out of the South American venture. He had had heavy expenses and had had to "fork up" large amounts for the Library, but after Lichtenstein left for South America on 12 June 1913, Coolidge began to have second thoughts, even though he was feeling the pinch financially. As a result, when Lichtenstein found that it was possible to buy the private libraries of Manuel Segundo Sánchez, noted Venezuelan bibliographer and librarian of the Venezuelan National Library, plus the collections of Donato Lanza y Lanza of La Paz, Bolivia — "rich in Bolivian pamphlets and Bolivian newspapers" — and of Blas Garay of Asuncion, Paraguay — "especially rich in the period of the younger Lopez" — Coolidge again stepped forward personally to make the purchases practicable.[132]

Coolidge emptied his own pocketbook as well as the Library's. "I never was in a position where I could do less to turn daydreams into realities," he confided to Lichtenstein on 24 March. "Even my private finances are crippled by the Sanchez purchase and other things, so I have not a cent to spare for you to get anything in Europe." Yet this was before the Lanza, Garay, and other finds came to light. Describing his Lanza treasure, Lichtenstein reminded Coolidge on 23 April 1914:

. . . only a year ago . . . you sent me a copy of a letter of Bingham . . . that has the following statement: 'We can say without unnecessary boasting that we have the best collection of books relating to South American history and geography in this county.' I think that this is past for all countries, except Peru. Harvard with the Sanchez, Lanza and Montt collections has the best working collection for South America in the U.S.A. . . .

Joyfully Coolidge answered Lichtenstein on 15 May 1914:

Your letters . . . filled me with jubilation. You have made a wonderful strike again, and ought to be feeling as proud as I am pleased. It does look as if Yale would have cause to sit up before we get done . . . We have every cause to rejoice . . . If only our luck and your skill hold out to the end . . . Harvard will have not only a good but a great South American library.

[132] The characterization of the three collections comes from William Coolidge Lane's *Eighteenth Report* as Librarian, 1915, p. 14.

Photograph by John Hopf, courtesy of the
Preservation Society of Newport County

"Miramar"

This Newport residence, designed for Mrs. Widener by Horace Trumbauer, is an ex
ample of the grandiose style which the Wideners' architect applied to most of his building projects, including summer places. It is noteworthy that "Miramar" was built
between 1912 and 1915, the same years during which Mrs. Widener was financing construction of Harvard's new library. On 6 October 1915 she married Dr. Alexander
Hamilton Rice (Harvard A.B. 1898; M.D. 1904; A.M. Hon. 1915), "the country's
first-ranking clubman," who listed "forty-three societies and twenty-six clubs in his
Who's Who autobiography," according to Cleveland Amory, *The Last Resorts* (1952),
p. 231. In this seaside palace Dr. and Mrs. Rice entertained "in the great Newport
tradition," and their annual Tennis Week Balls were "particular bright spots . . .
Shortly after midnight" Mrs. Rice "would disappear and take a nap. Early in the
morning she would reappear and, fresh as a daisy, cheerfully breakfast with the late
stayers"—Amory, *op. cit.*, p. 236.

Alfred Claghorn Potter at his desk in Gore Hall about 1912.

James Buell Munn

Lionel de Jersey Harvard

Turner and Western Americana

One of the most interesting developments bearing on the growth of the special collections in the pre-Widener period was Coolidge's part in bringing Frederick Jackson Turner back to Cambridge. A fast friend of Professor Charles Homer Haskins, Turner had had several terms of teaching at Harvard, but had stayed at Wisconsin as Haskins had not, and was understood to be unhappy with the attitude of the Wisconsin regents toward his preoccupation with research and graduate teaching. In the fall of 1909, Turner wrote, "I had been on the edge of accepting a call to U. of California; — in fact, had practically decided to accept, but had not committed myself, when I was asked by Harvard people to delay my decision."[133] Coolidge was then Chairman of the History Department, not yet officially connected with the Library. As Chairman he wrote President Lowell a long letter about Turner, personally pledging to guarantee Turner's salary for five years (1910–1915) at $5,000 per year.[134] Coolidge's letter to President Lowell illustrates the vigorous way he pursued every opportunity to strengthen Harvard's scholarly stature and how often he acted as the "banker" to make an improvement possible. Arguing for his financial proposal he wrote:

Busy as you are there is an important matter I must bring up as it will need to be quickly settled if we are not willing to let slip a chance which will hardly occur again. For some time some of us have been very anxious to improve the situation in American history here by getting Turner. Good as both Channing and Hart are there has been a great decline in our graduate students in American history and we have fewer of them than we did ten and fifteen years ago while Turner draws large numbers (he has usually about twenty-five in his seminary course) and draws them from everywhere . . . All Turner's pupils I have ever seen were enthusiastic about him. I believe him to be a very strong man, perhaps the strongest professor in history in the United States outside of Harvard. There is no younger man in American history who has so far really distinguished himself in the subject . . .

[133] *The Historical World of Frederick Jackson Turner with Selections from His Correspondence: Narrative by Wilbur J. Jacobs* (New Haven, Yale University Press, 1968), pp. 44–62.

[134] This commitment was conditioned on the Corporation's accepting responsibility for a $5,000 guarantee Coolidge had made toward the salary of another historian and on the Corporation's agreeing to reduce the Turner guarantee if other funds should come in to help bring him to Cambridge. See also Ray Allen Billington, *Frederick Jackson Turner, Historian, Scholar, Teacher* (New York, Oxford University Press, 1973), pp. 237–239 and 281–307.

Of course, it is a drawback that Turner has written so little, that he has founded a school rather than produced much himself. Much of what he has done, however, has been brilliant and I know that he is anxious to devote himself to writing in future. In Wisconsin he has been a great figure, constantly appealed to for all sorts of things. At Harvard he could lead a quieter life and produce more.

A consideration that affects me a good deal, though it is not a department matter, is that Turner is widely known in the West and has influence there. He is identified with the teaching of western history and his appointment here would be regarded as a proof that Harvard meant to pay more attention to western affairs. I believe it would be a very good stroke of policy, not only pleasing our western graduates but the West generally, and that it would draw students from there . . .

I am not sure that we can get him in any case and I feel certain that if he once settles in California he is lost to us. The place tempts him and the climate suits his wife who is rather delicate. The Bancroft library [of Western Americana at the University of California, Berkeley] is an attraction and he will not want at his age to uproot himself again a few years hence. It is now or never. He will be here next week and we shall have a unique chance to get at him then, before he has committed himself. We have no time to lose . . .

We now have the strongest history department in the country, but without Gross [135] it will be very seriously weakened. It seems to me that altogether the best thing we can do to maintain our primacy is by getting Turner to put ourselves head and shoulders first in American history, the subject that attracts most historical students . . . By this arrangement the Corporation will get the services of Professor Turner without incurring any expense therefor in the next six years . . ." [136]

Harvard's cordiality and admiration for his accomplishment (Turner received the honorary Litt.D. at Harvard's 1909 Commencement) overcame Turner's inclination to move to California. His decision to come to Cambridge resulted in a scramble on the Library's part to extend its already distinguished collections of American history to include more Western Americana. Turner was in the forefront of this effort, and his chief ally was a remarkable Massachusetts woman, Alice Forbes Perkins Hooper [137] — "a vast lady . . . whose substantial form

[135] Charles Gross (1857–1909), the medieval historian, a member of the History Department since 1888, had served only one year (1908–09) as the first Gurney Professor before being incapacitated. Regarded by Coolidge as "our greatest historian," he died 3 December 1909.

[136] A. C. Coolidge to A. L. Lowell, 28 September 1909.

[137] See Frederick Jackson Turner, "The Harvard Commission on Western History," *Harvard Graduates' Magazine*, XX:80 (June 1912), 606–611; [Frederick Jackson Turner], *The Harvard Commission on Western History, Charles Elliott Perkins Foundation*, Harvard University, Cambridge, Massachusetts, 1912 — a 15-

was not diminished by loose-flowing dresses and a multitude of scarves and veils" — the daughter of Charles Elliott Perkins, builder of the Chicago, Burlington and Quincy Railroad. Having been informed by Professor Turner that "the collection of material bearing on the history and development of that part of America which lies beyond the Alleghanies [*sic*] is incomplete," Mrs. Hooper decided to increase her annual donation to the Library to $1,000 a year — "as long as I am able to give it" — for the purchase of Western Americana. She requested the President and Fellows:

That I may be permitted to keep in touch with the growth of this particular collection of books, and when material of value & importance is to be had, beyond the aforesaid sum of one thousand dollars, that I may be given the first opportunity to present such material to the Harvard College Library, if at the moment it is in my power to do so, my wish being to gradually build up this collection of Western history & to make it as complete as possible.

That a Book Plate be designed for this particular collection and that the payment of the fund be made in January & July, five hundred dollars each month.

I do not offer this fund unadvisedly but with the knowledge & approval of President Lowell, Mr. Archibald Coolidge & Mr. F. J. Turner who agree that this addition to the Harvard College Library will be of benefit to young men & I offer it in memory of one, who, in his youth, went into the West alone to make himself, he dedicated the best years of his life to the opening up & development of the Middle & Far West, he took a keen interest in young men & believed that they should first of all, know the history of their own country.

He was Charles Elliott Perkins of Burlington Iowa & if I, as his daughter, can help young men to that end, through the Harvard College Library, I shall indeed be gratified . . .[138]

Mrs. Hooper's generosity resulted in 1911 in the creation of a Harvard Commission on Western History, of which both Coolidge and Turner were members, and Edgar H. Wells, the first secretary.

For several years the commission employed an archivist — initially, Professor Archer B. Hulbert of Marietta College from 1912 to 1916, and then Thomas Powderly Martin, Ph.D. 1922, from 1916 to 1918.

---

page pamphlet containing material reprinted from the *Harvard Alumni Bulletin*, XIV:27 (10 April 1912), 430–432; Ray Allen Billington, ed., with the collaboration of Walter Muir Whitehill, *"Dear Lady": The Letters of Frederick Jackson Turner and Alice Forbes Perkins Hooper, 1910–1932*, San Marino, The Huntington Library, 1970.

[138] Alice Forbes Perkins Hooper to the President and Fellows of Harvard College, 8 November 1910.

Although Coolidge played no large role in the work of the Commission except to give it his blessing and general support, Edgar Wells, Coolidge's money-raising associate, helped push the cause until he left Harvard in 1913. He was succeeded by Roger Pierce, A. B. 1904,[139] and it was Pierce who acted as middleman in the strange negotiations which eventually brought to Harvard from Salt Lake City the Eli Peirce collection of 2,653 books on Mormon History.[140] This was one of a considerable number of acquisitions[141] which came to the Library in Coolidge's time as a result of Mrs. Hooper's enthusiasm and generosity and the work of the Commission. Approximately 1,000 books on western history were purchased or donated in the period between 1913 (when the effort really began) and 1917, when the war hampered the Commission's activities.

The sad aspect of the whole enterprise was that, despite the labors of many and the irrepressible buoyancy of Mrs. Hooper, the campaign gradually slowed to a stop. The objective failed to achieve financial support in the East (in proportion to the energy expended) and evoked real hostility in the West, where numerous prospective donors felt Harvard was trying to wrest local treasure for itself. When the war came, the thoughts of all concerned turned to other things. Ray Billington has remarked that "the Harvard University Libraries could not have attained the important place in western history that they maintain to this day had the Harvard Commission . . . not been conjured into being."[142] Realistically he commented that the Commission's end seemed inevitable. "Most college presidents anywhere encourage prospective donors but few are ready to commit the general funds of their institutions to the peripheral 'pet project' of a donor whose gifts are inadequate." Billington concluded:

[139] Roger Pierce (1884–1959), a graduate of Harvard College in 1904, had married President Eliot's eldest granddaughter, Ruth Eliot. Pierce was an important wartime officer of the University, serving as Secretary to the Corporation (1914–1919) as well as Secretary of the Alumni Association, publisher of the *Harvard Alumni Bulletin*, Business Advisor and Business Director of the Medical School, and for one year (1918–19) Acting Comptroller. He was later President of the New England Trust Company.

[140] Billington, "*Dear Lady*," pp. 32–38.

[141] Others were the letter books of Bryant & Sturgis, a hide and tallow firm, the James Hunnewell manuscripts on the Hawaiian trade, the Marshall papers dealing with Hawaii, China, and the Pacific Coast, and the Villard papers and other railroad records. See *Nineteenth Report of William Coolidge Lane, Librarian*, 1916, pp. 9–10.

[142] Billington, "*Dear Lady*," p. 68.

Mrs. Hooper undoubtedly got her money's worth of amusement and self-esteem out of the Harvard Commission on Western History. President Lowell received the initial suggestion amiably enough, on the standard assumption that it could do no harm, would keep Turner happy, and *might* lead to something genuinely useful to the Harvard Library. But the president's lack of continuing enthusiasm was due not only to obfuscated provincialism but to the fact that a thousand dollars a year was not an important sum in the game preserves that he was hunting, especially when attempts to enlist western alumni had led chiefly to outbursts . . .[143]

A letter from Coolidge to John F. Moors,[144] a member of the Corporation, throws light on the successes and failure of Mrs. Hooper's "American History Crusade":

Turner . . . has come here from Wisconsin and is regarded all over the United States as the best-known authority on the subject. His pupils are to be found in almost every important university where it is taught, in fact, he has been the father of a School. He naturally has been deeply interested in the whole enterprise and has seen much of Mrs. Hooper with whom he is on the best of terms. He, too, sees big possibilities in this connection and feels that the opportunity ought not to be thrown away. On the other hand, temperamentally he is not of the "hustler" type — the kind to put much personal push into the enterprise. He is of the scholarly temperament and resents having to give too much of his own time to correspondence . . . He, therefore, has been — and rightly — keen for somebody who should be paid to look after just that sort of thing. But, that somebody must not be a mere clerk but a man of sufficient standing to correspond on even terms not only with presidents of Western Harvard Clubs but with the heads of Western historical societies, — all of which is right and sound in itself but costs money. Incidentally, Turner and A.L.L. [President Lowell] are not fitted by temperament to understand each other easily . . .

Your humble servant . . . has regarded the whole thing as clear gain but . . . is in no way a specialist about our Western affairs or has any great personal interest in them. I merely see that the idea is a big one and well worth while, but I am not the proper person for an evangelist in this connection. To tell the truth, I am sometimes driven nearly frantic between the various parties in a question which, at bottom, is not my affair.

The story of the Western History Commission which has been organized for this enterprise is about as follows. Mrs. Hooper has regularly given money with which we have bought large numbers of books for the Library with results which, from my point of view, are completely satisfactory. Besides this, there has been a general activity in the way of keeping in touch with Harvard West-

---

[143] *Ibid.*, p. 69.

[144] John Farwell Moors, A. B. 1883, was a close friend of Coolidge and his financial advisor.

ern Clubs, picking up documentary and other material and in general playing the Western game. At one time we attracted a good deal of attention and, in fact, provoked hostility. Western archivists began to feel that it was the intention of Harvard to try to get hold of things which they believed should be left in their hands. There has been some little friction and stir, in fact, I think there is no doubt that the existence of our Commission has tended to stimulate local enterprise in document collecting in the West. The more we have done, or tried to do, the greater has been the correspondence to look after and the things to be done hence by somebody, and that has been the difficulty. Turner can not look after it all and does not want to. The same is equally true of myself. The result is we have had various temporary assistants from graduate students and others, who have been paid with money given by Mrs. Hooper. And so matters have dragged on with ups and downs, some results, and much bother, for several years. The time has now come when most people feel that the thing had better be put on a more permanent basis. Either the larger side of it should be dropped altogether or else money should be found to set it on its legs. Mrs. Hooper has always hoped . . . that if the thing were put in an attractive enough form, some of our Western men would take hold of it and set it going. As for the President, he has been kindly and encouraging in his conversations with Mrs. Hooper, but I am afraid she has exaggerated the interest he has ever taken in the affair.[145]

The seeds planted by Mrs. Hooper, Turner, and others eventually bore fruit in a subsequent generation, and it is possible to suggest that such benefactions as that of Mr. and Mrs. Charles Warren [146] were to some extent inspired by Harvard's failure to stir more interest in American history in the 1920s.

There was, however, in the mid-1920s one more chance to strike for gold to enrich the Library's American collection when Harvard inherited the fortune of a great-grandson of General Artemas Ward.[147]

[145] A. C. Coolidge to J. F. Moors, 30 March 1920.

[146] Charles Warren, A.B. 1889, Overseer (1934–1940), and former President of the Harvard Alumni Association, was a lawyer and historian of the Supreme Court of the United States and of the Harvard Law School. He was deeply interested in the promotion of American studies in colleges and secondary schools. His widow, Annielouise Bliss Warren, whose brother and sister-in-law gave Dumbarton Oaks to Harvard, bequeathed to the University the Charles Warren American History Fund which supports chairs in arts and sciences, law, and education, and the American history collections in the Library.

[147] Artemas Ward (1727–1800) was a Revolutionary general whose father founded Shrewsbury, Massachusetts. Ward was prominent in town affairs, served as chief justice of the Worcester County Court of Common Pleas, and was a member of both the Continental and U. S. Congresses. His homestead came to Harvard by the residuary bequest of his great-grandson, Artemas Ward, who died in 1924. When the latter's son, Artemas Ward (A.B. 1899), generously waived his statutory right

Scenting a strong possibility for a major underwriting, Coolidge wrote to President Lowell on 14 January 1926 to express the hope that when Ward money began to come in a portion of it would be used for purchases in American history. "Since the Western History Commission came to an end, our special purchases in that field have almost dried out. Schlesinger and Merk, and doubtless Channing and Morison, would have liked me to ask for more but I believe in moderation." The Corporation, however, did not relish allowing an unrestricted bequest to escape their clutches at a time when the limited funds of the central university account were so badly needed for other more mundane objects such as salaries. Coolidge was "keenly disappointed" by the Corporation's decision. He wrote to Lowell on 26 January one of those long instructive letters which university officers find necessary from time to time to make sure that their particular situation is clearly understood:

I want to say a word more in regard to my application for money from the Artemas Ward Fund, which has just been turned down by the Corporation. I am doing this not in protest, though I am keenly disappointed by the result, but to make the reasons for my request perfectly clear. I realize, of course, the tremendous financial pressure under which the University is laboring, the innumerable and ceaseless demands for worthy causes from every side, and the paramount necessity of keeping whatever is possible for the payment of salaries in the College. I should, therefore, never have asked for any Artemas Ward money if there had not been such an explicit expression of desire on the part of the testator that the name of his ancestor should be widely commemorated. It has seemed to me that there was no way by which General Ward could be recalled to the minds of large numbers of our students more appropriately and permanently than by devoting a small portion of the bequest to the purchase of works on American history with book-plates that should bear his name.

Another point upon which I wish to touch is your apparent impression that, owing to the Dexter and other bequests, the Library is now in a position to purchase all necessary books. I admit that these bequests have made a difficult situation much easier, but apart from the fact that the cost of many books has gone up more than one hundred per cent in the last few years, we have to struggle with the results of our own enrichment. A generation ago the College Library had perhaps four or five specialties which might be called really first class. Today we have a great number and it is these that put us so high up among libraries. But they have been only in small part due to purchases from

to 50 percent of the estate, Harvard received the total remainder, which now amounts to more than $11,000,000. The fund is used University-wide as well as for the Faculty of Arts and Sciences.

any of our regular funds; they have come from a large if uncertain flow of gifts and legacies. Now gifts and legacies will make great collections, but they will not keep them up, and unless kept up to a tolerable extent they soon begin to lose in value. This means that far more kinds of books have to be got than was formerly the case and it is hardly more possible, without a much heavier expenditure than of old, to meet the demands for even the ordinary literature on the vast number of subjects in which the Library is strong and for which scholars consult it than it would be for the University or the College to meet present calls with the income of twenty-five years ago. Even as it is, the Library is not well ahead in a good many respects. Year before last, one of our graduate students went to New Haven instead of coming here because the Yale collection of English literary periodicals in the Eighteenth Century was, and is, so greatly superior to ours. Still, as I say, sorry though I am for the American History people who ought to have more material bought for them, I am not complaining, but merely restating my position which I hope you and the Corporation understand.[148]

Lowell, replying the same day, tried to assuage Coolidge's sense of frustration. "Do not think I do not value the Library or appreciate the need of constant expenditure upon its collections; but we cannot spend the same money in two different ways . . . For the present I feel that keeping up the salary budget in the Faculty of Arts and Sciences is of predominant importance."

Perhaps this decision left the President with feelings of guilt about disappointing the Library. At any rate, Coolidge, with suspicions in that direction, could report his surprise and pleasure to Wells (11 June 1926) when the Corporation decided to allocate to the Library for purchases, with no limitation imposed, the income of the Franklin Temple Ingraham Memorial Fund. This fund, received eight years previously, amounted to $35,000 with accumulated interest. "An amusing feature of the transaction," Coolidge confided to Wells, "is that I am told the suggestion for this use came from the President himself. Perhaps he wishes to console me for having thrown down my application for money from the Artemas Ward Fund for books on American history. I shall, however, keep this reflection to myself. If the American history people heard of it, they would promptly clamor for the goods."

Acquisitions During the War Years

It has been seen that the year 1914 was noteworthy for the South American collections acquired as a result of the Lichtenstein expedi-

---

[148] A. C. Coolidge to A. L. Lowell, 26 January 1926.

tions. The next year, 1915, was probably the most important in the history of the Library; it brought the move into the Harry Elkins Widener Memorial building and the receipt of Harry Widener's notable library of 3,000 volumes. This included some of the major monuments of English letters — a Caxton, the first four folios of Shakespeare, a first printing of *Purchas His Pilgrimes*, a first edition of Foxe's *Book of Martyrs*, and a particularly strong collection of nineteenth-century British authors and extra-illustrated books, many of them copies associated with the author or remarkable for their former owners. The Harry Elkins Widener Collection became — and still remains — the centerpiece and one of the chief glories of Harvard's library.

The year 1915 also brought to Harvard the theatrical collection of Robert Gould Shaw, A.B. 1869, with substantial financial backing as well. When the 35,000-volume theatrical library of Evert Jansen Wendell, A.B. 1882, was received in 1918 — "the largest gift of books in [the Library's] history," said Coolidge — it was possible to form the outstanding Theatre Collection, of which Harvard has been so justly proud.

In 1916 came the Frederick Lewis Gay collection of British and American political tracts, over 4,000 separate items, to be added to what Gay, as Curator, had given to Harvard in his lifetime. Many of these were "of utmost rarity," a total collection of about 6,000 titles. In this period Harvard also received the Lincoln collections of Alonzo Rothschild and William (the "Widow") Nolen, the Jeanne d'Arc collection of Francis Cabot Lowell, and many, many others.

This is but a sampling of a list which could go on and on. Many of the private libraries were the donations or bequests of members of the Harvard faculty and alumni — such as the Persius collection of Morris Hicky Morgan and the philosophy collection of George Herbert Palmer — and would have been given to Harvard under any conscientious director or librarian; but many were inspired by Coolidge's extraordinary breadth of interest and the enthusiasm of those who gathered, promoted, and purchased for Harvard under his irresistible influence.

In contrast to the memorable gifts that marked these years, the Library's foreign purchases were sharply curtailed after the outbreak of the European war in August 1914. Coolidge soon decided that it was time to call a halt to Walter Lichtenstein's activities. The latter, in South America, had been hoping to continue his acquisitions in Europe, but Coolidge was then short of money and the situation on the Continent was too chaotic to promise much from further book-buying at the moment. He wrote to Lichtenstein:

This brings me to the important part of my letter . . . our decisions as to book buying, decisions which I am afraid may not be entirely agreeable to you. We are going to draw in sail and straighten our affairs before entering into any new enterprises. I have to announce accordingly that after the receipt of this letter, you may consider your mission in South America as having come to an end as far as we are concerned, except for such things as you may have started upon before receiving this letter, or commissions that have been sent to you from here before this date. The decision, however, is not likely to affect you in reality. I feel confident that before reading these words you will have spent the funds you have for us, but at any rate you can now look on the job as done. I need hardly repeat that we are not complaining of the results . . .

Secondly what will affect you more directly is our decision not to spend any money whatsoever at present on special purchases in Europe even though you may be going there now. I believe that after the war would be a better time than at present, but whether that is so or not we have made up our minds that we are not going into the book buying business in Europe just at present. I fear this will be a disappointment to you, but it is merely repeating what I wrote to you a while ago.

When shall we see you in Cambridge? By the time you return we hope to have the Lanza books so arranged and looked up that we shall know definitely which ones we want to keep, both of them and of the Sanchez. The valuation of what we desire, and the distribution of the booty must wait for your return . . .[149]

Coolidge, with his many friends in Germany and France, felt the war keenly, and kept hoping that it would soon end. But he was too much of a realist not to make a prompt adjustment and concentrate on the digestive process which necessarily had to accompany the treasures of 1915. Internationally, the war had made book purchasing by mail next to impossible. Coolidge commented in his report of 1915:

The Library has suffered . . . as a result of the European war. Compara-tively few books have been ordered from abroad, and not all of these have come. One of our regular dealers has been killed, another has had to leave the country where he was settled; with another we have placed 196 orders instead of the usual couple of thousand. The number of European booksellers' catalogues that have appeared has been only a fraction of the ordinary output, though as yet the prices show little diminution and profits made on a more favorable

[149] A. C. Coolidge to Walter Lichtenstein, 31 October 1914.

rate of exchange are counterbalanced by increased cost of transportation and insurance.[150]

And in 1916 the story was the same:

The continuance of the war makes it difficult and often impossible to get books or periodicals from most of the European countries, notably from Germany. We do not even know what is written there . . .[151]

The single foray abroad was a buying trip made by David Heald in the summer of 1916, financed by a subscription fund of nearly $5,000 from eighteen alumni. With this sum Heald was able to acquire 1,700 volumes, mainly on English local history and topography and on English literature. He also purchased hundreds of English broadsides and Irish books and tracts and made arrangements for the purchase of works of Irish history and of the writers of the Irish "renaissance." He made contacts with British government offices, so that the Library might receive, for example, the Colonial Office's Official Blue Books and other such publications. Most of the Library's purchasing took place in the United States, however, although orders continued to go to Switzerland, Holland, and France, as well as the British Isles.

One of two library developments in which Coolidge took special interest was the opening of the Farnsworth Room on 5 December 1916, dedicated to the memory of Henry Weston Farnsworth, A.B. 1912, who enlisted in the French Foreign Legion in 1915 and was killed in the Champagne offensive on 29 September 1915. The room, intended for recreational reading, was the gift of Farnsworth's parents. The other development was the creation in 1915 of the Justin Winsor Memorial Room in Widener as a center for the Library's fine map collection, which at that time numbered some 30,000 sheets and 1,200 atlases and bound maps, and contained all the cartographical publications of the United States government and the major European ordnance and geological surveys.

As previously noted, Coolidge himself was on war service in 1917–1919, first as a member of "The Inquiry," the study group of academic and government specialists organized at the instance of Colonel Edward M. House to prepare background information for the use of the future

[150] Report of Archibald Cary Coolidge, Director of the University Library, 1915, pp. 3–4.
[151] Report of Archibald Cary Coolidge, Director of the University Library, 1916, p. 3.

peace conference; later as chief of the American Mission to Vienna and as a member of the Paris Peace Conference staff. He also made a trip to Sweden and Northern Russia for the Department of State in 1918 at a time which coincided unexpectedly with the Allied Expedition to North Russia. These responsibilities, while diverting him from Harvard for the moment, actually greatly helped the Library, for Coolidge always had Harvard on his mind and was constantly on the lookout for opportunities to acquire the documentary record of the prewar and postwar period. He made full use of his wide acquaintance, particularly among European officials, American specialists, and Harvard alumni to assemble as much source material as he could relating to this critical epoch of world history.

Immediately after the war the European money market was greatly upset and Coolidge and his staff suddenly found that the Harvard Library could take advantage of favorable rates of exchange "undreamt of before." Coolidge moved promptly "to make the best use of opportunities not likely to recur" (as he reported to the President in 1919–20) and ordered heavily and profitably in Austria, Germany, Italy, and France despite "violent fluctuations of exchange and . . . the efforts of sellers . . . to counterbalance unprofitable exchange by the imposition of special charges."

He was especially fortunate to find himself on leave from the Library in 1921–22 as a member of the American Relief Administration at a time when it was still possible to buy books and serial publications of the Russian pre-war era. As a result — with the help of associates like Frank A. Golder [152] — Coolidge purchased for Harvard several thousand books on Russian history, literature, and art, as well as priceless runs of scholarly periodicals which were to make the Harvard Library a hardly-rivalled center for Slavic research in the decades ahead.

As might be expected the Russian purchases were conducted under great difficulties, and the benefits which the Harvard Library, the Hoover Library at Stanford, and the Library of Congress gained were often achieved in the face of human turmoil and tragedy. Distinguished

---

[152] Frank Alfred Golder (1877–1929), Russian-born historian, graduated from Harvard in 1903 and was Coolidge's graduate student until Golder received the doctorate in 1909. Their paths crossed frequently thereafter. Both were members of the Inquiry and the A.R.A. staff. Golder became Professor of History at Stanford and later Director of the Hoover Library on War, Revolution and Peace. Thus he was also a rival collector in Coolidge's favorite field.

professors, confronted with exile and desperate for funds, parted with their scholarly libraries in the midst of an incredible inflation which steadily raised the price of the dollar in relation to the ruble.

Once back in the United States, Coolidge had to rely on Golder and others in the A.R.A. to help him locate through dealers and private individuals the scarce volumes he wanted for Harvard. It was a tricky business dealing in unstable rubles. At the rate of 1.5 million rubles to the dollar, American currency went a long way and Coolidge initially got good values. On 11 May 1922 he informed Golder:

> I have written to Adams [Ephraim Douglas Adams, Professor of History at Stanford and Director of the Hoover Library] suggesting that we give each other a first preference on Russian duplicates. He replies that the Library of Congress has a first lien on things bought for the Hoover collection but that he is willing to make an agreement in regard to things bought with other funds. I shall write making this arrangement with him informally . . . I am delighted to hear that our books were due to leave Russia on April 6th . . . The day ours reach this library I shall have the flags put up.
>
> I made out a check for $210 according to your directions . . .

But the economic chaos in Russia had a quick effect on book prices. Only a month later (10 June) Golder was telling Coolidge:

> Prices have gone crazy and you may congratulate yourself on your purchases. The dollar will now bring three millions, and a set of *Starye Gody* were offered me the other day for 600 millions, other books are equally dear and I am not buying. There is not much to buy anyway. You need have no regrets.

To complicate matters, Melgunov, one of Harvard's and Stanford's chief agents, was thrown in prison for two months. This was all a mistake, the authorities claimed, but Melgunov decided to be "done with socialism" and to sell out his socialist collection. He told Golder that "socialism is dead . . . at least the old socialism." "The work on hunting," Golder reported on 13 August, "can still be had if you are willing to pay the price, somewhere between forty or fifty dollars . . . Everything goes up except the dollar. It has been standing in the neighborhood of four millions and does not budge at all . . . Because of the high price of books I am not buying anything except the newer things and they are the most expensive of all."

Coolidge, however, was always willing to risk money for quality and since Harvard's requirements were somewhat broader than those of the Hoover Library he continued to send lists of his wants to Golder.

On 2 October 1922 he wrote:

I wonder if there is any chance that our people at Orenburg could pick up for me a set or any part of a set of the *Trudy Orenburgskoi Uchenoy Archivnoi Komissii*. The thing ought to be distinctly worth having and we have but one stray number (22, 1910). You see my appetite for good books remains unchecked . . . I am afraid I must owe you large sums of money which I shall be glad to pay at any time when I know just how and how much.

The regular contacts between Coolidge and his former student continued until early 1926 when the latter returned to the United States and wrote (in collaboration with Lincoln Hutchinson) his report on his A.R.A. experience, *On the Trail of the Russian Famine* (1927) and in the same year published his bibliographical summary of *Documents of Russian History*. Golder died a year after his mentor.

Collecting in the Twenties

Although Coolidge began in 1922 to be very actively involved in the editing of *Foreign Affairs*, he kept a major part of his time for the Library and its ever enlarging mission. Other than the ubiquitous Edgar Wells, few adherents of the Library were more active and helpful in the 1920s to Coolidge's acquisitions program than James Buell Munn, A.B. 1912. Munn first came to Coolidge's attention when he was still a graduate student. (He received the Ph.D. in philology in 1917.) Through the instance of Kittredge and Greenough, members of the Library Council, Munn was installed in 1916 as the secretary of that body. Although the University's official catalogue listed Munn as secretary for three academic years, in fact he did not serve as such in 1917 18 and 1918 19 because he was on military duty, first in this country and then in France. His interest in and helpfulness to the Library led to his appointment to the Visiting Committee in 1921. For the next six years, until Coolidge's death, the two men had a lively correspondence and many personal contacts.

As a Professor of English at New York University, Munn had a primary interest in strengthening Harvard's holdings in sixteenth- and seventeenth-century English literature, but building a great scholarly library transcended, for him, any special interest in book-collecting. The year 1924–25 had been an undramatic one, but still had brought its share of triumphs. "We are living along here much as usual," Coolidge told Munn in thanking him for a rare French edition of an essay on literature by Gibbon, dedicated to Lord Sheffield. "The Library happens to be worse strapped financially at the moment for the purchase of books than it has been at any time since I have been connected with it, but somehow or other we seem to manage to get things, and things worth while, so I am not complaining too much." [153] Yet the following year was a real sensation — the year in which Harvard inherited the Amy Lowell collection and in which anonymous donors gave Harvard a collection of the works of John Milton and other seventeenth-century poetry in memory of Lionel de Jersey Harvard, A.B. 1915.[154] It was a year of stellar acquisitions through the Clawson sale in New York. All in all, it rivalled in splendor the year 1915–16, in which were received the Harry Elkins Widener collection, the Robert Gould Shaw collection, and the Fearing collection. In the absence of a real Friends organization — then not much more than a hoped-for idea — Wells, Munn, and Coolidge formed an aspiring and tireless triumvirate, locating books, raising funds, and searching for donors. A selection from Coolidge's correspondence in this period provides a record of some of the high moments. Munn was just then in the final phase of completing his Milton collection for Harvard and every shipment of seventeenth-century books and pamphlets relating to Milton's era brought a warm response from Cambridge. Coolidge told Munn on 30 January 1925:

I have just seen the wonderful things which Lowes [155] has brought back here as a gift from you. I have also heard Kittredge burble and declare that they

[153] A. C. Coolidge to J. B. Munn, 2 December 1924. For the small staff of the Order Department, 1924–25 was a particularly difficult year. With Alfred Potter away on sabbatical the burden of running the department fell on "the two Gertrudes" — Gertrude Sullivan and Gertrude Shaw. Miss Shaw, whose responsibility was searching titles and approving purchases, then became Coolidge's right hand in the area of his greatest concern and pleasure. Bright and early every morning and every evening after hours Miss Shaw was kept busy trying to keep up with the flood of queries and recommendations from Wells and Munn in New York. "What are we going to do tonight?" Coolidge would ask Miss Shaw, and then stand by "like an errand boy" while she tried to determine at the highest speed consonant with care if Harvard had the John Milton items in which Munn and Wells were interested. (Interview with Gertrude M. Shaw, 5 November 1973.)

[154] "A beloved alumnus who bore the name of his Alma Mater with true humility and distinction," Lionel de Jersey Harvard (1893–1918) was a lineal descendant of John Harvard's brother. He graduated from Harvard *cum laude* in 1915. As a Captain in the Grenadier Guards, he was killed by shellfire at Arras.

[155] John Livingston Lowes (1867–1945) was Professor of English from 1918 to 1930 and Francis Lee Higginson Professor from 1930 to his retirement in 1939.

were just what we wanted most, "everyone of them a nugget." It is therefore not easy for me to thank you adequately. These days when there is so much foolish outcry about the Harvard of the future being nothing but a Business School, I am rather setting my teeth (though I am on excellent terms with and quite sympathetic to the Business School myself) in the determination to play the game for all I am worth in keeping up certain other sides of the institution with which I am more immediately concerned. We have got a first rate start in many respects and we must not lose it. Such aid as yours is invaluable to us and a real blessing to Harvard. Need I add that I feel a glow of personal pleasure that you are still so loyal to the place . . .

On the same day Munn was writing to Coolidge from his Washington Square office:

Very few of us can do what we would like because of insufficient financial means, but I know that the life-long devotion of men like yourself and Mr. Wells has made Harvard what it is, and I want to help in the library as much as I can. Just recently I wrote Mr. Potter about a campaign in the Elizabethan and Jacobean field for such books. If we lay down a policy for the next twenty years we ought to have a splendid collection, even though we receive no outside gifts, and of course I know your hopes in that regard.

By mid-May Coolidge was full of excitement about the Amy Lowell bequest [156] and wrote enthusiastically to Munn on 21 May, describing a preliminary examination of Miss Lowell's library:

Potter and I went over the other day to look at the Amy Lowell books. The Keats collection is of course superb. There are, besides, a number of interesting manuscripts. Kipling's "Without Benefit of Clergy" (to Mrs. Livingston's delight), Mrs. Browning's "Aurora Leigh," etc., and a large number of autograph letters or things of the sort which we did not have time to look at in detail. There is no list or catalogue of any kind nor is the material arranged in any order except that the most valuable things are in the safe and a good many of the best books are in one corner of the room. There must be a nearly complete collection of first editions of Scott (scattered in two or three places) besides many first Dickens's, Thackerays, Hardys (in great numbers), Masefields, etc. We saw a Milton. Potter thinks it was the eighth title page and that we have it already, but he was not sure. I ran across Johnson's own particular copy of "Rasselas," etc., etc., etc. Even many of the most commonplace looking books are likely to have the signature of the author in them or be interesting for some other reason. The money that we shall get ultimately is to be devoted primarily

[156] Amy Lowell (1874–1925), the poet sister of President A. Lawrence Lowell, died on 12 May, leaving the Harvard Library the privilege of selecting from her personal library any books and manuscripts desired as well as the income from a fund to purchase items related to Miss Lowell's wide range of literary interest.

to association books and manuscripts, particularly of poets. It will amount to quite a tidy sum . . .

On 22 June Coolidge was reporting to Munn a new success in an entirely fresh direction. "We have bought a lot of Bossuet at an auction sale in New York," he told his eager New York friend. "In fact we got so much that the man who got almost all the rest has lost interest and offers to sell us his, which we shall buy if we do not have to give up much more than our original bids. This puts us on the map for another author. We have also ordered a large number of Italian complete sets dealing with things in general, but particularly the Fine Arts . . . If we get them we shall soon be nearly as strong in Italian periodicals as in French and German." Coolidge added the news that John B. Stetson, Jr.,[157] Harry Widener's friend, who had just been appointed to the United States ministry in Helsinki,

tells us to go ahead and order any Portuguese material that we want at his expense. At our own, I have commissioned him to pick up a lot of 16th and 17th century French literature . . . in Paris on the way to his post in Finland. He wanted to do this before but we refused on grounds of poverty. He has, however, been so successful in a previous purchase of this kind and is so important a person to be on good terms with that I told him to go ahead this time. I mean to use Stillman money and perhaps Friends of the Library to help out . . .

On 27 June Munn again sent Coolidge (as he had in a handwritten note of 12 June) intelligence he had gathered regarding alumni support of the Yale Library:

Here is some gossip if I have not already written you. The other day I was introduced at the Brick Row Book Shop as of New York University. In looking over some books I saw one which should have been in the Library and I said to the head man — an Eli — why not put this in Yale? Then he blew up and said that while an occasional man had helped the Yale Library in the past there was no coordination and that it was a hit or miss policy — all of which I took in and hand on to you for what you will, with the addition that we will all play the Dutch game if you want it. I'll be glad to get the early plays as they arise . . . I believe we are going to organize here a very sensible auxiliary for your plans in the friends of the library . . .

Munn had waxed enthusiastic about the Amy Lowell collection and

[157] One of the most steadfast Library supporters in Coolidge's time was John B. Stetson, Jr., A.B. 1906. Though a busy foreign service officer, he was an interested and regular contributor to the Library, working to build a distinguished collection of Luso-Brazilian materials in memory of his Portuguese stepfather, the Count of Santa Eulalia. He frequently served Coolidge as a book scout in Europe.

bequest. On 23 June he told Coolidge, "You could feel justified in spending $10,000 or more for a Caxton Chaucer if the need arose. Some items we shall not get without paying high for them." Munn informed Coolidge that he had arranged to have his father, Dr. John Munn, give Harvard anonymously a first edition of Milton's *Comus* "in memory of Lionel de Jersey Harvard" on the tenth anniversary of the latter's graduation.

The summer of 1925 passed without appreciable dampening of Munn's ardor. "I've done another fool thing, perhaps," he wrote to Coolidge on 18 September, "in purchasing the Conrad notebooks, but I'd like to start up an interest in the modern field. There are many Harvard collectors of contemporary literature and we want to get them looking our way. I'm against mss. as much as you are, but by this we may swing a fine Conrad library in the near future."

A month later, on 19 October, Munn was giving Coolidge advance warning to expect a package of seventeenth-century poetry. "When it is entered in the Library books, I think it had better be entered not as my gift but as a gift from the Friends of the Library. I am going to try to raise most of the money to pay for this last batch, because I think it will be a good thing to have our Library contributed to in this field by a number of people."

Munn's package of "Caroline poetry," Coolidge told his friend on 22 October, "takes away not only the breath of myself but of all the other people who look at its contents, and hardly have I got over gasping than you begin to talk about Chaucer." Potter's ill health was making it difficult for Coolidge to find someone to help in the ordering, and he commented to Munn "the fact that Mr. Lane remarks without too obvious regret, 'we shall send off much fewer catalogue orders' does not entirely soothe me." Coolidge's delight over Munn's gifts led him to reflect to his friend the next day, "One thing that becomes clearer and clearer to me is that we must somehow or other have a librarian or curator in charge of the Treasure Room and its annexes, that is to say of all the rare books in the Library with the exception of the Widener collection."

On 24 October 1925 Munn sent Coolidge suggestions as to how to organize the effort to advance "our present needs and plans for the library" — more lists of wanted books in the field of sixteenth- and seventeenth-century English literature, allocation of special fields to interest graduates and faculty, enlarging the Friends of the Library.

He went on:

Let me again tell you how absolutely correct your idea of the Dutch collection is.[158] I have had occasion to investigate the price of Middle Dutch books, and while they are very reasonable now, I do not believe that they will continue to be so. We ought to make that killing within the next five years . . . I am attempting to get together some money for the Library from friends of mine, the tangible object being to provide $6,000 to purchase some Elizabethan quartos which we have here on consignment . . .

Mr. Wells . . . remarked to me . . . that one thing he would like to do for the library some day would be to serve as secretary to the Library Council, and help build up the Friends of the Library, the list of Harvard collectors, and our list of desiderata in many fields. Of course, I believe that most Harvard men who are interested in books have a deep admiration for Mr. Wells, and would be glad to help him in this position. But I also realize that his present occupation makes him feel that many people would regard him as rather guileful in taking on such a position.

All the above merely goes to show you that I am deeply, if not intelligently interested. At present, I think the Milton collection is pretty well on toward completion as far as the expensive items are concerned. It shouldn't take more than $500. a year to clean up everything else. I will work along on 17th century poetry until you get someone else who is deeply interested in it, and then I will be glad to take hold anywhere you want in English literature . . .

Your letters have made me realize the momentum which the library has gained, and we can't afford to lose it . . . I have never been as much impressed with the importance of a great library for a university as I am today, and it seems to me that such a library cannot be built up by the efforts of a few people as thoroughly as it can by the attack of a large number over a large front.

As was his habit, Coolidge responded promptly to Munn's comments in a long letter on 27 October — what he sometimes called "a talkee-talkee letter on a number of subjects."

Your letters are always stimulating and your last is particularly so and suggestive in several respects. I shall begin by taking it up point by point and shall wander therefrom as the ideas happen to come into my head.

[158] The Dutch collections in history and literature were very largely inspired by Coolidge and to a considerable extent financed through him. They were small in size until 1906 when an anonymous gift made possible substantial purchases of historical periodicals, society publications, and local history. The history collection was given in honor of John Lothrop Motley, A.B. 1831, the historian, and Coolidge's dream was to see it solidly endowed as a Motley Memorial. Coolidge also worked hard to build the rather sparse collection of Dutch literature, noted for the plays of the Renaissance dramatist Vondel and the nineteenth-century playwright Dekker (Multatuli), and he importuned every Dutch-inclined alumnus he could think of to help with the project.

1. We need lists and a great many of them, the more the better. Years ago I discussed with both Harrassowitz and Hiersemann [159] the fact that their catalogues tended to become less and less use to us owing to the ever smaller proportion of things they contained which we wanted and did not have. They agreed with me but asked what I had to suggest, to which I could make no reply. Lists are the best substitute for the decreasing value of any but the special book-seller's catalogue. The trouble is that they take time and work on the part of an expert. We have no such paid experts and can only grab enthusiastically whenever we can find an amateur who is willing to help us out. Of course one difficulty is the lack of knowledge in our staff. I may have told you that when I went through the list of the personnel of the then Royal Library in Berlin, I counted nearly fifty people who had the title of Ph.D. or something equivalent to it. I have no doubt they were miserably paid and many of them less competent than our Library School graduates but they did represent an impressive mass of available knowledge which could be called upon for all sorts of things. American conditions preclude that.

2. Only a small proportion of the members of the faculty are of any real assistance in ordering books. The others you can't either drive or persuade to do any work for you. The effort is wasted and produces little but vexation of the spirit. This seems to be a matter of temperament more than anything else. Some of the best scholars have no practical interest in building up in their own fields collections beyond what they and their students actually need. For instance in ancient history, Ferguson [160] is a thoroughly competent man and a good fellow with whom I have been on friendly terms for years, and yet though I regard our ancient history as being perhaps the only collection in history in the Library that is second rate, I have never been able to stir Ferguson up to do anything about it and I have ceased trying. All one can hope for is that in each department there will be at least one man who is keen about adding to our resources and when we find such a one we give him all we can. I wonder what the total of books ordered by Kittredge in the last thirty years would foot up to.

3. The institution of curators has been a success even if you admit that several of them have done nothing at all. The principle I have gone on is not that of having a lot of subjects and appointing a number of people who would probably do very little about them, but whenever I have known someone who I thought would take a real interest and be helpful I have created a subject for him. Even as it is, I would cheerfully drop half the curators I have. In some instances they are people who have actually asked for the place and have never done anything about it afterwards. In others my guess has turned out wrong and yet in both cases the men themselves would feel hurt if I were to suggest to them that they merely lumbered up a list which I should like to keep small

[159] Karl W. Hiersemann of Leipzig supplied the Library with European publications in the period from 1890 to 1928.

[160] William Scott Ferguson, then Professor of Ancient History, later McLean Professor of Ancient and Modern History.

in order to give it distinction. In spite of my desire, however, not to have too many names I am always ready to appoint a new curator offhand when a good one turns up. I should not at all object to having several for English literature and would snap at the chance to make you curator for the seventeenth century or anything else if you cared to accept the position. If, however, we had several curators for different periods of English literature, I think the centralization might perhaps be better done by someone like Lowes who is actually in the department and interested.

4. I quite agree as to the necessity of tying up the interests of men who are bookish and who have made collections. If we had what I should like to have, a man here of the right sort whose full time should be devoted to knowing about and looking after the rare books, he would be the person to keep track of all such things.

5. As you know, I am enthusiastic for the scheme for the institution of Friends of the Library but have so far been stumped in finding the right person to head it. I still think he should be a New Yorker, but I have not got much farther than that.

. . . at last the appraisers have released their hold and yesterday and today our portion of the Amy Lowell library has been brought over here. There is certainly some wonderful material in it and I am waking up to new interest and activity . . .

I shall end off with a promising bit of news that is making me quite cheerful. Roland Morris of Philadelphia (a Princeton graduate) has seen Edward Bok [161] as to the possibility of founding a John Lothrop Motley Memorial Collection in the Library of works on Dutch and Flemish history, literature and art. The sum I suggested was $100,000. Morris writes me that the suggestion met with a very favorable reception but that Bok said he had certain large commitments in connection with the League of Peace and the World Court which tied his hands for the moment, but Morris thinks that after the Senate debate, if all has gone well and if we have joined the Court, Bok will probably come to the point. I am writing to him today. I have told Lowes and Wells about this but don't want the news to go any further.

Munn decided to take the plunge on 23 October and wrote to Coolidge that he had decided to have the Caroline poets charged to his account and to take all the Friends of the Library money that he could get and allocate it to $6,000 worth of late Elizabethan plays. All this beneficence made Coolidge want to give Munn a curatorship of English literature in the Library but Munn replied on 28 October that he preferred "to be free to do whatever is necessary to do without title." Later in the year, with Coolidge's knowledge, President Lowell

[161] Edward William Bok (1863–1930), Dutch-born editor, author, and philanthropist, came from a family which included a King's minister, an admiral, and a Chief Justice. Derek Curtis Bok, 25th President of Harvard, is his grandson.

made an attempt to woo Munn from New York University for a permanent position with the Library, but here again Munn declined, largely because of his responsibility toward his elderly parents. He hoped "to be useful in a smaller way."

Then on 20 November 1925 there came from Munn to Coolidge a letter which surely now deserves to be on the public record, although during his lifetime Munn kept his great interest in the Library a relatively secret matter between him and those in the Harvard hierarchy who would naturally come to know it.[162]

When I started some time ago to complete, if possible, the Harvard collection of the work of John Milton, I carried it on with my own resources, and thought that little needed to be done. As you know the scope of the collection has grown until it embraces the field of seventeenth century poetry, and probably will take a lifetime to complete, if that is possible. Moreover the means at my disposal would not be adequate to do what is necessary.

You probably are not aware that my parents shared with me a deep affection for Lionel Harvard. Accordingly, when the Milton Collection grew, they offered to help, and the major part of the collection represents their aid. At first I thought that only a few of the minor seventeenth century poets would be needed, but today I have had the pleasure of forwarding to the Library some of the treasures of the period insofar as poetry is concerned.

It is therefore my wish slightly to alter the plan of the collection. As the bookplates have not been placed in the books, I should like the entire collection of Milton, and of seventeenth century poetry to be entered as in memory of Lionel de Jersey Harvard. Mr. Potter designed a beautiful bookplate, leaving off the name of the donor. Please substitute that plate for the one bearing my name, and cause to have entered on the private records of the library that these gifts are made by Dr. and Mrs. John P. Munn and their son James Munn 1912, in memory of Lionel de Jersey Harvard. It is an anonymous gift as far as the public are concerned.

Today, as I looked at the record of these gifts and the great poets they represented, I felt as never before how closely they expressed our affection for Lionel. He seemed to us and still seems the ideal embodiment of English young manhood.

It is impossible to close this letter without expressing to you how much the collection owes to Mr. Wells. It will be an oft repeated tale to you, but it is only a new example of his devotion to Harvard. Without his ever friendly and judicious guidance I would never have been able to undertake the work. It is

---

[162] So modest was Munn about his affection for the Library that he did not even mention a library connection — not even his membership on the Visiting Committee — in any of his autobiographical comments for the various reports of his College Class of 1912.

my wish and that of my parents that you know of this as a most significant part of the gift.

Four days after this magnificent letter Munn was back at Coolidge with more ideas concerning library strategy. Rare Elizabethan plays on the London market were his particular concern. He believed that with $10,000 to $20,000 Harvard could make a great impact in "shaking down" plays "which exist in pockets" in the book market. "Do you know anyone whom you could knock down," he asked, "or . . . anyone whom we could knock down for you."

When I started work upon the Milton and Caroline collections, I saw that two courses of action were possible: to collect a few books a year over a long period, or to make a sudden smash to clean up reserves on the market now, and then buy up slowly whatever came. I believe the second method is preferable and less expensive, although at first you have to spend quite a bit of money. For example, if anything happened to me now, you would have practically all the *great* books of poetry of the 17th century in their original editions. What remains to be added is a long and scattering list of rarities, many of which have little intrinsic value. I would like to see some method of making a similar smash on the play situation within the next two months . . .

In a letter of 30 November Coolidge was quick to take Munn up on his offer to help with a group of sixteenth- and seventeenth-century Dutch plays — "stray ones we can look after ourselves but for a considerable batch we might be glad of assistance." Commenting on Munn's strategic suggestions, he agreed:

Of course you are entirely right as to the way in which a great collection of books should be built up under the present circumstances. First get the big essentials and then steadily and patiently fill in till your result is really imposing. The only thing that worries me is how to find the $20,000. I talked to Harold Murdock [163] about it the other day and though he hemmed and hawed a good deal, he promised to interest himself in the matter and to speak to one or two people . . . I spoke of the need of getting $12,000 which was the figure given me by Wells, and should not venture at once to raise the amount to $20,000. Murdock thought we might make good use of a remark of Lowes's the other day that except for our lack of Shakespeare quartos, he thought if we could get the plays now in Wells's hands, we need not fear comparison with the Elizabethan Club at Yale. It would be amusing to equal them on their choicest

[163] Harold Murdock (1862–1934), the scholarly former Boston banker, served as Director of the Harvard University Press from 1920 until his death. He was the father of Kenneth Ballard Murdock, A.B. 1916, Francis Lee Higginson Professor of English Literature from 1939 to 1964.

specialty. To come back to what you say, all I can promise is to keep my eyes as wide open as I can, to jump at any chance I see, and never to despair.

For Munn, in this era of opportunity, one fresh vista simply led to another. Wells reported to Coolidge on 30 November that Munn had ordered all the books in Ellis' List IX [164] which were not already in the Harvard Library, a total of some forty titles. "He is ready to move on the broadest front and it is important that we should enlist other men to advance on other sections of the front," Wells asserted. Coolidge assured Wells on 3 December that he would "begin to worry Charlie Coolidge [165] before long." "My powers of epistolary gratitude are quite used up as far as J.B.M. is concerned," Coolidge confessed.

Overwhelmed by this new evidence of Munn's enthusiasm, Coolidge inquired of Wells just how definite Munn was about keeping the source of his gifts a secret. Wells responded on 9 December that "Munn wishes to preserve his anonymity as far as any public statements go. He certainly does not wish to preserve it from the President of the University, members of the Corporation, or other parties at interest." Accordingly Coolidge wrote to Lowell the following day that he hoped the President would make a point of speaking to Munn when he saw him at the annual dinner of the Harvard Club of New York, and tell him "under what deep obligations we are to him." Coolidge noted, "We shall soon have received from him and his family, which means of course at bottom from himself, something like $60,000 worth in the last six months and he is full of fiery zeal and the intention of contributing in the future to building up our collections, particularly in English literature of the seventeenth century. It is being done as a memorial to Lionel de Jersey Harvard, but the donors prefer to remain anonymous, at least to the general public. Munn is the most modest person in the world."

A Philosophy of Collecting

In early December 1925 the catalogue for the Clawson sale [166] be-

[164] The London booksellers.
[165] Charles A. Coolidge, the University's architectural consultant and an old friend of the Library, had been appointed chairman of the Visiting Committee as of 1 July 1925.
[166] The sale of the great library of John L. Clawson, distinguished particularly for its books printed in England before 1640, took place at the Anderson Galleries in New York, beginning on 20 May 1926.

came a matter of great concern to Wells and Munn, as well as to Coolidge. The task of going over the catalogue on the evening of 9 December with Edgar Wells inspired Munn to further thoughts about collecting books for a university, which he set down in some detail the next day in a letter to Coolidge:

The wealthy connoisseur usually makes his collection in literature rather than in the literature and history of a period . . . As he wishes to have something to show for his money, he strives for well known items, and for those which are rare because few exist, rather than for those which have intrinsic literary worth. From what I have seen of great collections in the past five years, I feel sure that few connoisseurs really know their libraries, but have them formed for them by dealers or by their own librarian upon the basis of what will make the best show. Between ourselves, if a man intelligently understood his collection and formed it for its intrinsic worth to himself, he would not sell it; it would be part of his life, and would pass from him only with his death.

A corollary of these beliefs lies in the knowledge that dealers artificially stimulate interest in certain periods where first copies of an item exist, and where the item has the value of being well known and rather aged. I have noticed that when there is no other way of keeping up the interest, the edition of an item is divided into "states," as much money being obtained for one state as would normally be obtained for any copy of the edition. This is distinctly unintelligent, to my way of thinking, unless a man is prepared to work out bibliographical details of printing, etc.

A university library ought to be glad to have all the items of a great collection of a connoisseur, but it should [not] stop there, in my opinion, because connoisseurs' collections are not based upon scholarly knowledge, upon a desire for completeness, and upon a recognition of the necessity for uniting history with literature. I will give you a case in point. There is not a connoisseur's collection which I know of which considers that the 17th century poet, Lovelace, has more than two items — namely, the 1649 Lucasta, and the 1660 Posthumous Poems. On the other hand, I know of at least three books not under the name of Lovelace which contain poetry of his, and which any collection should have to be complete. It would be possible for me to point out many other analogies, and you will of course recall many in the field of history. My feeling, therefore, about the university collections in literature is that we must not merely get the great and showy collections of the connoisseurs, but that we must build up in the other significant history and literature of a period, as we shall be enabled to do through the scholarly researches of our faculty.

A corollary of this belief is that while a connoisseur usually has reprints made of his rare books, you cannot obtain reprints of genuinely significant contemporary material which has not been raised to an artificial value by the connoisseur and the book dealer.

Consequently, in the 17th century, while I propose to get eventually as many of the rare items from the point of view of the connoisseur as possible, I feel it more significant for the university, and a more unique contribution to get equally significant but less known items which reveal the life of the time and complete our knowledge of the literary work of the period. No private collector does this; every university collector should.

Acknowledging receipt of a "fresh batch" [167] of Munn's "wonderful Christmas present" on 23 December, Coolidge directed himself to comment on Munn's ideas of collecting for a university. Coolidge wrote:

> I think we are quite agreed as to the general principles on which a university library ought to be built up. As you know, I have always believed in both quality and quantity, accepting cheerfully everything that comes our way but doing my best to guide carefully the expenditure of whatever funds I control or when I have any influence on the purchases of others. I am at one with you as to the necessity of background and filling in. A collection of a single author, no matter how splendid, cannot give his real significance for this cannot be understood without knowledge of his sources, of the influences which surrounded him and affected him and the results he produced on the minds of others. There is much truth, too, in the fact you point out that writings which are neither great nor fashionable stand little chance of being reprinted even when of considerable value. Therefore the originals are all the more necessary for us.

Munn conceived the not very practical idea that lacking another donor, Mrs. Rice might be persuaded to purchase the Clawson collection en bloc and merge it with Harry Widener's collection.[168] "Her son's collection is significant as an admirable beginning, rather than as a rounded achievement," Munn said. Such a "beautiful and touching memorial" could illustrate what Harry Widener "personally could have done." Coolidge was not about to irritate Mrs. Rice with an approach of this kind. In the end, with a collective effort from New York — backed by $40,000 in contributions from Munn, William A. White, A.B. 1863, J. Pierpont Morgan, A.B. 1889, Ernest B. Dane, A.B. 1892 and Thomas W. Lamont, A.B. 1892 — the Harvard Library made an impressive showing with the Clawson books, leading Coolidge to reflect on the successes of the year 1925–26 in a letter to Munn on 10 June 1926:

> Now that the music and the shouting of the Clawson sale have died, one can look back at the results more calmly. I don't find that time diminishes my ap-

---

[167] "Some twenty items, including The Domestick Intelligencer, eight revolutionary items, a Milton which is being returned as a duplicate and a couple of volumes of Conrad."

[168] J. B. Munn to A. C. Coolidge, 10 December 1925.

preciation of what we obtained there. Considering that we already had half the items in the Clawson catalogue, an addition of 130 represents a very good result, but it isn't merely the Clawson sale we have to look back upon, it is the total result for the last year and this is really big. I have a feeling of wanting to get away and think it over and get it digested in my general conception for the Library in its future, a conception which as you know is capable of limitless extension. Compared with what we have got for seventeenth century England, other acquisitions seem almost insignificant. At the same time Potter's purchases in Italian and French literature are notable in themselves, the additions in the Fine Arts are pretty considerable, and there have been a good many nice things here and there. Did I tell you that I have made a second attempt on Bok for Dutch history and literature and got thrown down very nicely but more decisively than before? I won't say I am discouraged but I am baffled for the time being. The idea of a John Lothrop Motley collection is too good a one to be dropped. Some Dutchman ought to take it up, and there is no one I know in the class with Bok, but there we are. I have had similar dreams in mind on a small scale for Scandinavia but luck has not played my way in that respect . . .

Looking back on a remarkable year, Coolidge could well tell the President in his annual report that the new acquisitions "alone would constitute one of the notable libraries in America." Coolidge declared:

The increase in number of volumes has not been unduly great according to our recent standards, but judged by their money value, which though not a scholarly test gives an idea of their rarity and the way they are sought after, we have had a year which can only be matched by the one in which we were given the Harry Elkins Widener, the Fearing [angling] and the Shaw collections. Besides keeping up with our normal growth in many directions, we have made a number of notable acquisitions in such subjects as early French and Italian literature and the Fine Arts; but everything else is thrown into the shade by the additions which have been made to our already rich possessions in the field of English literature . . .

The result of all these benefactions makes a splendid total for which we are devoutly grateful, but it should be remembered that all such works can come only from benefactions and from a few small special funds . . .[169]

All the while that he was urging on his enthusiastic friends, Coolidge in his quiet way was contributing impressive sums annually to help with purchasing and cataloguing. In 1924–25 came $7,200 from him for books and $3,500 for administration. In 1925–26 he gave $6,400 for books and $3,850 for administration. The scope of his library gifts ranged from Russian history and fine arts to French local history. In

[169] Report of Archibald Cary Coolidge, Director of the University Library, 1926, pp. 1–2.

1926–27 Coolidge contributed $2,800 for periodical sets, French poetry, and works on Russian art, as well as $3,550 for administrative expenses. In his final year as Director, Coolidge gave $2,470 for books on French history and Russian art.

The last two years with the Library were overshadowed by Coolidge's concern for obtaining the Fernando Palha library of Portuguese history and literature and the library of Count Alfred Boulay de la Meurthe relating to the French Revolution and the reign of the first Napoleon.

"My most immediate worry," he told Munn on 8 January 1926, "is the Palha collection. It takes a good deal of assurance on my part to tell Stetson that we can guarantee $75,000 when I have nothing but pretty uncertain hopes to fall back on, and yet I am terribly tempted." Ever the optimist, Munn urged him on (11 January 1926), emphatically advising, "$75,000 seems a lot to risk on raising for the Palha collection, but I should *certainly* do so. *The thing to do is to get these collections when they come up*, for they cannot be duplicated. If an emergency arose everyone would help out. I believe that you are in a position now to get such collections and that the graduates will help . . . " [170]

Munn, who had just presented a Bunyan item to the Library, warned Coolidge on 9 January 1927, "Don't let the Ronsard collection get away from you. If you call on a number of people I feel sure they would help. We know that for five years we can get good French books, but we must nail down the 16th & 17th centuries now."

As for the Boulay de la Meurthe library (10,000 volumes and 30,000 pamphlets), this was an opportunity not to be denied. The owner, a grandson of the Minister of Culture under Napoleon I, had been an historian of the Concordat, and his four-room library of religious and political history of the Revolution and Empire contained few duplicates on Harvard's shelves, despite the vigorous collecting which Coolidge had pushed forward. Coolidge wrote to Munn on 10 February 1927:

The chance seemed a remarkable one. The pamphlets alone must have a great mass of valuable material and as our already existing collection of French history deals chiefly with political and military affairs, the duplicates ought not to be too many. The price (80,000 francs) struck Potter and myself as a decidedly low one. We accordingly determined to risk the venture, trusting to

[170] J. B. Munn to A. C. Coolidge, 11 January 1926.

get back a considerable part of the expense by the sale of duplicates and to manage the rest somehow.

In the end Coolidge money helped bring the collection to Harvard, just as Coolidge's generosity had secured two collections of Revolutionary French newspapers some months before. It was thus particularly fitting that in 1931, three years after his death, anonymous gifts made possible the acquisition of the 3,500 volumes and pamphlets of the Aulard library of French Revolutionary and post-Revolutionary subject matter as a memorial to Coolidge.

There were problems other than building the collections which caused Coolidge much concern during the final years of his tenure. The reading rooms were filled almost to the limit of their comfortable capacity, professors were waiting for studies, many graduate students could not have stalls to themselves, top-floor working space had begun to encroach on the "through passages used by sight-seers," The stacks were nearly full. In his report for 1922–23 Coolidge pointed to the fact that "not four percent of the rows are wholly vacant to act as a reserve." He warned that "before many years we shall be in urgent need of making use of our two stack floors in the cellar which, though austere as a place of study and not quite so easily reached from the desk as the floors above the ground, will make an excellent store-house. Unfortunately, the mere equipping them with shelves and the other requisites will probably cost about $75,000, a fact we shall have to face some day." This same warning he repeated in his next annual report, 1923–24, and the subsequent one. He hoped that Mrs. Rice (the former Mrs. Widener) might take note of the need and fill it, but he was prepared if necessary to issue a more general appeal. While Mrs. Rice and her family had provided in 1920 a $150,000 fund for the Library's annual administrative expenses, Coolidge constantly bemoaned the fact that he and President Lowell had never struck a bargain with Mrs. Rice for a maintenance fund. "It costs $25,000 a year just to keep this place cleaned," he confided sadly to one of his graduate students.[171] But space for people, and especially books, had to take precedence.

"I am puzzling over what I had better put in my report this year," he divulged to Wells on 14 September 1925. "We have been in Widener for ten years and it would seem to be a good moment to in-

[171] Interview with William L. Langer, 31 October 1973.

dulge in smug retrospection at the same time as in piteous appeals for the future. I must touch the heart of the graduate without angering Mrs. Rice."

Was there hope of interesting any other large donors in the Library's physical needs? Coolidge had added William L. Clements to the Visiting Committee with some such purpose in mind, but Clements had not attended the organizational meeting of the Friends of the Library and was spending so much on his library in Michigan "that it is no use looking to him for something large anywhere else," Coolidge told Wells realistically. "The question is now where next to turn, for we need badly as soon as possible a special building for our treasures here. I believe nothing would help us more in the acquisition of just such things as we have been getting lately and confirm us in our superiority to almost all rivals in this field." This special building for rare books and manuscripts eventually came into being in 1942, when the Houghton Library was opened.

The Director as Diplomat

DISRUPTING THOUGH the effects of the first World War were, they did encourage the central Library to turn inward, settle immediate problems, and assess accomplishments. The first matter on the docket was to supplement Mrs. Widener's gift by furnishing the building with such necessary items as 28,000 label holders, 39,000 book supports, tables and chairs for 300 stalls, furniture for 72 studies, and new furniture for the principal offices "to accord with the dignity of the Library." [172] All these were quickly obtained, thanks to the prompt generosity of J. P. Morgan, Jr., and others.

The new building had brought with it a host of minor problems for the Director and his staff. Some of the questions so solemnly settled in 1915 have an aura of unreality in today's world. The matter of appropriate dress, for example:

It should be remembered that the Widener Library is open to visitors who come in large numbers from all parts of the country. This makes it the more necessary to maintain a proper decorum in the reading rooms. Readers are requested not to put their feet on the chairs or to sit in shirtsleeves, although in really warm weather outing shirt and belt without a coat are permissible.[173]

In the Library of 1915 the place reserved for Radcliffe College students was close to total exclusion. By prevalent theory the Library was a male sanctuary, financed by Harvard College and therefore rightfully the scholarly resource of Harvard students and faculty. Anything Radcliffe got came by cautious negotiation. L. B. R. Briggs, Dean of the Harvard Faculty of Arts and Sciences and President of Radcliffe, had recognized Radcliffe's obligation to give something in return for her modicum of privilege. When Coolidge asked

[172] W. C. Lane, Undated "Memorandum of Items Still Needed for the Equipment of the New Library" [1915].
[173] Undated memorandum [1915].

Radcliffe in 1911 to pay a small annual sum to Harvard for its occasional use of the Library, President Briggs officially acknowledged that Radcliffe's use of Harvard's books and of the so-called "pen" (where Radcliffe students waited in Gore until a library page got them what they wanted) was worth something on the order of $500. As President Briggs wrote:

> When a certain use of the Harvard Library was allowed to the girls, it was a use the inconvenience of which to Harvard was reduced to the very lowest terms. Radcliffe did its best to keep the girls out of the library . . . and got returned books by its own messenger . . . Such use of the Library as Radcliffe has is purely a matter of courtesy and good will on the part of Harvard. Even courtesy seems to have been carefully guarded; for one Radcliffe graduate employed in University 9, who went to the girls' room in the Harvard Library after lunch to read, was locked in and had to ring up a boy before she could get out.[174]

Briggs reminded Coolidge of the "desirableness of a suitable provision for Radcliffe students in the new library" — not merely a room but "opportunities in the stack." [175] Coolidge would not promise this. It was a question not of architecture but of regulation, he said. "Without undertaking to prophesy what we shall do, it seems to me that the stack will be freely opened to graduate students, but [as in the case of students in Harvard College] not to undergraduates." [176]

So it turned out. The new regulations governing Radcliffe students in Widener limited undergraduates to the Radcliffe study on the second floor adjacent to the General Reading Room, where Radcliffe staff and students could use reserved books, reference books, and titles temporarily borrowed for reading in the building. Other books, as in the past, were to be borrowed through the Radcliffe Library. On the other hand, Radcliffe graduate students (like those of Harvard) could use the stacks "on recommendation of their instructors, when such access is essential to their work." They could also attend "seminary courses" in the Library not open to Harvard undergraduates.[177]

[174] L. B. R. Briggs to A. C. Coolidge, 29 September 1911; L. B. R. Briggs to A. C. Coolidge, 8 November 1911; A. C. Coolidge to L. B. R. Briggs, 11 November 1911.
[175] L. B. R. Briggs to A. C. Coolidge, 15 November 1912.
[176] A. C. Coolidge to L. B. R. Briggs, 18 November 1912.
[177] Untitled, undated memorandum headed "Harvard College Library," relating to Radcliffe arrangements [November 1915].

The sticking point was the evening. Coolidge queried Briggs as to whether he thought it desirable "that Radcliffe students, even graduate ones, should use the Widener Library in the evening." He had been told there was a student who had to do work in the evening in the history seminar room on the top floor. "This does not seem to me advisable, especially as the Library exercises no general supervision of that floor at night." [178]

Briggs countered with the information that the girl's only time for work was in the evening. "She goes home at half-past nine," he said. "Also she is near a good many persons and apparently quite safe. On the whole it seems . . . better to let the matter go on." He added, with seeming fatalism, "Whatever happens, I thank you for calling our attention to the situation." [179]

Coolidge did not feel he could let the subject drop at that. "The general question is too large for me to feel competent to settle on my own responsibility." He proposed to refer the problem to the Library Council, "though I am not sure," he said, falling back on higher authority, "that the President will not think it should go to him as a matter of University policy." [180]

The question was ultimately settled by the Library Council, which met on 10 November 1915. Coolidge reported the results to Briggs the next day:

> It was voted:
>   that, visitors shall not be admitted to the Library after six o'clock.
> There will be obviously a certain amount of discretion in enforcing this rule.
> It was voted:
>   that, the Radcliffe Reading Room shall be closed after six o'clock.
>   that, all women be excluded from the stack after six o'clock.
>   that, under the existing conditions, seminary rooms, special libraries, offices, and studies shall not be open to women after this same hour; but that the Director shall have discretion in applying this rule to fixed appointments in University courses.
> This last provision was put in for the benefit of the Radcliffe student who . . . may . . . continue to come, and I shall give directions that she be admitted. If there are any other cases of the same kind, I should be glad to be notified of them.
>   Given in this form, it may seem to you that the Council sat down to make

[178] A. C. Coolidge to L. B. R. Briggs, 16 October 1915.
[179] L. B. R. Briggs to A. C. Coolidge, 22 October 1915.
[180] A. C. Coolidge to L. B. R. Briggs, 26 October 1915.

rules against Radcliffe. This was not at all the spirit or the intention. We had to make rules and such rules have to be restrictive. Perhaps the main difficulty in the way of more liberal action is that after six o'clock, in fact, after five-thirty, we no longer have any supervision of the top story, or of any part of the stack, or even of the entries, above the first floor. It is better, too, that we should begin with a less liberal policy and, perhaps, be able to broaden it later . . .[181]

Coolidge, never truly comfortable with most women, and painfully conscious of his speech impediment, showed a certain social awkwardness with the opposite sex. He shunned lecturing at Radcliffe, and his women associates, no matter how much they admired him, were sensitive to the fact that he avoided expressing interest in their personal lives outside the Library. He did not dislike women but, other than the women in his family of whom he was naturally fond, the opposite sex played no part in his life. Even if space and cost considerations had not been governing, Coolidge was scarcely likely to lead a crusade for Radcliffe library facilities at Harvard.

Yet the women who worked with him seem without exception to have been devoted to him. One librarian, a cataloguer, who remembered her Harvard experience as the richest of her professional life, attributed this in large measure to Coolidge. "We had such a good time, working like beavers, but having so many laughs, and I remember my final day, when he kept me long after everyone else had gone, and at last I said that I really must go, as I had a dinner engagement, he said, 'Oh, do let's finish Siberia!' and then waved good-bye as I rushed down the steps." [182] For another, it was "the contagion of his enthusiasm." Even with an unappealing subject, "when you worked with him . . . he managed to infuse you with his own interest to such a degree that its progress became a personal matter to you." [183]

Cooperation — Within and Without

As Director of the University Library, Coolidge was concerned with encouraging a cooperative spirit and mutual understanding among the College Library and the independent satellite libraries of the Uni-

[181] A. C. Coolidge to L. B. R. Briggs, 11 November 1915.

[182] T. F. Currier, *op. cit.* (note 53), p. 170.

[183] *Ibid.* One of his closest associates, Gertrude M. Shaw of the Order Department, categorized Coolidge as "the most impersonal man" she had ever known — one whom she esteemed highly and "thought I knew well, but who didn't know me" (Interview with Gertrude M. Shaw, 5 November 1973).

versity Library. In such matters as the elimination of duplicate purchases and the introduction of a reasonable interchange of volumes and even collections which logically belonged in one library rather than another, Coolidge was assiduous, persuasive, and above all patient. Since his goal — and President Lowell's — was to simplify and eliminate unnecessary expense, Coolidge knew he could always call on the President for backing. If necessary, presidential influence could sometimes overcome the pride and independence of the uncooperative.

As a matter of tradition the larger units, like the Law School Library, were accustomed to acting as independent entities, and officers of even smaller ones, like the Peabody Museum Library, had the pride of specialists who knew their subjects thoroughly and what was required, without the need for coordination with, much less advice from, a unifying authority — no matter how mild.

Concerning the purchase of books, there were two stipulations made by the Corporation in 1880, modified in 1892. The first provided that no "books, manuscripts, maps, or other objects naturally included in a library shall hereafter be purchased by any department of the University, except the Law School . . . unless through the Librarian of the University . . ." And the second specified that such materials acquired by any department "by purchase or gift" be sent to the College Library for cataloguing and insertion of the University stamp or bookplate before being sent to the library of the department.[184] Coolidge reported to Lowell that, of the so called departmental libraries, three were exempted from the first regulation, "a fourth is petitioning for an exemption; two others have violated it for years; and one other observes it in part." As for the second rule, Coolidge found it was "hardly observed by any of the departmental libraries and, if it were, it would simply break down the College Library from the amount of work put upon it." [185]

Coolidge's way of dealing with this uncontrolled situation was to get the Corporation to vote on 30 January 1911 to require departmental libraries to send to the central library duplicate cards recording their new acquisitions, so as to build up a union catalogue of all Harvard holdings.

[184] Votes of the President and Fellows of 13 December 1880 and 31 October 1892.
[185] A. C. Coolidge to A. L. Lowell, 7 December 1910.

Another problem of cooperation among the parts of the University Library related to the treatment of duplicates within the system and the transfer of books from one library to another when appropriate. Although the statutes defined the University Library as consisting of "all the collections of books in the possession of the University," it was not possible to insist that they be located where they would be most useful. Coolidge pointed out in his annual report to the President in 1911 that the departmental libraries and most of the special reference collections had their own budgets and "not unnaturally regard their volumes as their personal property." [186] Even so, Coolidge asked "whether the different parts of the University Library might not do more to help one another than they sometimes have." The new Director urged a broad liberal policy — generosity without injustice and an absence of "an attitude of bargaining."

By early 1912 Coolidge had reason to seek presidential support for his efforts. The great Olivart collection of international law, which Lichtenstein and Coolidge had located for the Law School, contained numerous books of general and historical interest that Coolidge believed should be transferred without charge to the College Library. He implored President Lowell to make the point clear at the Law School faculty meeting of 9 January.

> What I am afraid of is that they will simply propose to sell to the College Library certain works. This seems to me all wrong in principle, and I hope they will understand that it is a broad, general question of the interests of the University and not a mere deal between two libraries.[187]

Coolidge told Lowell that the Gray Herbarium had just asked him to transfer from the central collection a work worth fifty dollars. If he were to decide to transfer the volume he would not have the College Library offer to sell it to the Herbarium. "This sort of thing comes up here often, but the Law School are unused to cases of this sort and their traditions are rather against taking broad views of such matters."

A month later Coolidge was again appealing to Lowell because Professor Joseph H. Beale had ordered a list of Italian medieval statuti "in the usual ignorance of the fact that we have been buying on that

[186] *Report of Archibald Cary Coolidge, Director of the University Library*, 1911, pp. 5–6.
[187] A. C. Coolidge to A. L. Lowell, 9 January 1912.

subject during the last year." It seemed to Coolidge that "this brings
out pretty clearly the evils of the present system."[188]

Coolidge used his annual report to the President in 1912 as a chance
to do further preaching on the subject.

As the various branches of the University Library increase, the tendency
will be for them to spread out and to enrich their collections without asking
whether the books they desire are already to be found in some other part of
Cambridge. Considerable duplication is doubtless inevitable, for many works
are useful to scholars in several subjects and should be represented at Harvard
by several copies conveniently located. The professors in charge of the Departmental and of the special libraries are naturally quick to resent any suggestion that they are not the best judges of their own needs and of those
of their pupils, and that they should be limited in their disposition of funds,
which in many cases are due to their personal efforts. And yet from the point
of view of the proper use of the University's resources, it is not satisfactory to
have several departments buy copies of expensive books . . . rarely used in any
of them.[189]

Coolidge pointed to the overlapping purchases in the four or five
botanical libraries, the thousands of titles in the Olivart collection du-
plicating works in the College Library, and the duplicate collections
on such topics as Morocco, Cuba, or Latin American border disputes.
Even between the Divinity School and the College or Law School
Libraries, where there was a natural division of interest, there could
be overlapping in subjects like church history or canon law. "Every
one of our libraries," Coolidge remarked, "thinks first of its own
readers and wishes to possess whatever may be useful to them, regard-
less of conditions elsewhere. It is not always an easy matter to re-
concile this natural and legitimate feeling with the broader policy
of the University."[190]

In the face of autonomously inclined library officers, Coolidge
moved slowly and tactfully, as with the Hancock Professor of He-
brew, David Gordon Lyon. Coolidge explained to Lyon that he was
considering which books should go from the College Library to the

[188] A. C. Coolidge to A. L. Lowell, 12 February 1912. Joseph Henry Beale (1861–
1943) was at that time Carter Professor of General Jurisprudence, later Royall Professor of Law.
[189] *Report of Archibald Cary Coolidge, Director of the University Library*, 1912,
p. 5.
[190] *Ibid.*, p. 6.

Andover-Harvard Library at the Divinity School and thought the Semitic Museum collection should be considered at the same time.

> Will you kindly give me an idea what your policy is in building up your collections, whether you wish to add to them beyond the limits of what your room will hold, how much attention you pay to the question of whether a book already is or is not in the College Library, and other things of the sort . . . It seems to me . . . that the time has perhaps come when you could plan out with some definiteness just what sort of things you wish to have and to keep . . . and that this may affect your purchases . . . The Corporation is very anxious to reduce duplication in purchases to a minimum, and I am trying to see whether we cannot have a little more coordination between the different libraries of the University . . .[191]

It was slow work, but quiet discussion and firmness in developing a rational policy produced results. On 24 March 1914 Coolidge could report to Lichtenstein, "I have transferred to the Law School all the material in our South American collections relating to Boundary Disputes. In return I hope they will give me their miscellaneous material about South America in the Olivart collection, and in time, various other things."

Coolidge was profoundly conscious of his "indefinite" relationship to the various libraries and his relatively weak position as a coordinator, despite Corporation authority. He told his counterpart, W. Dawson Johnston, Librarian of Columbia University,[192] in a letter dated 25 February 1913:

> The Corporation . . . have put me in as their representative, but for many reasons it would be most unwise for me to provoke any conflict that can be avoided, and I am therefore feeling my way gradually. You see I am perfectly frank with you. It is only this year that (between ourselves, at my own suggestion) I have been made an ex officio member of the various library councils. The part I take in debate varies according to circumstances, but I am satisfied so far and believe that when the various Schools get used to having an outsider in their sacred midst, I shall be able to get a good many things done. I had thought of asking the Corporation to vote that no School should have a right

[191] A. C. Coolidge to D. G. Lyon, 23 December 1912. Hollis Professor from 1882 to 1910 and Hancock Professor from 1910 to 1922, Lyon was the first Curator of the Semitic Museum, serving from 1891 until his retirement thirty-one years later. He died in 1935.

[192] William Dawson Johnston (1871–1928), an historian who knew Coolidge from a graduate year at Harvard, was Librarian of Columbia University from 1909 to 1914. He later served as Director of the St. Paul Public Library and of the American Library in Paris.

to purchase works over my veto, a veto that would only be rarely exercised and would be used only to prevent duplication, but no question of this kind has as yet come up, so that I do not intend to run the risk of a row over a merely theoretical right . . .

I am not a regular member of the joint library committee of the Andover-Harvard Divinity Library, but by courtesy I am invited to attend its meetings, which comes to a good deal of the same thing.

As for the Medical School — The library question there is in such a mess that there is no information about it that would be helpful to you. There has been no central Harvard Medical Library. At one time there were fifteen separate ones. These have now got down to five and there is a strong movement which I believe will be successful for combining these five into one. This will mean all sorts of changes of practice. Until now the Harvard Medical School has not tried to keep books that were not immediately useful and has turned over all the older ones to the Library of the Boston Medical Association.[193]

To Theodora Kimball of the Library of Landscape Architecture, Coolidge reiterated his view about the idea of one part of the Library system selling duplicates to another part.

I quite disapprove of it as a principle. It will not do to have our various libraries dealing with each other in that way. The College Library is continually sending over books to the other libraries without a thought of asking them to pay for them, and we cannot allow the special libraries to act differently. We are all parts of the same institution and the thing we are aiming for is that with as little waste and duplication as possible our books should be put where they are most useful.[194]

Sometimes there were contretemps, such as the slip in May 1914 which led the Corporation officially to include the Law School among "departmental libraries" in the revised statutes, an inadvertent classification which Coolidge quickly disavowed in the face of wounded pride and a long letter to Lowell from Dean Ezra Ripley Thayer.[195] Coolidge was also prepared, when it seemed appropriate, to avoid acquiring books or manuscripts which obviously belonged in a library

---

[193] Coolidge worked earnestly through most of his administration to bring the Boston Medical Library and the various collections of the Medical School into one entity, but this goal was not accomplished until thirty-three years after Coolidge's death. The Countway Library building made it possible.

[194] A. C. Coolidge to Theodora Kimball, 8 May 1913.

[195] A. C. Coolidge to A. L. Lowell, 23 May 1914; A. L. Lowell to A. C. Coolidge, 25 May 1914; E. R. Thayer to A. L. Lowell, 26 May 1914; A. L. Lowell to E. R. Thayer, 27 May 1914.

that contained almost everything related to that subject. When Harvard was offered the manuscript of George Ticknor's *History of Spanish Literature*, Coolidge deemed it appropriate to turn down the opportunity because the Boston Public Library had Ticknor's research collection and funds to support it. "Great as are my acquisitive instincts," he told President Lowell, "in this case I should prefer to have the booty go to its rightful place rather than coming into my clutches." [196]

Coolidge and Lane sought in every reasonable way to avoid competition with other libraries, when such competition made no sense, but were quite willing to compete when a real advantage to Harvard was involved. Coolidge hedged and hesitated over the question of buying South American books in competition with Yale; he finally decided to compete, but in countries where Yale was not strong. In pursuing books on the list of European history titles prepared by the Princeton librarian, E. C. Richardson, Coolidge went to great pains to make sure that Richardson received careful corrections of every error and discrepancy, so that the valuable list would be as accurate as possible. When cooperation was proposed by Harry M. Lydenberg of the New York Public Library, Coolidge saw little advantage to Harvard and much expense in supplying information on Harvard's serials and periodicals for a union list of such items in American research libraries. Mr. Lowell showed no real enthusiasm for the project, and Coolidge was tempted to decline participation. In the long run he saw the question as one of friendly cooperation among comparable institutions. Coolidge obtained special funds to underwrite Harvard's share and went ahead with the work.[197]

He perceived merit and much good will for Harvard in such helpful deeds, and he was on excellent terms with his university counterparts elsewhere. Yet he steadfastly refused to become involved in professional library organizations. He avoided the pose of a profes-

[196] A. C. Coolidge to A. L. Lowell, 18 February 1915.

[197] See Lowell folders in Coolidge Papers for 1922–1923 and 1923–1924, Harvard University Archives, for the background of this episode. Lowell's statement was characteristic. "I have always felt," he wrote to Coolidge, "that the time might possibly come when some system would be developed whereby a catalogue of every library would be in every other; but until that becomes possible, it seems to me hardly worth while to distribute partial catalogues, like those of periodicals. However, you understand the problem better than I."

sional librarian. Lane, Currier, Winship, and others were the ones who attended the annual meetings of the American Library Association and reported in the columns of the *Library Journal* on operations of the Harvard Library. With one exception, Coolidge managed to wiggle out of opportunities to speak at gatherings of his professional colleagues.[198] He even declined participation on the governing board of the American Library Institute, which E. C. Richardson of Princeton was trying to build "on the lines of a learned society" — representative of "those who know the problems of the great reference and research library." Coolidge replied:

> I am sorry to say I do not see my way to accepting. The fact is I am not a librarian and I lack much of the technical knowledge that one should have . . . More important still from a selfish point of view is that I am Professor of History at Harvard and am supposed to give nearly half my time to work in the Department which pays a corresponding share of my salary. As you may guess, the Department has been shabbily treated by me for the last few years and has got nothing like its fair share of my attention, and my lectures have not been at all as freshly prepared as they should have been. I am hoping now that we are beginning to get shaken down in our new quarters that I may be able before long to devote myself more to academic and less to library work . . .[199]

Diversionary Influences

The war was a kind of watershed in Coolidge's library career. Not that his interest or energy ran down after the achievement of Widener. But, beginning in 1917, Coolidge's public side began to absorb more and more of his time and effort.

[198] The one exception was on 21 June 1921 when, at the Swampscott meeting of the American Library Association, Coolidge delivered a "paper" on "The Objects of Cataloging" — *Library Journal*, XLVI (15 September 1921), 735–739. It is not recorded what Coolidge thought of the procession of 500 automobiles, loaded with more than 1,000 delegates, which drove through Cambridge on Harvard's Commencement Day, headed for Lexington and Concord. Presumably Coolidge was safe within the Yard. Thomas Franklin Currier's article on Coolidge, *op. cit.* (note 53), p. 167, refers to a Coolidge "address before the conference of the American Library Association at Magnolia" but presumably this is a slip. The national meeting at Magnolia in 1902 was addressed by President Eliot ("The Division of a Library into Books in Use and Books Not in Use . . .") but the only Coolidge recorded attending was J. Randolph Coolidge, Jr., brother of A. C. Coolidge and an active trustee of the Boston Athenaeum and other libraries.

[199] E. C. Richardson to A. C. Coolidge, 4 February 1916; A. C. Coolidge to E. C. Richardson, 15 February 1916.

The first diversion was his membership in "The Inquiry," a group working with Colonel E. M. House, President Wilson's confidant, to prepare background information for the future peace conference. "One of the first to join us," James T. Shotwell has recounted, "was Professor Archibald Coolidge of Harvard, recognized as the outstanding authority in the American academic world on the history of Eastern Europe and a master of the literature of European diplomatic history."[200] The Library's resources were put at the staff's service, with publications going back and forth to Washington and New York.

In 1918 Coolidge's war service became literally active when he was appointed Special Assistant to the Secretary of State and to the War Trade Board.[201] The latter position took him to Stockholm in the summer of 1918 and then to Murmansk and Archangel "to study and report upon the economic and commercial conditions in Russia." Coolidge's visit to North Russia was brief and necessarily superficial since it coincided with the Allied intervention. He went back to Washington to report and then sailed again for Europe in November. He at first had intended to go to the Balkans, but when he arrived in Paris he was appointed head of an American mission of inquiry to be stationed in Vienna to collect information concerning Poland and the various parts of the former Austro-Hungarian Empire. This assignment lasted only about five months, but it provided an opportunity to acquire some 4,000 works relating to the late Dual Monarchy. He then returned to Paris in May 1919 with the Austrian peace delegation to work with the American Commission to Negotiate Peace.

A further interruption of his Harvard life came in 1921–1922 when Coolidge served as political advisor and chief of the liaison division of the American Relief Administration in Russia to help with the task of alleviating famine conditions affecting 15,000,000 people. He and President Lowell both felt that Herbert Hoover's invitation could not be turned down, even though Coolidge's teaching and library responsibilities would be affected.

"I have asked the University to count this as a sabbatical year for

[200] James T. Shotwell, *At the Paris Peace Conference* (New York, The Macmillan Company, 1937), p. 6.

[201] His biographers suggest that the commission may have been "perhaps merely a cover for the real purpose . . . to go to Russia for the State Department." Coolidge and Lord, *op. cit.*, p. 174.

me with half-pay," he wrote to his brother, Harold Coolidge, on 2 September 1921.[202]

I rather hated to do this, as they are so hard up, but after all I had not had a sabbatical for sixteen years, that is to say more than twice the time that entitles one to it, so I think they might as well help out. My half-salary is to be $4,000 [the amount he received for his Library post] and I have suggested . . . that the Treasurer should simply keep it and count it towards four of the five thousand dollars of my payment this year to the Endowment Fund.[203] You will thus have only to find a thousand dollars, which may make things a little easier for you.

Coolidge's service as liaison chief with the A. R. A. lasted from late September 1921 until March 1922. It was an exciting experience which enabled him to see or meet Trotsky, Kamenev, Chicherin, Rakovsky, Radek, Litvinov, and others of the "old Bolsheviks."[204] He also avidly collected published documents and books, particularly books on Russian art, which he had shipped back to Harvard.[205]

[202] Noted in Coolidge and Lord, *op. cit.*, p. 272. Coolidge gave his brother power of attorney to act for him in his absence.

[203] When asked to subscribe to the Harvard Endowment Fund campaign of 1919, Coolidge had hedged. "I should like to eat my cake and have it too," he had told Thomas Nelson Perkins (1870–1937), Boston lawyer and member of the Harvard Corporation for over thirty years, in a letter dated 30 September. "That is to say, that I should be glad to be numbered among the contributors for a good sum but I believe the best use I can make of such pennies I can spare the University is in meeting current wants in these difficult times until our situation is changed. By 'wants,' I mean, of course, the Library, which needs not only all it is receiving and all I am going to ask from the Corporation, but also all the contributions it can get." Having delivered himself of this, Coolidge offered to subscribe $5,000 annually for five years "provided I could spend it just as I wanted." Coolidge's proposal was accepted, even though his gift could not be construed as for "endowment." He suggested that it might be considered as a kind of "advance from income" of the eventual "mobile" fund with which the University hoped to provide the President.

[204] Initially Coolidge was responsible for liaison with the USSR Government, with other missions, and with the Russian and international press. When the A.R.A. established a communications division on 30 January 1922, the liaison division dealt mainly with repatriation cases. See H. H. Fisher, *The Famine in Soviet Russia 1919–1923: The Operations of the American Relief Administration* (New York, 1927), p. 446.

[205] An interesting summary of Coolidge's successes, together with excerpts from some of his letters giving an account of his difficulties is contained in *Harvard Library Notes*, No. 9 (December 1922), pp. 203–208. "All told, this book buying business is proving too complicated for my peace of mind," Coolidge commented. "If I can pull this through successfully without some big smash I shall retire from the profession contented."

The third interruption — although this was only partial — was his cautious acceptance of the editorship of the new quarterly journal, *Foreign Affairs*.[206] The invitation came to him a matter of days after his return from Russia in March 1922, and he agreed to consider the post only on condition that he have a managing editor to carry on most of the business of the publication. He told his friend and colleague Edwin F. Gay: [207]

> I do not feel ready to give up either my teaching at Harvard after doing it, though with interruptions, for nearly thirty years, or my management of the College Library, though I believe I could very considerably reduce the amount of time I give to this last. I have not even broached the matter to President Lowell, but I feel pretty sure he would be strongly opposed at least to my severing my connection with the Library.

Coolidge assured Gay that he would accept the editorship if the Council on Foreign Relations could find an intelligent younger man with knowledge of the world, capable of taking part in all activities connected with the magazine. Then there might be some advantages to having the editor in Cambridge, Coolidge thought.

> The office and the work of administration would be in New York and I should go down from time to time when it was necessary . . . In no place in the world could exactly the right magazines and books (though not newspapers) be so conveniently near to my hand as they are in the Harvard Library. I have built up the collections on these topics for many years and I can put my finger on a given magazine or recent book or work of reference of any kind with the least possible delay. The saving of time is, therefore, great. I believe too that there are some advantages in comparative seclusion

---

[206] The idea of a journal devoted to international affairs had emanated from a meeting on 30 May 1919 in Paris, attended by a group from Britain and America, including Coolidge, who wished to establish "institutes . . . to furnish a better fund of information on policy as well as mere facts." Out of this sprang the Royal Institute of International Affairs in London and the Council on Foreign Relations in New York. "In the case of the American organization," James Shotwell has noted, "a plan had already been started in New York, which, however, did not work out successfully until it was reorganized to meet substantially the plan drawn up in our meetings in Paris, Professor Archibald Coolidge of Harvard taking the initiative." See Shotwell, *op. cit.*, pp. 346–347, 356–357.

[207] Edwin Francis Gay (1867–1946), LL.D. 1918, who had been at Harvard since 1903 and was the first Dean of the Graduate School of Business Administration (1908–1919), had left the University to become editor of the New York *Evening Post*. At the time of the founding of *Foreign Affairs* he was a Harvard Overseer. He returned to Cambridge in 1924 as Professor of Economic History and was elected Henry Lee Professor in 1935.

for more detached thinking . . . Influenced by my experience in supervising the Library here, I rather dream of the new job as one where the machine should be complete enough to run of itself and produce a good magazine without my continual direction, and that the most important part of my strength, energy and whatever ability I have should be devoted to making it something more than a good magazine, an absolutely first-rate one in every respect . . .[208]

Gay enlisted Hamilton Fish Armstrong as a managing editor for Coolidge, and Armstrong proved to be an ideal choice. For the next half-dozen years Coolidge and Armstrong worked together on unusually compatible and intimate terms. The new publication met with instantaneous success and quickly attained a solid circulation of more than 5,000, easily exceeding the wildest dreams of the founders. Coolidge's contribution to the first issue was the "editorial statement" and an anonymous article on Russian affairs signed "K." Coolidge wanted anonymity to avoid the possibility of criticism directed against the editorial board. "An article by me, if cussed out, might hurt the whole Review." Coolidge also laid down the condition that the article be placed last in the magazine because he felt in that position — especially unsigned — it would attract attention and make the point that readers should digest the whole of the issue. He reported to Armstrong, "By sitting up to two o'clock for the last couple of evenings I have managed to get theoretically to the end of my Russian article. At the present moment I have very little idea what it is about." [209] The piece attracted much attention, however, when it appeared, and not least in Russia where Lenin, Trotsky, Bukharin, Radek, and others of the Bolshevik hierarchy were found to have read it. "We must have plenty in Foreign Affairs about Russia first and last," Coolidge told his managing editor. "First and last" over the forty-five years of Armstrong's editorial career, *Foreign Affairs* printed 248 articles on Russia, several of them by Coolidge, and some 2,000 book reviews and comments on Slavic topics. Since Armstrong was something of a Slavic expert himself with a background of service in Serbia and other places in Eastern Europe, Coolidge had touched a sympathetic chord.

[208] Coolidge and Lord, *op. cit.*, pp. 310–311.
[209] See Hamilton Fish Armstrong, *Peace and Counterpeace: From Wilson to Hitler* (New York, 1971), pp. 185–197. Armstrong, a graduate of Princeton, was connected with *Foreign Affairs* for half a century. He succeeded Coolidge as editor in 1928.

Although Coolidge did most of his work for *Foreign Affairs* from his post at the Library, Armstrong has recorded that Coolidge "found trips to New York exhilarating and frequently made excuses, connected with *Foreign Affairs* or otherwise, to come down, and, usually, spend a couple of nights with me." Coolidge's editorial work, his biographers related, was divided into two kinds of effort.

The first was the securing of writers and subjects that would maintain the standard set at the beginning, together with the tactful rejection of numbers of proffered articles from men (often personally distinguished) whose primary interest seemed to be the chance to get their names before the public. The second was the very careful supervision of the text of all articles before they went into print.[210]

While it was true that Coolidge found "a source of pleasure and interest" in his frequent trips to New York, Harold Coolidge has recorded that his brother "never . . . quite got over the irritation caused by having to pack his bag and take a night train in order to see someone whom he could not be sure of putting his finger on when he got there." [211]

Coolidge and Armstrong were in almost daily communication, by letter, telephone, or trips back and forth. Armstrong "learnt constantly from him" and relied on Coolidge's "wise judgment and advice, his knowledge of what men are like and how the world they live in may be made more pleasant, more peaceful and more intelligent." [212]

At an earlier time Coolidge had expressed to his father the fear of becoming a dilettante. His whole career — as book collector, library director, scholarly expediter, foreign affairs adviser, editor, and teacher — was that of the most effective kind of generalist in an era not yet overwhelmed by the need for specialization. Coolidge was always ready to recognize that his pioneering work in international studies and in the building of scholarly collections was a kind of "stop-gap," as he said. For lack of financial support he would find, lend, or give the money; for lack of scholarly materials he would see that they were acquired; for lack of teachers he would teach himself. He was modest about his own contribution and though a talented teacher was

[210] Coolidge and Lord, *op. cit.*, p. 316.
[211] *Ibid.*, p. 309.
[212] *Ibid.*, p. 319.

all too conscious of the constant effort needed to keep abreast of advancing scholarship. Coolidge substituted for Robert Howard Lord one day when his colleague was ill. He explained to the class that he had once given the course. "Since then," he remarked with humorous self-depreciation, "much has been learned about Russian history — but not by me!" [213]

In a letter perhaps intended to secure support for Far Eastern Studies at Harvard, he wrote to his friend Charles R. Crane:

Since my early days here, that is some twenty-five years ago, I have been very keen on the idea that the subjects I was personally most anxious to see taught by the History Department at Harvard were, besides Slavic countries and the Balkans which I tried to do myself and most of which Lord now does, Latin American History and the History and Conditions of the Far East. I have dreamed, fussed and schemed about these two for many years but I have felt that they could not be established in the way they should be without a definite special foundation. A few years ago we were given $125,000 for a Chair in Latin American History and Economics. It took us some time to get the right man [Clarence Henry Haring, A.B. 1907] but I believe we have succeeded at last and this matter is taken care of.

As for the Far East, where I have been able to specialize a little myself, I have never looked on my own courses as anything but a stop-gap which I would give up with pleasure any time we could get a real authority on the subject. In the meanwhile I have built up the literature on the topic here, as you know, and since my return from Paris I have again twice given my half course on the Far East. I have done this quite unwillingly because I have lost touch and am not likely to specialize on the the Far East again, but it seemed to me so shameful that Harvard should not have some instruction that I have filled the place as best I could . . .[211]

Coolidge's efforts resulted in 1923 in an anonymous fund to support a lectureship in the history of the Far East for a five-year period, the beginning of a more securely financed scholarly program in an area to which Coolidge attached singular importance. Coolidge also played some part in the establishment of the Harvard-Yenching Institute, set up at Harvard in 1928 by the trustees of the estate of Charles M.

[213] Interview with W. L. Langer, 31 October 1973.
[214] A. C. Coolidge to C. R. Crane, 3 February 1921. Charles Richard Crane (1858–1939), whom Coolidge had known since 1891, was scion of the plumbing fortune, civic reformer and devoted internationalist. He had been a member of the Root mission to Russia in 1917, a member of the Inter-Allied Commission on Mandates to Turkey, and, for a brief period, American Minister to China. Crane's son, Richard, was the first American Minister to Czechoslovakia and his daughter, Frances, married Jan G. Masaryk, son of the chief founder of Czechoslovakia.

Hall (1863–1914), bachelor philanthropist and discoverer of the first commercially successful process for making aluminum. Although the real leader of the effort from Harvard in the early stages was Dean Wallace B. Donham of the Business School, Coolidge was a member of the organizing committee and was instrumental in the trustees' decision, prior to final agreement, to give $5,000 to Harvard for the purchase of Chinese books and to underwrite the salary of a curator.[215]

The Stalwart Advocate

Despite his absences and outside interests, Coolidge was almost always on hand in time of need, and the Library officers found him a just mediator in internal matters and a mighty advocate when the Library's integrity seemed threatened. President Lowell was not always understanding of Library problems. Coolidge had to take his case time and again to the President — and sometimes the Corporation, explaining patiently in elementary terms why the Library personnel needed higher salaries, why the book funds were insufficient, why additional University appropriations were required for cataloguing, why the budget could not be cut.

Coolidge encouraged an attitude of self-reliance on the Library's part and only bothered Lowell and the Corporation when the cause seemed to him extraordinary and just. One senses that this had not always been so in the days of Lane, who did not have Coolidge's bold decisiveness when it came to Library money matters and had wearied — even irritated — Lowell with his appeals for help with library problems which exceeded his very modest budgets. A sample was Lane's request in 1909 for an additional University appropriation to help with part of the cost of "classifying our books on Church History." Ephraim Emerton[216] had been urging Lane to do something about this important collection because, as a result of the death of John Harvey Treat, A.B. 1862, the Library was to receive a bequest

[215] A. C. Coolidge to E. H. Wells, 3 January 1927. The curator was Dr. Alfred Kaiming Chiu, who was to serve with distinction as Librarian of the Harvard-Yenching Institute until his retirement in 1964.

[216] Ephraim Emerton (1851–1935) was Winn Professor of Ecclesiastical History, an historian of the papacy and of the Renaissance and Reformation. He was graduated from Harvard College in 1871 and taught in the University from 1876 until his retirement in 1918. Emerton's *An Introduction to the Study of the Middle Ages* took a cultural approach to the subject and was widely influential.

of not only Mr. Treat's considerable collection in the field of Christian archeology and church history but also a fund for further acquisitions. Coolidge had underwritten the services of T. F. Jones [217] to work on the bibliographical collections of the library during the summer and had volunteered to continue with this expense if Lane would put Jones on the task of arranging the books on church history. "There can be no question, I think," Lane argued in a letter to Lowell, "that we ought to take advantage of Mr. Coolidge's offer, but the library must provide for the clerical work necessary." Lane explained in detail how he proposed to carry out the project and what it meant in rearrangement of books.[218] He estimated a clerical cost of "forty to fifty dollars a thousand titles. No very large sum, as you will see, even if it turns out that we have four or five thousand titles to put into the collection. This sum will have to be provided in addition to our ordinary running expenses . . . I hope you will feel justified in approving . . ." From Squam Lake, N.H., Coolidge added a word of his own, in expectation that another Library request for extra money from the Corporation might irritate the President. "I greatly hope," he pleaded,

that you will not refuse Lane the money he needs for reclassification of Church History. It does not seem to me a suitable point at which to call a halt on him, for it is in no sense an idea of his own. It is all my doing, indeed it was I that got Emerton, who has wanted the rearrangement for years, to go and talk to Lane as a preliminary. A few years ago I calculated that the Library wasted about five hundred dollars a year on its classifications, that is to say it will cost that much to change to their permanent numbers the volumes which (at equal cost) are now given temporary ones. The sooner the new classifications are made the more money will be saved in the end.

As a further practical argument Coolidge contended that it "may be long before we can get so good a man as T. F. Jones," who "knows a

[217] Theodore Francis Jones, A.B. 1906, Ph.D. 1910, Litt.D. (N.Y.U.) 1951, who was associated with the Harvard Library from 1909 to 1910, worked on Bibliographical Periodicals and began a classification of Church History and a reclassification of British History. Later he spent some time with A. C. Coolidge in France and helped him with local travel arrangements. Coolidge's letters to Jones detailing motoring difficulties, the perils of road and engine troubles and the need for new tires, are an amusing contemporary sidelight on a pioneer automobile driver. Jones became Director of the University Heights Library of New York University in 1922. He also served as Professor of History. He retired in 1951 and died in 1968.

[218] W. C. Lane to A. L. Lowell, 13 August 1909.

great deal of history and several languages" to carry out such a "complicated" classification. "The ordinary member of a library staff would putter over it indefinitely." [219]

Apparently the Coolidge argument of spending money to save it won out with Lowell, for Lane got his special appropriation and moved on with the work. However, Coolidge recognized that he could not often go back to the well for an extra portion beyond what had been rationed. One of the first things he did after becoming Chairman of the Library Council was to warn the Council that the Library must be cautious in its dealings with the President and Fellows:

> As far as the chairman is able to make out, the Corporation has been irritated by a number of small demands for money which, though not considerable even in their total, have come frequently. This has been due to the fact that there has been no regular budget account with fixed estimates. Therefore each little extra expense has had to be provided for by a fresh appeal to the Corporation, while economies (and there have been many of them) have received little or no credit. The chairman believes that it would be most unwise for the new management to begin by asking some fresh small subsidy, especially in view of the present financial condition of the University. For the time being we must get along with what we have and console ourselves with the hope of obtaining substantial and needed increase of our resources at a later date.[220]

The remarkable fact about Coolidge's financial administration of the Library is how rarely he had to appeal to the President and Fellows for extra help — and when he did so, it was usually only as part of the annual budgeting process, contrary to what seems to have happened before he took charge. His first major appeal was for assistance in cataloguing reform in 1911. First he asked for an annual budgetary increase of $4,400, which was granted. Then he requested that money already in hand — the balance of a gift, most of which had been used to pay for the 1907 addition to Gore Hall — be assigned to cataloguing. He expressed gratitude for "the kindness of the Corporation in making some increase in the Library budget," but pointed out that "catching up with arrears . . . must demand an extra subsidy." The Yale Corporation had recently granted the Yale Library $10,000 a year for five years to correct their cataloguing deficiency — "a situation which it is admitted there was not as bad as our own." Coolidge recognized

[219] A. C. Coolidge to A. L. Lowell, 10 August 1909.
[220] A. C. Coolidge, "Abstract of Statement made by the Chairman of the Library Council," 26 January [1910].

that he "could not properly appeal for even a much smaller gift of the same sort from the current income of the University." But the capital fund in question was "not [in Coolidge's words] large enough to count much towards a new building." [221] Since Coolidge had already secured "the complete assent and approval of the donor" [William Amory Gardner, A.B. 1884, Coolidge's first cousin], the Corporation found it easy to grant Coolidge complete discretion in the use of Mr. Gardner's money.

The second major instance of a special appeal came in connection with the move into the new Widener Memorial Building. Coolidge had obtained in 1913–14 a grant for book moving, the same appropriation ($41,000) which the Corporation had agreed to give him in 1910–11, plus the income of the Amey Richmond Sheldon Bequest (1909) originally given for the rebuilding or enlarging of the Gore Hall library ($16,200). This, together with miscellaneous income, came to a total of $58,123.86 — an amount "obviously far from adequate to meet the requirements" for operating in the new Library building in 1915–16.

Coolidge felt that salaries, purchasing, accession and cataloguing costs would not be affected by the new building.

What does and will affect them is the steady growth of the institution and in particular of the Funds and Bequests devoted to the special purchase of books, not to speak of gifts of books themselves, sometimes thousands of volumes at a time. This growth we could not stop if we wanted to. All the books that come have to be attended to, and even the looking up, handling and getting rid of great numbers of duplicates is a costly matter.[222]

Coolidge warned that circulation costs would be bound to increase as would superintendence of the various rooms and keeping rooms open at night, care-taking and cleaning, heating, light and power. Coolidge had been able to save one salary by not replacing a deceased employee [223] but "a successor . . . will be a prime necessity in the

[221] A. C. Coolidge to the President and Fellows of Harvard College, 27 September 1911, with a covering note to "dear Lawrence": "I enclose a rather important screed for the Corporation, I think it explains itself and have only to add that the idea is not a new one but one that I have been nursing for some time."

[222] A. C. Coolidge, "Memorandum to the Corporation on the Expense of Running the Library in the New Building," 26 March 1915.

[223] Thomas J. Kiernan, for thirty-six years Superintendent of Circulation and a veteran of fifty-nine years in the Library's employ, died on 31 July 1914 at the age of seventy-seven.

new building." He proposed that "in this difficult situation" the Corporation allow him the same budget for 1915–16 as in the previous year but including the salary of the Superintendent of Circulation. "With these sums allotted to me and with what I can save on cataloguing and various extras and present expenses, I will do my best to meet the heavy increased charges." He asked only that the Corporation assume the cost of heat, water, light and power — "an item of unknown magnitude that under the present circumstances I cannot fairly be expected to determine or control except that I shall seek to avoid waste." [224] Coolidge recommended that the Inspector of Buildings and Grounds accept responsibility for this part of the Library's operation. As with other instances of a well presented, carefully argued, almost prearranged plan, Coolidge received the assent of the President and Fellows.

Coolidge was a careful and close-fisted budgetary officer and a firm but fair bargainer, willing to beg piteously for more money from the President and Fellows but realistic when he was — or surely would be — turned down. In response to a hopeful request from T. Franklin Currier that Coolidge ask the Corporation for money to help with the acquisition and cataloguing of scientific books, Coolidge's hand-penned edict (14 November 1917) was loud and clear: "All idea of asking the Corporation for any further grants may be dismissed without an instant's hesitation at the present time."

The Director took pains to encourage a practical and pragmatic outlook on the part of his staff; he told his department heads on 5 September 1919:

> Please remember in making out your estimates of expenses for the coming year that besides the statement of what you consider as indispensable, you should be ready with a statement of what you should recommend in case, as is practically certain, the Corporation refuses any increase of the subsidy that it pays to the Library.[225]

There was a recurring necessity to remind the Corporation how fortunate they were that the Library was not a complete dependent. In a long memorandum of 1920 discussing the practicality of putting the Library budget on a more "rational footing . . . providing I do not lose anything in the process," Coolidge remarked to Lowell:

---

[224] A. C. Coolidge, *op. cit. supra*, note 222.
[225] A. C. Coolidge, "Memorandum to Department Heads," 5 September 1919.

The Library is of course a great charge on the general funds of the University but I do not believe the Corporation realizes how well off they are in this respect. I believe there are very few, if any, college libraries in the country where all the books are got from special funds and none at the expense of the general budget of the University. The special funds also for running the Library, though quite inadequate of themselves are still a useful contribution lacking in most libraries . . . We have an annual income of about $41,000, which must be spent on the Library in any case and therefore costs nothing to the Corporation and the general funds. The income of the $150,000 given by Mrs. Rice and her children will add to this amount . . .[226]

The Fellows, despite their desperate searching for ways to cut expenses, were never able to cut back the already hard-pressed Library. Coolidge was always a staunch defender of his case and could retreat to higher ground, with the argument that he himself was contributing heavily, both for acquisitions and for the running expenses of the Library. The President never ceased to try to cut costs — as he did on 7 July 1922:

Dear Archie:

The University is poor, and we are now running a very heavy deficit; and it has been necessary to cut down wherever possible. It seems to me that it is possible in the Library. That you are managing it with extreme efficiency I do not for a moment doubt; but it does seem to me that it could be managed more economically when it is necessary, as it is now. I am asking Mr Mead [227] to talk with you about it.

But Coolidge was ever ready with a straightforward response and his own little reminder about the true state of the Library's resources:

Dear Lawrence:—

All right, I appreciate how bad the University's financial situation is and that your own position in the matter is most difficult, not to say painful, and I shall meet Fred Mead in that spirit. But there are certain essential facts to which I shall call his attention as being fundamental.

1. The books purchased by the Library come from gifts and restricted funds which cannot be applied for other purposes. At present they are being used with particular profit, as owing to exchange there are wonderful chances to get books of permanent value from Europe oftentimes at ridiculously low prices. Other acquisitions come from gifts; for instance, I profited by my stay in Russia to buy and present some 2,500 volumes to the College Library and perhaps 1,000 to the Law School. The opportunity to get these works was

[226] A. C. Coolidge, "Some Reflections Suggested by Reading the Treasurer's Report on the Library," 28 December 1920.

[227] Frederick Sumner Mead, A.B. 1887, served as Comptroller from 1920 to 1926.

unique, there will be no such chance again and they put us in a class by ourselves on Russian history, art and law, but even if we do not catalogue them
the cost of handling them is considerable and I have no idea what to do about
binding. We are always liable to get valuable unforeseen gifts which have to
be looked after somehow.

2. I am expending yearly $2,500 given me by Jack Morgan to help out in
emergencies, and $5,000 out of my own pocket not on books but on admin-
istration.

Nevertheless:

3. According to the statement of July 1st we have some 17,000 volumes and
as many pamphlets still uncatalogued, not to speak of countless reports, etc.
This statement also includes a list of eighteen of the most important things in
the way of back work which need to be attended to. We are continually receiving requests from departments and professors for the making of useful
special lists or improvement of existing ones, requests which are legitimate
in themselves but to satisfy which requires money and we need perhaps $20,000
to catch up with our binding and rebinding. From this you will see that I
am not swimming in plenty.[228]

Fortunately for posterity Coolidge set down on paper before his
conference with Comptroller Mead the story of the library budget
under his administration. From the time of the move into the Widener
building, he had, he asserted, "only asked twice for an increase of appropriation, an increase rendered inevitable by the growing size of
the machine and much greater expense of wages and everything else."
He reiterated the inevitability of the Library's costs and made some
reasonable suggestions as to simplified accounting procedures. He
then declared:

I wish just to mention without emphasizing two or three points which
bear on the general situation of the Library. To begin with we are really
living considerably beyond our regular income. The $5,000 a year that I
have given for the Endowment Fund for five years is, as you know, by special
agreement devoted to the expenses of the Library. Two years hence it will
come to an end. Also what rather troubles me, I am spending just now $2500
a year which Jack Morgan gives me for extra expenses for something very much
like regular ones. Then there are such details as the fact that I pay for my
secretary out of my own pocket though the greater part of the work she does
is for the Library. It is true that on the other side, I help myself to stationery,
stamps and telephone wires without giving any account for them. The thing
that troubles me most is that I am desperately up against it on the subject of
binding. We need at least $5,000 to catch up with the regular binding and
repairing, and as much more to bind the rest of the Wendell books and plays,

[228] A. C. Coolidge to A. L. Lowell, 10 July 1922.

and finally the gift of Russian books we are just receiving will probably need $5,000 more and I haven't the faintest idea of how to get the cash for these objects.

I do not wish to bother you with my troubles, you have enough of your own but I will end with a small compliment to myself, although it is particularly foolish at the present time. Since I have been in charge of the Library, I have never gone to the Corporation at the end of the year and said that I had miscalculated and must be helped out, though I have been pretty close to the line. I call this compliment to myself particularly foolish just now as a month or so hence my expenses for this year have got to be summed up and who knows what accident may happen.[229]

Needless to say, Coolidge's budget was allowed to stand unaltered.

Two years later, however, Coolidge found he had to increase his normal budget request by $10,000 "though it will be far from meeting all the demands." To the President and Fellows he pleaded:

It has been only possible to keep up as well as we have for the last four years by all sorts of expedients, and particularly by devoting to expenses of administration the five thousand a year which has formed my contribution to the Endowment Fund, and by also devoting to what have really been current expenses an unwarrantable part of the twenty-five hundred a year which Mr. J. P. Morgan has sent personally to me to expend at my discretion for desirable extras or to help out in tight places. It must be my endeavor in the future to use this money, which might cease at any time, not as a part of the regular budget, in whose preliminary estimate it should not appear, but as an extra in the way the donor intended. Also my own contribution to the Endowment Fund will come to an end in a month or two and though I hope to be able to make gifts to the Library in the future for things in which I am particularly interested, I am not prepared to bind myself in advance to contribute a fixed sum to purposes of regular administration.[230]

Although concurring with Coolidge's request, the President was not above delivering his own little dig in the interest of economy and efficiency, for he was ordinarily rather well informed and, as a noted walker, made a point of inspecting most of the outposts of his domain during the course of a year. His powers of observation and assessment were quick and sharp. It was not often that he could catch Coolidge in a budgetary miscalculation and, into the bargain, give fatherly advice on administration, such as the following:

[229] A. C. Coolidge to Frederick S. Mead, 8 June 1922.
[230] A. C. Coolidge to the President and Fellows of Harvard College, 14 March 1924.

Your budget has come in, and I shall recommend to the Corporation to make the increase of $10,000 that you ask for. I shall, however, change the total, because the lighting this year is to be furnished to you by the University for $5000 instead of $8000, as you put it in your budget. Therefore this makes the total $157,000, which, with the reduction in the charge for lighting, will be $10,000 more than for last year.

As I wrote you the other day, I think that we have a right to ask for more administrative efficiency in certain directions. I recognize the difficulty of this with a librarian who is not in vigorous condition [meaning Lane, then in his mid-sixties], and yet I am well aware that some pressure from the top often improves conditions. Mr. Carney [Superintendent of the Buildings of the College Library], I think, ought to do his job better. He never gets there early to see that his cleaning force is on time. He ought to do so at least occasionally. Then, as I go through the catalogue room, it seems to me that the work there — which is badly in arrears, — could be speeded up. A little pressure from you, without the expenditure of much time or nervous force, would not fail of its effect on sluggish subordinates.[231]

Handling President Lowell, Coolidge found, was a skill to be specially developed. The ever enthusiastic James Buell Munn proposed to Coolidge that he [Munn] try to impress on President Lowell the importance of Harvard's acquiring an important collection of Elizabethan and Caroline literature and of interesting either Clarence Dillon or Vincent Astor in putting up the necessary money — provided Lowell had no other plans for seeking their help. Quelling Munn's eagerness, Coolidge gave a candid picture of how to deal with Lowell:

I think [your suggested letter] would be a decided mistake . . . The size of the sum needed for the collection . . . would take his breath away, especially as he has hardly the faintest natural appreciation of things of that kind. I doubt if anyone, for instance, had less knowledge or sympathy with the books his sister collected than had her brother, a fact by the way of which she was fully aware. All this I have had for years to take into account. He is not a good person to argue with but he has at least a very satisfactory appreciation of results. It is no use trying to persuade him that your hobby is as worthy of support as his, but if you can put the thing through successfully without having to appeal to him, he is the last man to quarrel with the results. In the fifteen years or so in which I have been trying to run this shop, I have acted in an infinite number of cases in a way that would not have met his views in that particular instance, but I believe he is content with the total achievement. I do not feel that I have a right to do things that would interfere with his

---

[231] A. L. Lowell to A. C. Coolidge, 4 April 1924.

Charles Chauncey Stillman, first chairman of the Friends of the
Harvard College Library.

THE HARRY ELKINS WIDENER MEMORIAL LIBRARY

CAMBRIDGE, MASSACHUSETTS

August 19th

Dear Mrs. Rice:

Mr. Wells has told me over the telephone of the latest instance of the splendid generosity of you and yours. It is impossible for me to convey to you an adequate expression of my thanks, both official and personal, yet I must try to do so as perhaps no one has been in a better position than myself to appreciate not merely the present difficulties which you are so generously helping us out in, but still more the vast benefaction you have bestowed upon Harvard and upon generations to come of American students and scholars. In the five years since this library was opened I have had opportunity to know the building in every corner and to realize how marvellously satisfactory it has proved itself to be. It is a great monument and a great laboratory. Many years ago President Eliot once asked me if I regarded the college library as the most important thing at Harvard. I answered him "Yes, perhaps not at some one moment, but as a permanent factor in the value and success of the University". In those days we

Letter from Archibald Cary Coolidge to Mrs. Rice, 19 August [1920].
[page 1]

merely had our collection of books which served as the indispensible nucleus but which we were unable to make profitable to the fullest extent. Now, thanks to you we have unrivalled facilities in a magnificent setting. I have been in a position to observe the wonderful assistance that this building renders to students of the most different kinds and the unique advantages it gives to Harvard among American universities. I have also heard from the lips of many how those advantages are appreciated and how much gratitude they as well as we owe to you. Naturally, the expense of running this library as it should be run is not and can not be slight. We have struggled with the task to the best of our abilities, and as you do not need to be told, the fearful rise of all costs has rendered it hard for us to keep up the proper standard of efficiency and to make both ends meet. All the more do we appreciate this fresh instance of your kindness and generosity and that of your son and daughter. I can only hope that the work done here may be such as to make you feel that your gifts have been well bestowed.

I remain

Most truly and gratefully yours

Archibald Cary Coolidge

Letter from Archibald Cary Coolidge to Mrs. Rice, 19 August [1920].
[page 2]

Edgar Huidekoper Wells, Coolidge's "confidential man of all work."

general plans but in following out my policies I go my own way unless I have to appeal to him for assistance, which fortunately is seldom.[232]

The same year in which he had to explain the budgetary facts of life to Munn, Coolidge was forced once more — "most unwillingly and after scaling down demands" — to tell the President that he needed $5,000 more for general expenses in the Library's 1926–27 budget. A twenty-percent increase in book fund income and the receipt by gift of "so great a number of valuable works, probably a hundred thousand dollars' worth for English Literature alone," meant increased costs of handling and cataloguing. The "greatest care is essential when the wrong arrangement of words in the title or a misfiling may result in the purchase by some generous benefactor of a duplicate costing hundreds of dollars," he explained to Lowell. "Owing to the extraordinary pressure we have been under and of which I see no prospect of immediate diminution, both the Ordering Department and the Cataloguing one have fallen very seriously behindhand and are losing ground steadily." The new McKinlock Hall library for freshman would mean additional work, he predicted. "As for special collections [like that of Miss Amy Lowell] they are simply shoved to one side till we can find time and means to take care of them, which is hardly encouraging for future donors." The rate of book circulation, Coolidge reported, had increased "by thirteen percent in the last three years," and routine expenses had continued to mount with greater Library use. "It should be noted, too," he cautioned the President, "that though the budget has much increased in recent years in spite of all efforts to keep it down, this has been due to the growth of the Library and to higher prices, not to branching out in new directions."[233]

Again the determined Coolidge prevailed in argument and received approval for the budget he recommended.

The Founding of the Friends

Throughout its history the Harvard Library has depended on its friends to support its objectives and fill its frequent special needs. Perhaps as much as any Harvard institution the Library has been a

[232] A. C. Coolidge to J. B. Munn, 16 February 1926.
[233] A. C. Coolidge, "Memorandum to Accompany Budget Statement of the College Library," 30 April 1926.

favorite "cause" for the alumni and others interested in the College. One has only to read in Quincy's history the compilations, prepared by Andrew Eliot, of gifts to restore the Library after the destructive fire of 1764 to realize that that storehouse of knowledge, the University's book collections, was regarded as a community resource of prime importance.

The efforts Harvard officers made over the years to augment the meager funds available for purchasing scholarly collections or individual items of importance had a haphazard and disorganized character. When a catalogue came or an opportunity to bid at auction, Harvard's librarians rarely had enough money to spare from the limited purchase funds. It was not good policy to take the chance that money might be forthcoming from alumni and friends after the decision to purchase or bid had been made. So, lacking confidence, they waited impatiently but prudently while they tried to dig up the funds by personal appeal to prospective donors.

When Archibald Cary Coolidge became Director and enlisted Edgar H. Wells [234] as secretary to the Library Council, he encouraged Wells to carry on an extensive correspondence with Harvard graduates and friends who might be able to help Alfred C. Potter and the Library secure important additions to its collections.

Wells never held a formal position with the Library, except for his honorary curatorship of Modern English Literature (1903–1913). When Lane proposed a more formal tie, Coolidge vetoed the idea, telling Lane:

> I do not see any object in making Wells a technical member of the staff and though I have said nothing to him I believe he would prefer to remain a free lance, neither receiving orders from, nor giving orders to any member of the staff save such as are put under him for a specific purpose. My own position in the past has been not unlike this, especially when I have been putting through some particular job . . .[235]

But in the years subsequent to his Harvard period Wells never for a moment lost his interest in the University or the Library, and he was of immense assistance to Coolidge during the latter's entire directorship. Initially Wells, as Secretary of the Library Council, worked on

[234] See note 33. "Not only has he got large amounts of money for the Library in the past ten years," Coolidge commented to Walter Lichtenstein on 19 May 1913, "but his advice and still more his stimulation to me cannot easily be replaced."

[235] A. C. Coolidge to W. C. Lane, 15 April 1910.

what today would be called "development" — undertaking to raise funds from the Library's friends, in Coolidge's behalf, wherever a special want needed filling. While Lane signed most of the routine acknowledgments of gifts received, Coolidge relied heavily on Wells to conduct the more delicate correspondence with important alumni, for Wells through his Alumni Association connections was on familiar terms with scores of Harvard men interested in books.

For instance, when the great book collection of Robert Hoe came up for auction in London in 1910, Edgar Wells accepted the responsibility of rounding up alumni who might help Harvard acquire some of the important items of English literary value. Since only $800 was given for this purpose by a group of six alumni, among them Robert Bacon, A.B. 1880, James A. Stillman, A.B. 1896, George Wigglesworth, A.B. 1874, and Lucius Wilmerding, A.B. 1901, the Harvard bids did not make much headway in a sale where the prices were (in Potter's words) "exorbitant," (and in Lane's) "from three to ten times what we were willing to pay." Perhaps it was just as well, for later in the year most of the money was "applied with great advantage to the purchase of original issues of English poetry of the seventeenth and eighteenth centuries, in folio form, offered for sale by Pickering and Chatto in London." [236]

Later, when Wells had completed his war service with the Red Cross, he reentered Harvard's service in a voluntary capacity as vice chairman of the Harvard Endowment Fund drive of 1919–1920. Following this venture, he formed a business partnership with Mrs. Phillips Blagden Thompson (wife of a classmate) for the sale of books and prints. In this role he was of continuous help to the Library, particularly in searching out important books and collections and finding the donors to buy them for Harvard. Further, he was perhaps the most active member of the Visiting Committee and a leading promoter of a scheme to establish a Friends organization for the Harvard Library.

One might of course argue that the institution of honorary curators for the various special collections was a kind of Friends organization. This system antedated the Coolidge administration but he brought it to full flower. As Coolidge explained its rationale:

[236] Fourteenth *Report* (1911) of William Coolidge Lane, Librarian of Harvard University, p. 32.

The curators are appointed annually by the Corporation and are interested in some particular side of the Library. It is not that we divide up the various topics and appoint a curator for each; on the contrary the list depends on the hazard of circumstances and I try to keep the number down. When some good heeler comes along who is really interested in a particular subject . . . and who would like to feel that he has an official connection with the University . . . I see if I can create a place accordingly.

There are no fixed duties . . . a kindly eye on the special collections . . . suggestion, advice, or any other assistance . . .[237]

But as to a formal Friends organization the Library was a relative latecomer. The Fogg Art Museum had organized its "Friends" in 1913, modelling the group on Les Amis du Louvre. As a starter the Fogg had used the class registrations in past Harvard art courses to compile a list of prospective members and had set a scale of membership fees to provide additional free funds for purchases and exhibitions.[238]

Coolidge had long wanted to organize a small group, each member of which would agree to give on a regular basis a certain sum for book purchases. The tradition is that Coolidge too during one of his leaves in Europe after World War I "became interested in the work of the Société des Amis . . . at the Bibliothèque Nationale [and] . . . was convinced that such an organization would have value for Harvard." [239] The Library, unlike the Fogg, had no basic list that could be used to initiate subscriptions from friends. Thus the scheme was slow in taking shape and it was not until the spring of 1925 that the practical details were worked out in correspondence among James Buell Munn, Wells, and Coolidge. Charles Chauncey Stillman, A.B. 1898, and one or two others were signed up prior to a dinner which Wells arranged in Coolidge's honor at the Harvard Club on Friday, 10 April. The plot was to have the Director discuss library problems and the idea of a Friends organization would be broached.

During that week — a time of better postal service — letters went back and forth between Coolidge in Cambridge and Wells in New York regarding Coolidge's part in the dinner and the best way to enlist members of the Friends. Wells wrote on 7 April 1925:

[237] A. C. Coolidge to J. B. Stetson, 1 March 1921.

[238] See "Friends of the Fogg Museum" by Edward W. Forbes, *Harvard Graduates' Magazine*, XXII (September 1913), 213–214.

[239] Mary C. Hyde, "History of Library Friends and the Phoenix Story of Columbia," *Columbia Library Columns*, XX:3 (May 1971), 3–8.

. . . a dinner jacket is the thing. Cannot you tell how long to talk as you feel out your audience? The men will be naturally interested in everything you say. I would suggest talking not more than forty minutes and then let the rest of the material be used as questions are asked. If there is anything you wish brought out by inspired questions, please instruct me or James Buell Munn.

And on the following day [8 April] Wells sent Coolidge further thoughts on the matter.

By all means let us hear of the weak spots as well as the strong spots of the Library. Have your thoughts clarified on the "Friends of the Library"? If organized, will they receive the warrants from the Corporation or simply from the Library Council? May a man become a "Friend of the Library" without a gift of either books or money? . . . I am sure that the Library can be richer by a good many thousands a year if you start on a systematic campaign of enrolling people, by persuading, inspiring, or otherwise inducing people to make annual contributions for special objects.

Coolidge responded on 9 April:

It is perfectly easy to speak about the weak spots of the Library. I had intended to touch on them as well as on the strong, the only question being that of the proportion between the two. . . .

As for the Society of the Friends of the Library, my own feeling so far is that it would be better to have it outside of and independent of the Library authorities, although in close touch with them, nor should there be anything to do with the Corporation. The suggestion should come, not from me, but from someone else at the dinner. The Society could be run by a small committee who should feel free to invite and gather in such members as they chose and on such terms as they chose. It might seem as if this were an amateur effort to duplicate the Visiting Committee, but the Visiting Committee is an official body whose primary duty is to inspect, report upon and indeed condemn the object of their inspection whenever it is necessary. Visiting Committees have raised much money but some of the members have always resented any suggestion that this was part of their function. . . . Members of the Visiting Committee would naturally in many if not all cases be Friends of the Library and the managing committee of the Friends would be obvious people to put among the Visitors. The Library itself should be ready to furnish all possible information to the Friends and it might be best for the committee of the Friends to keep control of the funds raised by them, in which case whenever the Library saw a particularly tempting offer that it was unable to meet itself, it might be sent down to the Friends to see how it struck them.

Invitations had gone to some thirty people, of whom seventeen attended, in addition to Coolidge and Wells. Apparently it was Wells and not Charles Chauncey Stillman who acted as the initiator by putting the question to Coolidge about the Friends.[240] Stillman must have been a quick seconder, for he was already an enthusiastic proponent and had predicted to Wells on 7 April that, if a group could be signed up, "in no time you will have an annual contribution amounting to $10,000.00 for the library, without it being burdensome on any one of the givers. Go to it!" The original nineteen Friends were (in addition to Coolidge, Wells, Munn, and Stillman) James Byrne, A.B. 1877; Thomas W. Slocum, A.B. 1890; Frederick Roy Martin, A.B. 1893; Jerome D. Greene, A.B. 1896; Harry M. Lydenberg, A.B. 1896; Grenville T. Emmet, A.B. 1897; Phillips Blagden Thompson, A.B. 1897; Langdon P. Marvin, A.B. 1898; Bridgham Curtis, A.B. 1899; Edward Mallinckrodt, Jr., A.B. 1900; Harold R. Shurtleff, A.B. 1906; James Lloyd Derby, A.B. 1908; William G. Wendell, A.B. 1909; Franklin E. Parker, Jr., A.B. 1918; and the New York bookseller, Lathrop Harper. A number of key donors such as Norton Perkins, A.B. 1898; Junius Spencer Morgan, A.B. 1914; and Henry Sturgis Morgan, A.B. 1923, were to Coolidge's disappointment among the missing. But it was a start.

Coolidge was profoundly grateful to Wells for having arranged the affair and told Wells on 13 April, "It was really a rare chance for me to meet and talk with that crowd, and it cheers one up to feel that there are such people interested in the enterprise which is dearer to one's heart than anything else." Apparently the company reacted favorably to Coolidge's remarks, for Shurtleff wrote to Wells the following week [15 April] that he thought "Professor Coolidge's speech one of the best expositions I had ever heard and the dinner an ideal one." Franklin Parker recalled that "in his informal discussion of that evening Professor Coolidge described so clearly the tremendous demands which were made upon the Library that each one present left with the conviction that he and every individual could perform a valuable service to the University in helping to supply the ever recurring Library needs." [241]

How to launch the organization? Wells was of two minds in his letter to Coolidge of 13 April:

[240] Edward Mallinckrodt, Jr., A.B. 1900, mentions this fact in a letter to Coolidge, dated 15 May 1925.

[241] Franklin E. Parker, Jr., "The Friends of the Library," *Harvard Graduates' Magazine*, XXXVI (March 1928), 368.

As far as the Friends of the Library are concerned, it seems to me there are probably only two ways of going ahead: either to have the invitations or suggestions proceed from the Library, or to have some active person outside recruit the force. Perhaps the whole idea is too formal and we could accomplish the same results by dropping the idea of the Friends and simply going out to get more annual contributions for the purchase of books. In any event, I am convinced there is money to be had if you ask for it.

Coolidge continued to favor a Friends organization. On 30 April he wrote to Wells, suggesting Jerome Greene as "a possible person to run the business of the Friends of the Library." When Wells agreed, Coolidge wrote to Greene on 19 May, outlining the purposes of the organization and explaining:

Between my trying to put it through and somebody running the thing from outside, there is the difference that there is between asking alms for yourself and suggesting to a friend that he might like to subscribe to a worthy charity. The Library should keep track of what is being done and should be ready to furnish all requisite information to the Friends at any time, but ought not officially to invite anyone to join the sacred band.

Of course the person who could and would make a success of the enterprise is Edgar himself. Unfortunately, I fear he is right in his strong feeling that his present occupation renders it impossible for him to carry out the plan. It might well happen that some of the money received would go for purchases made through his firm and he has got to avoid what would even suggest a suspicion that his business interests would profit by a thing that is solely for the benefit of the Library . . .

Greene did not refuse outright, but observed that "I have had so many Harvard irons in the fire that I am not sure that I can be as effective as if I came fresh to the task." He added that "we are going to have some difficulty in making the methods and aims of the Harvard Fund understood and I am a little afraid of muddying that situation . . ." [242]

Munn continued to remind Coolidge of the Friends proposal and worked to supplement it, despite vigorous personal collecting activity at the same time. On 23 May he wrote to Coolidge:

I feel that my job at present is to complete the Milton and work on the 17th century English poetry.

However, a vastly more important job is to mobilize the men who are interested in books and get them to work all along the line. There is a great deal in the *Friends of the Library* scheme, and we can do something with it,

[242] J. D. Greene to A. C. Coolidge, 20 May 1925.

I am sure. A constant and intelligent interest in our problems will build up the library from generation to generation . . .

Then, after months of indecision, Jerome Greene concluded that he could not take on the Friends of the Library. Coolidge cast about in a number of places for a possible chairman, only to be disappointed. One of his ideas was to try Henry James, member of the Harvard Corporation and later the biographer of President Eliot. After lunch with James on 12 September 1925 he reported sadly to Wells that the prospect had

held forth on the topic that we must find some way sooner or later to get rid of dead books. There is something to be said for this point of view but it did not encourage me to sound him out as to whether he would be the active chairman of the Friends of the Library; indeed it made me doubt his qualifications.

In order not to lose more time, Coolidge carried on his own private donor enlistment and re-enlistment program, although he thought it wrong for the Director to be continually begging for assistance.

To the current Friends, he sent out standard, individually typed letters, dated 16 February 1926, like the following:

Although you are one of the Friends of the Library, you may not be acquainted with the great service which this organization is rendering to the Harvard Library. It is true that we have certain funds with which to meet the usual needs of increasing our collections, but it is impossible for us to take advantage of special opportunities to purchase rare and very important books or collections of books. It is for such purposes that the money of the Friends of the Library is expended. Next month, for example, Mr. A. C. Potter, the assistant librarian at the head of the ordering department, will be in Paris. His visit will offer us a particularly favorable opportunity to pick up early editions of French literature at reasonable prices, and a list is being forwarded him of what we already possess. Under these circumstances it would be a favor if the Friends of the Library would send us their subscriptions for this year or whatever they wish to contribute in time for Mr. Potter to make use of the money. Please make checks payable to the Treasurer of Harvard College and enclose them to me at the Harvard College Library. Your subscription for 1925 was $50.

Such letters were a temporary measure, and Coolidge authorized Munn to ascertain whether Stillman would head the Friends. Munn found Stillman receptive, to Coolidge's relief. On 17 March he wrote to Munn:

It is very good news that Stillman is willing to undertake the scheme of the

Friends of the Library. As you know, I have always felt strongly, in spite of Wells's opinion to the contrary, that the organization should be an outside one run by people who have an interest in helping things along and getting others to help, and not merely a list of names like the countless ones made out for professional purposes, to whom the Library should send out begging circulars, as often as we think we can get something out of them. What the Library can and should do is to keep in close touch with the chairman or secretary of the Friends, furnish any information that is asked for and report when particular chances turn up which may seem to warrant a special effort. It was only because matters had reached a deadlock and under pressure from Stillman that I unwillingly sent out a circular signed with my own name. In all this, mind you, I am not criticizing Forbes and Sachs and the way they handle the Friends of the Fogg Museum which seems to me splendid. The Library problem is a different one.

During April, Munn and Coolidge drafted a circular; but Stillman departed for Europe before his assent could be obtained to publishing it over his signature, and apparently it was never used. Much to Coolidge's regret, Stillman failed of election to the Harvard Board of Overseers at Commencement 1926, and it was a tragic blow to the Friends' scheme when he died on 31 July. His loss was "calamitous" (Wells's words in a letter to Coolidge of 11 December), particularly because Stillman had agreed to give money to support part of the salary of George Winship in his new capacity as Assistant Librarian in charge of the Treasure Room.

Disappointed in his efforts to get the Friends organization out of the Director's office and into the hands of a responsible alumnus, Coolidge confided to Roger Burlingame, A.B. 1913, the writer and editor, on 2 November 1926, "The Association of Friends is rather halted now owing to the death of Chauncey Stillman who was at the head of it. I trust we may find a good successor." Lacking that paragon, Coolidge labored hard to maintain interest and engage fresh support. Every suggestion of a possible helper he followed up vigorously. In a letter to one such he wrote on 11 March 1927:

The facts of the case are that though we have considerable funds and make many purchases, the field of books which we should like to have, and indeed ought to have is illimitable. Our regular resources have to go for the most part to meeting every day wants but there are countless opportunities of acquiring the sort of things which give distinction to a library and make it a really great institution. For these, we have to rely on accidents and the generosity of graduates and friends. We have much to be thankful for in this respect but every book counts, and counts permanently, and we therefore welcome particularly the association of "Friends of the Library" which has already helped us to purchase a good many worth while volumes which we should otherwise have missed. We are also grateful for the assurance that our graduates are interested in maintaining and, as far as in our power, in fortifying our present position of leadership among university libraries and our no small place among the libraries of the world.

For this handsome appeal Coolidge received a firm pledge of ten dollars per year! Like a Rembrandt forced to sell a masterpiece for a pittance, Coolidge questioned his own capacity as a fund-raiser:

> As a beggar, I have always been a failure. I suppose one reason is that it is hard and disagreeable to me and therefore I do it badly. I don't dislike it because I disapprove. On the contrary I have a frank admiration for people . . . who do it so unselfishly well but I know that I am not born for it and the older I get the worse I become . . .[243]

Coolidge, Wells, Munn, and Parker did most of the soliciting for the leaderless Friends; adherents numbered only about fifty in the first years. Finally, as a stopgap measure, at Coolidge's request, Franklin Parker accepted the position of Executive Secretary of the Friends of the Library.[244] To back him, a Committee of Sponsors was organized composed of Francis R. Appleton, A.B. 1875; George Lyman Kittredge, A.B. 1882; William Cowper Boyden, A.B. 1886; Chester Noyes Greenough, A.B. 1898; E. Hubert Litchfield, A.B. 1899; Edwin F. Gay, LL.D. 1918; William R. Castle, Jr., A.B. 1900; Edward Mallinckrodt, Jr., A.B. 1900; Thomas Barbour, A.B. 1906; James B. Munn, A.B. 1912; T. Jefferson Coolidge, A.B. 1915; and Owen D. Young, LL.D. 1924.

In a description of the founding and support of the Friends, the Executive Secretary declared, shortly after Coolidge's death:

> The Friends of the Library welcome large contributions, but the association is not greatly interested in the size of a gift. What it particularly wants is a membership composed of sincerely interested persons who are watching and

[243] A. C. Coolidge to E. H. Wells, 17 March 1927.

[244] Only a year before, Coolidge had expressed his fear that Parker was too young for the job. He told Munn on 23 December 1925, "Franklin Parker, my former secretary in Europe, lunched with me here Saturday. He is keenly interested in eighteenth century English literature and is beginning to collect. I intend to make him an honorary curator of the Library in that subject and I think he will be really helpful. If he were not so young and were not just starting things, he would make an excellent secretary of the Friends of the Library."

following the Library and who will preach its mission among their friends, for if this membership is large enough and spreads throughout the world, the aggregate of contributions will be sufficient to carry out that which the association seeks to do. And the interest of this membership will be the inspiring force that makes the administration of the Library accomplish miracles. If those in Cambridge who guide the destinies of the Harvard Library knew that a group of ten thousand persons were actively and directly behind them in the task of keeping the Library in its position of prestige, there is nothing within reason, or even a little beyond it, which could not be accomplished.

He added:

Professor Coolidge's death was an inestimable loss to the Library. Since he became Director in 1910, he had an inspired vision. It was his dearest interest in Cambridge. A five-minute conversation with him would have been sufficient to implant in the most complete bibliophobe the seeds of real devotion to the Library's work. There could be no more fitting memorial to Professor Coolidge than a large, active and efficient Friends of the Library, and those who knew and loved him can pay respect to his memory, in the way which he himself would prefer, by membership in this association.[245]

Whatever the founding priority of Friends organizations among American libraries, Harvard seems to have been at least slightly in advance of her traditional rival in New Haven, for Munn provided intelligence (12 June 1925) that, "wealthy Yale graduates are not organized, but contribute hit or miss, and . . . additions to the Elizabethan Club are not being made — all of which persuaded me that we are on the right track with the Friends of the Library idea."

[245] Franklin E. Parker, Jr., *op. cit.* (note 241), 368–372.

The Man and the Tradition

ALTHOUGH THE written record tells much, some personal testi-
mony recreates a picture of Coolidge life-size. Armstrong has
left us the image of a man "of medium height, square shoul-
dered, broad chested" suggesting a "sturdiness more to the eye than in
fact." One might dispute the "medium height," for Coolidge was only
five feet six inches tall, and for his stature perhaps a little overweight.
There was a certain rotundity to his waistline. Armstrong remembered a "countcnancc frank and tranquil" and "blue-blue eyes" which
"looked at you steadily whether benevolently or in exasperation,"
rather sparse hair brushed forward and faintly parted in the middle
and cut short in such a way as to give "an old-fashioned fringe effect
across his broad and high forehead." [246]

This, combined with his general physique, gave him a Napoleonic
look which some thought he intentionally cultivated. There the re-
semblance ended, however, and in no other way could this shy and
kindly man be thought an imperial figure. Instead, there was a refreshing quaintness about him. One recognized him almost instantly as a
unique product of a special environment. He had "a rather funny
walk" with feet turned out (as W. L. Langer remembered), "a kind of
strut," his secretary called it, but a very quick step and an overly
straight carriage, almost leaning over backward.[247] Coolidge was one
of those persons who have more important things to think about than
the trivia of personal appearance or manners. Yet he could be utterly
confounded if he caught himself, through his own absent-mindedness,
wanting in courtesy or consideration of others. He spent money on

[246] Hamilton Fish Armstrong, *op. cit.* (note 209), p. 186.
[247] Statements of W. L. Langer (31 October 1973) and Helen G. Powers (7
November 1973).

his clothes, yet never really looked well dressed. He was always just slightly rumpled, or his tie — in those days of stiff collars — was not cinched up above the stud. He was simply unconscious of such things, and Langer remembers how horrified he was to observe that Coolidge rarely if ever wore an overcoat even in the coldest weather, although always a hat to cover his thinly thatched head as he hurried from the library to class.

There was also the speech defect which added to the quaint impression. People joked about his inability to pronounce the letter R. Ever current, ever retold, was his supposed response to the inquirer who asked the source of Coolidge's amazingly wide knowledge of the world, "Oh, I wead and I wewead and I bwowse awound."

Some of those who knew him well, like Langer, felt that the speech handicap was a serious embarrassment to him, particularly in lectures before large groups of students.[248] Yet once the initial contact was passed, the students got used to him and forgot his somewhat eccentric manner, sensing only his obvious command of his subject and his fairness of judgment, respecting his high standards and revelling in the way the subject came alive under his guidance.

There was no doubt that he was at his best at the graduate level. The devotion and gratitude of a generation of distinguished scholars of diplomatic history attest to that, but he was also one of those undergraduate teachers who, fathers told their sons, should not be missed. In his rather dry and straightforward manner he had something to say,

---

[248] His nephew and namesake thinks that the speech peculiarity can be overemphasized. Certainly it made no apparent difference to Coolidge in his ordinary dealings with people. He did once tell his nephew that he had contemplated early in life calling himself Cary rather than Archibald, but he had been discouraged by the fact that he had difficulty with the letter R. One family legend attributes to a childhood nurse the business of pronouncing R like W. She is said to have consciously drilled into the five Coolidge brothers this manner of speech because she thought it elegant — something like the Yankee affectation of dropping the final "g" when talking of "fishin', shootin', huntin', and nothin'." Whatever the cause, the peculiarity seems to have had little effect on Coolidge's fluency in French, Russian, German, or any other of the seven languages he knew well. At the time of his wartime "trade mission" to Sweden, under State Department auspices, his nephew asked him whether he spoke Swedish. Coolidge replied that he was taking a Swedish grammar book with him and planned to study the language on the boat. "One knew perfectly well," his nephew commented, "that he was going to get by with it." In diplomatic matters he always wanted to speak the other fellow's language because, as he often said, "I want to be the one who makes the mistakes." (Statement of Archibald Cary Coolidge, A.B. 1927, of Cambridge, Maryland, November 1973.)

and one of his basic teaching principles, often reiterated, was, "If you notice your auditors' attention wandering, don't try to be eloquent — throw in a date and everyone will jot it down."

Langer's first exposure to Coolidge was in the fall of 1920, with three other students in Coolidge's research seminar on the eighteenth- and nineteenth-century history of Continental Europe and Asia. They met on the top floor of Widener in one of those rooms "which I came to think of as the greatest abomination for there was nothing in them except the tables and the chairs, and the rooms were so resonant that you could hardly understand what the fellow on the opposite side of the table was saying to you. Archy was talking about the war and the peace conference and so on, and I was immensely impressed almost immediately with the humanity of the man." When the class discussed the mistakes of omission and commission made by the leaders of the time, Coolidge "was always very alert to the circumstances of the case. He would say, 'Have you thought how little sleep those men were getting and how easy it is to make a slip when you're tired?' All the way through there was an extremely humane quality about him, a tremendous wisdom, and his influence could not help but rub off on all of us." He had a knack for stirring his auditors and for jolting conventional opinions. Jane Revere Coolidge Whitehill, daughter of Archibald Cary Coolidge's brother Julian (later the wife of Walter Muir Whitehill, A.B. 1926), remembers how startled she was "when he suggested the to me unthinkable idea that the Allies might lose World War I and when he compared the Bolsheviks to the Revolutionary French of 1793 who were at war with the rest of Europe and carrying on the Revolution as well." [249]

As with anyone who has touched constructively the lives of many people and several institutions, Coolidge evoked a variety of memories. To the student of the 1890s he was a junior lecturer with an awkward way of inflecting sentences, who twisted his feet nervously around the rungs of his chair — and even in later life went through the tortures of the damned in the hour preceding his opening lecture. For others he was the genial, well-informed, widely-traveled man of the world, the conversational host of Randolph Hall who could be found reading the St. Petersburg (Leningrad) daily papers over his breakfast eggs and toast. For still others he was an enthusiastic young clubman, keen as

[249] Jane R. C. Whitehill to W. Bentinck-Smith, 11 April 1974.

a Teddy Roosevelt about the fortunes of the varsity football team and the crew.

But this was the Coolidge of a youthful period.[250] As time passed his direction became more purposeful, his determination more unrelenting, his pace more intense, his attitude more statesmanlike. His clubbable qualities, which in mid-life were of the intellectual sort, brought him warm academic and international friendships and a wide range of acquaintance among men of his own cast of mind in the larger community of Boston and New York. Otherwise for him society and social life were of small interest. Social functions were to be loyally tolerated rather than enjoyed. He avoided them whenever he could. He hated to waste time on non-essentials.

Coolidge struck many of his staunchest admirers as a fundamentally self-sufficient, perhaps even lonely, man. As one of Coolidge's most devoted graduate students, Langer could not help but note the solitary nature of Coolidge's life.

He didn't have many people to talk to about the subjects that most interested him and began to count on my looking in on him every day at his office in the Library. He loved to talk to me about some book sale or purchase and if I had noted the appearance of some new book about European policy, I would tell him about it, and he would say (leaning forward and pointing at me with his index finger), "Have you ordered that for the Library?" That was always his first question. But he would also love to talk about books in general and about the recent events of European diplomacy, and if I did not look in on him some day, he would ask, "Where were you yesterday?" I really saw him almost daily, and sometimes it was a little bit of a burden because graduate students are very busy. I still can't go in the front door of Widener now without looking down the corridor where his office was.[251]

Members of the Coolidge family have long thought that the broken engagement of his youth seriously affected Coolidge's relations with others.[252] To have his love and intimacy rebuffed unexpectedly was

[250] By 1920 his early interest in athletics, augmented by his service on the Athletic Committee, had waned in favor of weightier matters. To his friend Bingham in New Haven, he wrote (9 November), "Thanks for . . . your invitation to stay with you at the time of the Yale game. To tell the truth I did not take the trouble to apply for tickets. I have no doubt it will be a fine spectacle if the weather is good but I am not quite as keen on football as I once was."

[251] Interview with William L. Langer, 31 October 1973.

[252] The lady in question was Corina Anna Shattuck, twenty-year-old daughter of George Brune Shattuck, A.B. 1863, Boston physician and Harvard Overseer. Whatever the reason for the rupture, it appears not to have been the presence of an immediate rival. Miss Shattuck did not marry until five years later. She then became

a shock from which he did not quickly recover. He told his sister-in-law Mary Hamilton Coolidge [253] that, after failing to patch the rift with his fiancée (following his hurried trip to Boston from St. Petersburg), he threw his revolver out the window of his bedroom lest he be tempted to use it on himself. Such an overly dramatic gesture gives some measure of the depth of his despair, which members of the family felt colored his relationship with other people for the rest of his life, driving him into a fundamental reserve and solitude. "I think he shunned intimacy," said his nephew Archibald Cary Coolidge II (son of his brother Julian). "A great many people were very much devoted to him, but I think he was mistrustful of ever letting himself go, of expressing emotion. He felt he had been burned, and badly burned, once. He was never going to run the risk again of getting involved."

Coolidge never referred to his own love affair, except obliquely. Once, because their names were the same, the elder Coolidge mistakenly opened "a fairly amorous letter" from a lady friend of his nephew. "I think this must be for you," he said, handing it to his nephew. "It has been some years since anyone addressed me in quite such terms." On another occasion he remarked that it was a mistake not to get married because it tended to make one selfish. He was particularly devoted to his brother Randolph's wife — "a remarkable woman of warmth and benevolence" who, in Jane Whitehill's words, "managed to combine a universal, affectionate motherliness along with an attitude of deference to the learned attainments of her brother-in-law." Mary Hamilton Coolidge "was such a wonderful person, such a truly magnificent person that she alone would have been enough to discourage a bachelor brother-in-law from marrying. He would know right off he couldn't possibly do as well as my Uncle Randolph, and I really think this may have entered into my Uncle Arch's attitude toward marrying." [254]

The family circle in which the five brothers had been brought up was not especially conducive to an easy relationship with the opposite sex. As Mrs. Whitehill put it:

---

the wife of one of her father's classmates, more than thirty years her senior. (Statement of Archibald C. Coolidge, November 1973, and *Report of the Secretary of the Class of 1863 of Harvard College*, Cambridge, 1903).

[253] Wife of his elder brother, Randolph. (Statement of Archibald C. Coolidge, November 1973.)

[254] Statement of Archibald C. Coolidge, November 1973.

A.C.C.'s father had grown progressively deafer from the age of twelve. Having married a woman with sufficient money to maintain him, he gave up the struggle to compete, and retreated within himself, cut off from easy association with other people by his deafness, and compensating for his disabilities by being strictly formal, entirely conventional in outlook, and convinced of his own aristocratic superiority. His wife was a plain, unassuming, dumpy woman, without an atom of "side," and with a paralyzing shyness that made it difficult for her to go outside her family circle. She had an affectionate nature, and a healthy sense of humor, with a store of wisdom; all her five sons loved her dearly. There were no daughters. Had there been, or had Mrs. Coolidge been of a gregarious disposition, women, young, middle-aged, or old, might have flocked to the house. As it was, A.C.C. and his brothers grew up in a household woman-less but for their mother. To them women were exotic specimens, on pedestals higher even than was usual to the Victorians. At least this was true for the two shyest brothers — A.C.C. and Julian. As he grew older A.C.C. appreciated women who were pretty, graceful and vivacious — a pleasing adjunct now and then to life, but scarcely a necessity.

The painful shyness in expressing his feelings, even to those he loved most, approached inarticulateness. One of those of the younger generation who had been closest to him was his namesake, Archibald Coolidge. To the latter, Uncle Arch was a kind of second father, an advisor and friend all his youth. In June 1927, on his wedding day, the nephew last saw his uncle.

A few hours before the ceremony, he came up to me and said, "Well, if there's anything — if you ever need anything — well, if there's anything anyone can do, you know to whom to turn." I made no oral reply, simply put my arms around his shoulders and squeezed them. Embarrassed, he said some seconds later, "Well, as I say, if you ever need help, you know to whom to turn." This remark cost him considerable effort. He was the exact opposite of people who say things and don't mean them. He meant them and couldn't say them without a tremendous struggle.

And so, more than most, Coolidge was married to his work, and the Library was both vocation and avocation.[255] It was a devotion which filled a large portion of his days, occupied many of his evenings, and went with him on his vacations or his trips abroad. He was never in spirit far from the library and he did much of his writing and lecture preparation in a small study in the stacks where he was safe from intrusion. Knowing his conscientiousness no one could be surprised to

[255] To Mrs. Flanagan of the Library staff who was leaving for a yachting trip one summer Saturday and wished him a good weekend, he commented, "The Library is my yacht." (Mary McIntire Flanagan to T. F. Currier, 7 February 1928.)

see him at the end of the day carrying out of the library a tray of cards to work on in the evening or on Saturday or Sunday in his rooms in Randolph. For the average librarian [256] this was not a practice to be encouraged — what if some of the cards got lost? But it was one of the ways Coolidge cut through established procedures to get things done. However, he never permitted himself to shortcut his commitments to teaching. Not even the prospect — much as he desired it — of hearing Ramsay MacDonald, the British Prime Minister, speak at the Council of Foreign Relations in New York could persuade Coolidge to absent himself until he had secured W. L. Langer's assent to drive the two hours from Worcester to take his place in the classroom.[257]

Coolidge's life was a life of books. He was seldom without them. In his younger days he traveled across Asia with a little trunkload of them. In later life, even in the garden at Tuckahoe,[258] he read as he walked up and down the mile-long "cedar lane." More than a writer or a talker, he was a reader. Although he was never at a loss for words, he had a distaste for public oratory. He liked the small audience rather than the large. In view of the breadth and volume of his library activity and outside responsibilities, the total of his published work was relatively slight — slight at least for so distinguished and influential an academic figure, but not surprising considering the busy character of his life.[259] Yet at least one of his books was an extraordinary achievement, showing a "prescience" (as Langer has put it) which makes it worthy of note in American intellectual history.[260] In this life of

[256] The term is used generically. One of the few times the younger Archibald Coolidge ever saw his uncle "blow his top" was when the latter, having heard his nephew apply it to him, exploded, "Don't call me libwaywian!"

[257] Langer was then Professor of History at Clark University. After this incident Coolidge asked him several times to take his place.

[258] Tuckahoe was the Randolph family plantation on the James River, one of the boyhood homes of Thomas Jefferson, an estate going back into the early years of Virginia history, which Coolidge, his father and brothers acquired in 1898. Coolidge owned a quarter interest in the property. He was also always ambitious to preserve his great-great grandfather Jefferson's "Monticello."

[259] His principal published works were *The United States as a World Power* (1908), *Origins of the Triple Alliance* (1917), and *Ten Years of War and Peace* (1927).

[260] Coolidge's book *The United States as a World Power* (New York, The Mac-Millan Company, 1908) originated as a set of lectures written for delivery in 1906–07, when Coolidge was exchange professor at the Sorbonne. Since Coolidge's aim was to inform a non-American audience about American historical development and American attitudes, the book is written with a deceptive simplicity and directness which are particularly attractive. So perceptive was Coolidge of the principles and

books — books as the foundation stones of learning — the Library was the focal point. As one staff member put it:

> It was funny about Mr. Coolidge, and some people might have thought it looked like he was snooping around, for he was always turning up all over the building, looking up the books he wanted himself; and he would come in at night just as we were locking up, on his way home from a dinner party or something like that, wanting to talk about the things we were planning to do. We wouldn't have stood it from anybody else, but you never minded it from Mr. Coolidge; you could tell him everything and you knew he'd be perfectly fair, and that he cared more for this Library than anything else in the world.[261]

His closest friends, outside of his own family, were those who made his work possible and successful. Although colleagues might work side by side with him, there was that ultimate shyness and reserve that for most precluded real intimacy. Coolidge did not readily give himself to others and did not expect others to give themselves to him. His intimates at Harvard were primarily History Department colleagues like Roger Merriman and Charles Haskins — or the breezy, good-humored Bruce Hopper, the war-time flyer whose great walking trip across Asia appealed to the romantic side of Coolidge's nature. But for others of his close associates — even one as close as Langer, who was his doctoral student, his assistant, and ultimately his successor — no matter how much they admired and loved the man and how much they shared common interests, there was never truly personal intimacy.[262] Langer has ventured that at least in his case the age difference and the widely disparate backgrounds were contributing factors.

---

problems affecting the United States in its relations with the other major nations that most of the viewpoints expressed hold as true today as seven decades ago. Essentially a liberally minded conservative in the best sense of the term, he was a man of forward-looking, refreshing common sense, alert to the possible and the practicable.

[261] Quoted from George Parker Winship, "Archibald Cary Coolidge," *Harvard Library Notes*, No. 20 (April 1928), p. 157.

[262] One would have thought, for example, that there might have been a close friendship between Coolidge and the man who became his biographer, Robert Howard Lord. But in point of fact Lord was "three times as buttoned up as Coolidge" (Langer's words) and, though an excellent lecturer, clear and well-prepared, and a frank and perceptive critic, Lord was an "armored person." Coolidge had immense admiration for Lord, but Lord was not the kind of man to call forth Coolidge's real affection. When Lord became a Roman Catholic and took holy orders, his former associates wondered if he would go on to a career in church history, but Coolidge perceptively remarked, "Make no mistake, Lord doesn't want to be an historian. He

Coolidge's shyness and the withdrawn quality of his personal life might suggest a kind of aristocratic exclusiveness. Nothing could be more unfair, for he got on well with all kinds and conditions of men. He was simply a solitary soul, shunning close ties. Because his work took him to many places and brought him many acquaintances in various parts of the world, he enjoyed constantly changing scenes and thoughts. As his brother Harold commented, "If his close intimates were few, his family affections were, on the other hand, very deep-rooted." He was very close to his brothers, particularly his brothers Harold and Julian. He made a regular practice of dining with the Julian Coolidges on Thursday evenings and was meticulous in having dinner every Sunday evening with his parents and others of the family circle whenever he was home.

The wide range of Coolidge's interests and knowledge was not immediately apparent to the younger generation of his family when listening to his conversation, but the young could not fail to be aware of what Jane Whitehill has called "the razor-like cutting edge of his mind." As for herself, she "tended mentally to step aside, much as I should today keep at a respectful distance, physically, from a man working a power saw."

Alongside the consciousness of his sharpness [she added], went the awareness of A.C.C.'s devouring nervous energy. At our house he did most of the talking, while the rest of us listened, and Father put in a comment or a question now and then. He spoke rapidly, and even in an upholstered chair sat hunched forward, giving the impression that his arm and leg muscles were tense. I never saw my father relax except in a sailboat, and as I never saw A.C.C. in a sailboat, I never saw him relax at all.

Coolidge's filial or fraternal letters, written with dutiful weekly regularity when he was away, have about them the ring of love and intimacy which he did not easily show to others. Yet he had the capacity to evoke from teaching colleagues, students, and library associates an exceptional quality of admiration and devotion which seems naturally to characterize one with the teacher's gift — a teacher whose standards are "exceedingly high" (Langer's words) but based on sound knowledge; a teacher who influences by example (an admirer called it "the contagion of his leadership, his sober but lighthearted insistence on all that is true" [263]) and calls forth the very best in those who come

wants only to be a humble priest scrubbing the floors of the church." (Interview with W. L. Langer, 31 October 1973.)

[263] Henry Goddard Leach to Harold J. Coolidge, 17 January 1928. A graduate

into his sphere of influence; who shares his wisdom with his pupils and treats them as adults; who inspires them and gives them incentive — that "twist of the wheel" [264] so important to all human activity.

"It is not too much to say that most of the best men in the younger generation of university teachers of modern European history in the United States have been moulded to a greater or less extent by his influence and precepts," Roger Merriman declared. Langer felt his "whole career hinged on this man. He was the one who taught me, the one who inspired me — the one who set my mind."

All the voices of the past seem fully agreed on the wisdom and intellectual breadth of the man and the attractiveness of his personality and disposition. Witness after witness speaks of his composure and good humor. Only those closest to him knew that he had a hot temper also, and that the price of self-control sometimes came hard, so hard that in a strange puritanical effort at self-discipline he would stuff a handkerchief in his mouth and turn away shaking with rage until he gained sway over his passion.[265] This childlike gesture served to cover his embarrassment as well as his annoyance. It sometimes seemed to be prompted by his not knowing quite what to say, and he usually blushed very easily under such circumstances. As Merriman said:

The dominant feature of his character — the moral complement as it were to the immensely wide range of his intellectual interests — was an abounding and affectionate sympathy for his fellow men. Every one was perpetually running to him for advice, on all sorts of subjects; and invariably received it in full measure, shrewd, humorous, and wise. He had a multitude of friends, of all sorts and conditions of life, and was unswervingly loyal to each and every one of them; if ever they were in trouble or difficulties he was the first to hear of it and speak words of encouragement, and if it were possible to do so, to give generous and devoted help. He had a remarkable faculty for discovering the good, the strong points, in every man he met, and emphasizing and capitalizing them to the utmost; not that he was blind to their faults — for he was an excellent judge of character — but he often affected to ignore them, for he acted upon the principle that the good drives out the bad. He was always a positive, never a negative force: he believed in "getting things done," and was impatient

---

of Princeton and a Harvard Ph.D. (1908), Leach was long the leading spirit of the American Scandinavan Foundation and from 1921 to 1931 held the curatorship of Scandinavian history and literature in the Library.

[264] T. F. Currier to A. C. Coolidge, 25 July 1919, "I have been holding off hoping that you would suddenly drop in on us and give the necessary twist of the wheel."

[265] Gertrude M. Shaw to Rene K. Bryant, Associate Editor, HARVARD LIBRARY BULLETIN, 29 October 1973.

of the waste of useless friction and misdirected strength; but his energy was held in leash by shrewd and cautious planning, and he never tried to carry a program into effect without careful consideration of all its possible consequences. He was almost pathetically modest — at least in all essentials — and utterly unconscious of the place that he held in the hearts of his friends; but with that modesty there was coupled a very keen sense of personal dignity, nay, more, a harmless and really charming vanity about little things, which occasionally cropped out . . .[266]

Coolidge was one of those hyperactive beings[267] who are forever building. First it was his own career. Then Randolph Hall, the private dormitory — his concept — designed by J. Randolph Coolidge, Jr., financed by four of the five brothers, his home for more than two decades.[268] Then it was his department, then the Library collections, then the catalogue, then the Library building itself, then *Foreign Affairs*, and then the organization of the Library Friends. One further project — an eight-year undertaking — was a personal one. This was the big country house of native stone and timber which he erected near Squam Lake on a New Hampshire hillside on the tract of land that he had gradually accumulated over the years.[269]

Coolidge in his later years had become more and more of a landowner — indulging in what his nephew John in friendly exaggeration has called a "seigneurial tendency." At the urging of his children, J. Randolph Coolidge, Archibald's father, purchased in 1893 a 350-acre New Hampshire farm on the shores of Squam Lake in Sandwich, but

[266] Roger B. Merriman, "Archibald Cary Coolidge," *Harvard Graduates' Magazine*, XXXVI:144 (June 1928), 556. Helen G. Powers, Coolidge's secretary from 1920 until 1928, cites two instances. One Class Day, J. P. Morgan came to call on Coolidge and smoked a cigar in his office. For some reason this amused Coolidge immensely and for years he kept Morgan's cigar band in his desk as a souvenir of the mountain's coming to Mahomet. On another occasion, when Coolidge visited the State Department in Washington, he was deeply impressed that the doorman greeted him by name and he assured Miss Powers with surprised and strangely naive relish that such an honor was reserved for only the most important people.

[267] "I sometimes wonder if my own temperament isn't entirely too mercurial," Coolidge told Munn on 16 February 1926, "as I seem to have a good many moments of optimism and despondency which often succeed each other with too great rapidity. In general, I think the optimism prevails except when I am a bit tired."

[268] Coolidge used to say that his brother Randolph's original design did not include staircases. ("Just the sort of thing that delightful guy would have left out." Statement of Archibald C. Coolidge, November 1973.) Julian Coolidge chose not to participate in the fraternal project because he did not approve of luxurious dormitories for undergraduates.

[269] See Coolidge and Lord, *op. cit.* (note 2), p. 334.

the senior Coolidge, though he added to the holdings, never really liked the place and finally gave it to his sons in 1908. Archibald took his share of 268 acres and over two decades purchased more and more land, at first "absurdly cheap," later "the opposite," until he became the proprietor or co-proprietor of 4,600 acres of mountain, lake, and forest, maintaining eight farms, a camp on Hoag Island, and a modest timber and sugaring operation which never really paid.

The place at Squam was about as much of a hobby as Coolidge ever had. The people who kept him company there were more likely to be family and family connections rather than academic friends. Coolidge was particularly conscientious in sharing it with his nephew. His namesake was "the bad boy with the good name," as he insisted on calling him until the labored humor became painful. Despite the four decades of difference in their ages, their friendship — though principally a summer matter — became fast and enduring.

Beginning in 1913, there was hardly a summer until his uncle's death when the younger Coolidge did not spend at least two weeks at Squam. From 1915 onward he went, usually unaccompanied, as the express guest of his uncle. They lived at "The Farm," a house owned jointly by the brothers, and Uncle Arch devoted a very large part of his limited summer vacation to seeing that his nephew had a pleasant and profitable time. In those early years, when the boy was only nine or so, the usual routine after breakfast was to walk from "The Farm" to whatever place his uncle had selected as a point of interest. The eleven miles of roads were then in the process of being built, culverts were being laid, and there was a sawmill in active operation. The sawmill was almost always included in their travels.

Archibald Cary Coolidge, senior, had "absolutely no gifts with his hands," and what he could not do himself for lack of skill and experience he enjoyed watching others do. His sawmill might have been more profitable in another location but Coolidge wanted it where he could look at it. He had no particularly deep interest in forestry, conservation, or lumbering. His main interest was "in saving rundown New Hampshire farms and providing good housing for the men who worked on the place and in encouraging their native skills." To such an extent the sugaring and syruping, the sawmill, and even his brother Harold's tree-planting and sheep-raising were matters of continuing interest rather than activities in which he played a personal part.

The morning walk of uncle and nephew ended at a portable house which the elder Coolidge had erected on the site where he later built his big "Stone House." Here, while the uncle wrote letters and worked, the nephew amused himself with boyish pleasures, until just before lunch, when the pair were reunited for a swimming lesson. Uncle Arch seemed no swimmer in his nephew's eyes. He had never learned to dive, and his style was limited to the breast-stroke. But he was a patient and long-suffering instructor whose efforts were crowned with success on the day young Arch, out beyond his depth, grew panicky, and his uncle told him with characteristic calm to "swim back!" He found he could.

For one who had been a modestly successful boxer and wrestler in his college days, a cyclist on European travels, and a hiker of necessity through the Burmese back country, Archibald Coolidge was strangely clumsy in his physical movements. Early in his career he had an interest in Harvard athletics, heightened perhaps by his service as member and chairman of the Athletic Committee, but he played no games for fun, and he had no time for them anyway, nor any special skill. He found exercise in tramping the roads and paths of his New Hampshire property. In the late winter he might even take to snowshoes to supervise the syruping operations. But Uncle Arch's antics with snowshoes were such as to reduce the younger generation to near hysterics. "He was absolutely hopeless on them, yet the job was absolutely hopeless unless one had them," so deep was the snow.

In one trick with his hands, however, he was singularly adept. He always wore boots, never shoes, and gave as the reason that with shoes he was constantly kicking himself in the ankle. His nephew, Archibald Coolidge, remembered:

In those days men's boots had little hooks instead of eyelets on . . . the last three or four "holes." Uncle Arch could, and habitually did, lace his boots with one hand. This, believe me, was no mean performance. I tried vainly to master the art at odd times, but unlike such manly skills as whistling through one's fingers, the necessary practice was such that the result hardly seemed to justify the effort.[270]

Coolidge was not above laughing at himself, such as the time he and his manager, James Rogers, walked long hot miles through heavy brush to inspect a recently acquired piece of land. When at last Rogers announced that they had arrived at the northwest corner of the Atwood

[270] A. C. Coolidge to W. Bentinck-Smith, 30 January 1974.

The official portrait of Archibald Cary Coolidge by Marie Danforth Page,
painted posthumously for the Harvard Faculty of Arts and Sciences.

The Coolidge brothers ca. 1904

Left to right: (standing) John Gardner Coolidge, Harold Jefferson Coolidge, and Joseph Randolph Coolidge, Jr.; *(seated)* Julian Lowell Coolidge and Archibald Cary Coolidge.

The Coolidge brothers in 1924

Left to right: (*standing*) Archibald Cary Coolidge and Harold Jefferson Coolidge; (*seated*) John Gardner Coolidge, Joseph Randolph Coolidge, Jr., and Julian Lowell Coolidge.

Randolph Hall, the dormitory financed by
four of the five Coolidge brothers.

The Coolidge house at 130 Beacon Street.

property, Coolidge responded cheerfully and breathlessly, "I have the gweatest wespect for the northwest corner of the Atwood pwoperty."

Though his correspondence shows Coolidge to have been a person of warmth and good humor, he was not in any sense a wit. His humor was of the facetious variety, and he abhorred frivolity.[271] "Stop the kidding, stop the kidding," he would tell his nephew, using the term not in its usual sense but as if it meant, "stop being childish!" His teasing was well meant, but its effect could be crushing. Jane Whitehill remembered vividly an instance of her uncle's facetiousness:

> There had been a French-speaking governess at our house every summer of my youth, so that my brothers and sisters and I had acquired a better than usual proficiency in French, and I think our father was pleased with our accomplishments. But recently turned seventeen, I was a Radcliffe freshman, a singularly unprepossessing, and immature one, of moderate attainments, not pretty, not neat, and not gaudy either. One morning my father was accompanying me to Widener Library to help me in starting on a paper that I was excited about, that, with very little encouragement, I should have been glad to discuss. On the steps of Widener whom should we meet but A.C.C. "Jane is going to write a paper on Molière," my father explained. "Can you spell his name?" asked A.C.C.[272]

The big "Stone House" — although in today's terms highly impractical for a single man — provided pleasurable distraction from the time its foundation was laid in 1919. Coolidge insisted that no work take place unless he was on the scene, and all the materials came from the Squam property — "smooth-faced stone quarried from nearby mountain ledges" and wood cut on his own forest land. He was in no hurry — "even the long delays while local materials were being selected and assembled were more pleasurable than frustrating." His usual routine, as has already been noted, "consisted of sleeping at the family farmhouse a mile away and spending most of the day in a small glass portable house which . . . gave him the chance to look at the marvelous view and oversee his building operations, while at the same time pegging away continually at literary or some other work." [273]

[271] Though he was far from being a prudish person, his conversational code, at least with the young, did not include matters related to sex. The younger Archibald Coolidge had a feeling that this topic would have acutely confounded his uncle. "He never smiled at a broad joke, let alone repeated one and would have been embarrassed had one been told in his presence, which must have happened occasionally." (A. C. Coolidge to W. Bentinck-Smith, 30 January 1974.)

[272] Jane R. C. Whitehill to W. Bentinck-Smith, 11 April 1974.

[273] Coolidge and Lord, *op. cit.* (note 2), p. 334.

The building was far more pretentious than its owner really desired — "somewhere between English and Polish baronial" in the eyes of the architect's grandson, Joseph R. Coolidge, 4th. "The great hall, 25 feet by 30 feet, was sheathed in oak panel, went up two stories into the roof trusses, with hand-hewn ten by ten inch oak beams on view everywhere." Throughout, it was "built of the best (and most expensive) materials, so that it was imposing and enduring. A.C.C. cared that it should be so," his niece Jane Whitehill recalled.

The Stone House was finally completed in August 1927 but by that time Coolidge was already hopelessly ill. He lived there only five weeks — helping abate his physical pain by reading detective stories — but he had the pleasure of achievement and, as his brother said, "full measure of satisfaction during the . . . years of planning and building." [274]

Another acquisition was the big old-fashioned double-fronted Boston house at 130 Beacon Street — the water side — on the corner of Berkeley, where he had lived with his father in the old man's last years. Although he knew his purchase of the property from his father's estate in February 1926 had expensive and ridiculous aspects, it was, he told Hamilton Armstrong, "the place I love, and life in it looks far more attractive to me than any other spot I can think of." [275] Everything about it was familiar. He loved the high-ceilinged elegance and attractive proportions of its rooms, particularly the second-floor library, with its river view, where he worked at his big ebony desk. He took

[274] Joseph R. Coolidge, 4th, A.B. 1938, who in later years became the owner of the Stone House, gave a touching recollection of that last summer of his uncle's life. "He had two Irish ladies to do for him. They required their regular Friday fish, but there was no local fish market, so A.C.C. commissioned nine-year-old me to catch some each week for them. I did so, leaving my tally @ 10½¢ a pound. At the end of the summer he was too sick a man . . . for anyone to bother him with minor details, and I soon forgot our deal. He died a few months later, and in the following February, I was in hospital with an appendectomy. To my utter astonishment, his executor appeared at my bedside and solemnly produced a check for $11.40."

[275] Jane Whitehill happened to be in the room the evening when her uncle announced to his brother and sister-in-law, Professor and Mrs. Julian Coolidge, his intention of buying 130 Beacon Street. "My father," she said, "was skeptical. It was obvious to him that for A.C.C. to buy and live in that large house would be uneconomical. Yet Father was fond of his brother, and wanted to be tactful, and so he tried to do what for him was nearly impossible, to speak moderately and indirectly about his objections. To my surprise A.C.C.'s tone of voice and manner softened appreciably as he spoke of the house, and he remained firm in his intention." (Jane R. C. Whitehill to W. Bentinck-Smith, 11 April 1974.)

pride in the handsome staircase with its graceful white bannisters and mahogany rail and the big hall rather daringly decorated in red silk with white trim. Pierre la Rose [276] chose the colors and materials, and Coolidge considered the result a great success.

On the first floor was the more or less formal drawing room with its bay window and the family portraits by Gilbert Stuart, Chester Harding, Anders Zorn, and lesser artists. This was the gathering place before dinner or at tea time where old Mrs. Coolidge or Miss Helen Neill presided. Coolidge always had his tea Russian style in a glass with a silver holder, and was uncomfortable if it were given to him in any other way.

Helen Neill ran the household and was the companion of old Mrs. Coolidge until the latter's death. In Jane Whitehill's eyes:

> Miss Neill endeared herself to every member of the family, from the youngest child of the clan to old Mr. Coolidge, who, when he was 97, found her indispensable. She was the admired and beloved friend and confidante of all. A Scotswoman who had studied at Edinburgh University, she was a highly educated woman, a keen reader, and a delightfully responsive conversationalist with a quick mind and a ready sympathy. Not in the least intimidated by A.C.C., with whom she shared an interest in the political problems of the time, she came, I believe, to have a warm, affectionate regard for him, and he for her, very likely never expressed in words. A.C.C. once paid a visit to the Neill home in Edinburgh, and my mother at any rate believed that A.C.C. had marriage in mind, but was frightened off by the thought of Miss Helen's unmarried sisters (to whom she was devoted).

At the end of the first-floor drawing room double doors opened into what was known as the music room, with gilt chairs and handsome chandeliers, a place used occasionally for such family affairs as a magician's performance at Thanksgiving time, but scarcely ever for music, at least in Coolidge's lifetime. Coolidge had no special ear for music and delighted in the story of his grandfather, Joseph Coolidge, who in later life decided to become a patron of the arts in Boston, following a somewhat spotty career in the China trade. The old man, Coolidge used to recount, had no musical discrimination but he played host at many musicales and after the concert would invariably answer those

---

[276] Pierre de Chaignon la Rose (1871–1941), A.B. 1895, is perhaps best known in Harvard annals as the designer of the Tercentenary emblems and of the arms of the several faculties and of most of the undergraduate Houses. For the greater part of his life he lived in the neighborhood of the Yard, devoting himself to literary work and decorative design.

who asked him how he liked it, "I was disappointed." In this way, if the concert had been bad, he was perfectly safe. If good, it showed he had tremendously high musical standards.[277]

If Coolidge's interest in music was limited, so too was his interest in art. After becoming master of the property he did not change the pictures on the walls, he simply lived on with the decorations and furnishings that were there. Upstairs, there were a number of "perfectly bloody pictures which Uncle Arch knew were bloody." A particularly memorable one (once owned by Thomas Jefferson) focused on a gory head of John the Baptist, presumably borne aloft on a silver tray by Salome. Coolidge himself owned a number of Detailles[278] which he had purchased on one of his European trips. These apparently appealed to his romantic nature and to his interest in the military and diplomatic maneuverings of nineteenth-century Europe.[279]

The big house had been his home, and he proposed to accept it as it came to him. It was easier to stay than to move and so he rattled around there "in a curious combination of luxury and spartan bachelorhood" (as Armstrong remembered it) with a domestic staff to sweep and dust and supply him "with 'picked-up codfish' for breakfast and a cream clam chowder for at least one other meal."[280]

On 27 September 1927 Coolidge wrote to Lowell about his health problems. He had, he said, been "badly out of health the last three months and more" and thought it might even be possible that he would not be able to return to his work in the Library. "Two abscessed teeth" in August, a painful case of "sciatica," and a generally run-down condition had led him to conclude that he must follow a light schedule. "I shall be at the Library every day," he told the President, "but avoid

[277] Statement of Archibald C. Coolidge, November 1973.

[278] Jean-Baptiste-Edouard Detaille (1848–1912) was one of the most popular painters of the French school of the 19th century. He specialized in romantic scenes of military life — particularly evoking the military glories of the Napoleonic era.

[279] It was more an absence of early training than a lack of sensitivity that limited Coolidge's interest in art. He had the essential discrimination to recognize the importance of things artistic but felt no deep pull in that direction. When he told Jane Whitehill about seeing his aunt "Mrs. Jack" Gardner inspecting in Italy a group of artworks sent to her by European dealers, "he gave . . . absolutely no indication what these works of art were . . . What had stayed in his mind, he said, was the extraordinary swiftness with which the lady had made up her mind in each case, deciding at once to keep certain objects, and immediately rejecting others." (Jane R. C. Whitehill to W. Bentinck-Smith, 11 April 1974.)

[280] Hamilton Fish Armstrong, op. cit. (note 209), p. 186.

staying all day, as there is no rest to be found in one's office chair. If you and the Corporation are willing to have me loaf on my job, though I trust not for very long, I shall go ahead accordingly."

The President hastened to assure Coolidge that "your loafing will be more valuable to us than other men's work. Take it easy by all means — as easy as you want."

Coolidge never regained the strength to return to his office in the Library, even on a part-time basis. In late October he "took a turn for the worse" and (as he wrote to Armstrong) "the doctors prescribed complete rest, which . . . meant going to bed and lying in one place on my back." Through all of November and most of December he could see visitors, read, and carry on correspondence, much of it concerning the January issue of *Foreign Affairs*. Although he tired easily, he kept in "mentally good form" and almost to the end maintained his intellectual acuity.

His friends and associates in Cambridge kept him informed by personal visits or letters. He continued to "read, dictate letters and see people every day," as he told Armstrong, valiantly inviting the latter in December to stay with him, and promising to give him a room on "the floor above all the fuss of the male nurses, etc." "I get rather easily tired, that is to say a conversation of a couple of hours is about all I am really good for, but I pick up again immediately afterwards and am presently ready for another."[281]

His interest in library affairs continued unabated. The chief problem plaguing his daytime thoughts was the need to finish and furnish the uncompleted bottom two floors of Widener. Although he had several times publicly stated the need in the hope that Mrs. Rice might rise to the bait, it now seemed imperative to Coolidge to force the issue. He sent Lowell a proposed draft paragraph for the Director's annual report which would frankly urge alumni support. It was clear, however, that Mrs. Rice ought first to be consulted, in the frank expectation that she would not approve a public appeal and might decide to do the whole thing herself. By 12 December Coolidge had received word that "Mrs. Rice did not like the report a bit" but she indicated that she would come to Boston soon with Trumbauer to "talk over the matter." Coolidge recognized that, because of his illness, he could not "meet the Rices here and go about with them," but Dr. Rice's letter

---

[281] Coolidge and Lord, *op. cit.* (note 2), pp. 342–343.

filled him with "excitement." He commended the matter to Lowell's "skillful hands" and was "full of hope for the results."

As to costs, Coolidge guessed that the project might require an expenditure of $70,000 and, "if Mrs. Rice is going to have Trumbauer look after the whole thing . . . no doubt . . . a good deal more."

"It seems to me," Coolidge commented, "that however nicely we put it, Mrs. Rice is against the situation. She did not give us a finished building and she has no right to complain of our turning to the graduates, and if need be in the most public way, to do the finishing." [282]

With Currier he conducted a lively correspondence, full of queries as to the accuracy of card counts, the appropriateness of catalogue designations, the progress on accessioning Slavic items, the amount of duplication in the Boulay de la Meurthe collection, or the eventual location of Amy Lowell's library.[283] Currier reported that the man who was the source of the set of Russian Duma documents had been "imprisoned," and Coolidge expressed the "hope it was not on our account." [284]

Though flat on his back, he continued to pursue the classification of books in which he had a special interest, telling Currier, "I have not given up my intention of going to the end of the alphabet in the work I have done, in fact I have accomplished a little even here lying in bed, but looking at cards and sorting them is rather clumsy when one is on one's back. It is a slow business."

Coolidge kept pressing Currier through the fall "to get . . . the Alsace books cleaned up as part of our general drive on French history and literature," [285] and was relieved to hear a month later that the work was finished. "It has been on my mind for some time," he said.[286] He suggested that "the long closed case with the specimens of the work of the French Academicians" be opened so as to see what it actually contained. Disposition of the items could wait until he returned

---

[282] A. C. Coolidge to A. L. Lowell, 12 December 1927.

[283] A. C. Coolidge, Memorandum headed "Notes and Queries," 13 October 1927.

[284] Bolan, the Russian dealer in New York, had told Currier that the U.S.S.R. authorities were "even now tightening up their restrictions, and are making it very hard for dealers out of Russia to get the old books." (Currier to Coolidge, 6 December 1927.) Prices were reported much higher in Moscow and Bolan's agent could obtain only 60 to 70 percent of what he had been able to acquire the year before.

[285] A. C. Coolidge to T. F. Currier, 11 November 1927.

[286] A. C. Coolidge to T. F. Currier, 7 December 1927.

to the Library — "as long as they have lain in the Library for two years, a little longer will not hurt them."[287]

Lane gave him a quick report on 17 December, describing the contents of the cases and how he proposed to arrange the portfolios in drawers and on the shelves. He also sought Coolidge's comments on some of the trouble he was having in finding study space for a number of professors. With a mind as sharp as ever despite his illness, Coolidge saw the need to resort to principle as a guide out of the dilemma: "The question of studies is a good deal of a mess," he responded on 19 December.

The worst of it is, the difficulty is likely to get greater every year. We must for self protection maintain the principle that we own the studies, and not the departments or the professors . . . We had better cling to the principle that the rooms in Widener are studies, not offices. That is one reason why I have held so desperately to the idea of not having any telephones in the ones in the stack. I wish I were in a position to discuss matters with you, but heaven only knows how long I shall be glued to my backbone.

Coolidge's last letter to Currier — and one of the last he wrote to anyone — was dated 22 December; it came in response to "some cards of yours and also an old list of Bolan's[288] which Miss Powers thrust on my notice." He told Currier:

You may go ahead with the things indicated if you want, subject to the chance that I shall be so poor that I shall never buy another Russian book again. Remember that, barring our list of magazines which I may cut off at any time, I have no interest in Russian reviews or much literature of any sort after 1917; that is to say as far as I am personally concerned, I am definitely building up an old, not a new, collection of Russian books.[289]

By New Year's Day 1928 his brother, Harold Jefferson Coolidge, was writing President Lowell that "Archy gets no better in spite of the efforts of many doctors. This of course means steadily worse — and it looks as if his power to carry on as he has been doing latterly was gone."

Archibald Cary Coolidge died on 14 January 1928, a little over a month before his sixty-second birthday. The malady which struck

---

[287] Helen G. Powers to T. F. Currier, 20 December 1927. Miss Powers served as secretary to three of the Harvard Library's Directors — Coolidge, Blake, and Metcalf.

[288] Simeon J. Bolan, the Russian book specialist in New York. See note 284.

[289] A. C. Coolidge to T. F. Currier, 22 December 1927.

him down and caused him such suffering was eventually diagnosed as cancer.

In Coolidge's absence from the Library, Lane and the other principal officers had carried on smoothly, as they had on other occasions when the Director was away. But Coolidge's death presented the President with a major problem of future staffing. Lane was almost sixty-nine years old and at that age obviously not a candidate for the directorship. Potter was sixty, Winship fifty-seven, Briggs fifty-seven, Currier fifty-five. Although accomplished in their specialties, none of them had the faculty standing to recommend them to Lowell.

There is no written record in the Lowell papers that the President made an extensive search for a successor.[290] Three or four names were suggested to him — Franklin Parker, A.B. 1918, Executive Secretary of the Friends of the Harvard Library; Harold Murdock, A.M. Hon. 1916, Director of the Harvard University Press; Robert Pierpont Blake, Ph.D. 1916, Assistant Professor of History at Harvard and member of the Library Council; and James Buell Munn, A.B. 1912, Dean of Washington Square College, New York University. Because of Munn's record of enthusiastic and generous help to the Library in the years since the World War and no doubt because of Coolidge's high regard for him, the President lost no time in deciding to sound out Munn ("I fear we cannot get him"[291]) on the day of the New York Harvard Club meeting on 27 January. Unfortunately Munn was not able to meet with Lowell at that time, but the President finally wrote him on 15 February, formally inviting him to become Coolidge's successor. After five days' reflection Munn declined the post. He felt compelled to remain in New York to be close to his eighty-one-year-old father.[292] Lowell then turned to Robert Pierpont Blake, who ac-

---

[290] In addition to Nelson Perkins and others of the Corporation, the President consulted Gay, Kittredge, Haskins, Lowes, and Grandgent.

[291] A. L. Lowell to T. N. Perkins, 4 February 1928.

[292] Coolidge had tried to persuade Munn to join the Library staff at the end of World War I but Munn had decided, partly for family reasons, to take an administrative and teaching position at the Washington Square campus of New York University. "Now that five years have passed [Munn wrote to Coolidge, 21 March 1924], I can look facts in the face and tell you honestly that while the position there would have been much happier, the position here is much harder. My job seems to be to take care of approximately two thousand boys, chiefly the sons of foreign born parents. The boys are trying to obtain a college education and learn what America means. It is a hard task. Moreover there are more candidates available for

The Stone House and its view of Squam Lake.

The Coolidge Family in Brookline, ca. 1909

Back row, from the left: J. Randolph Coolidge, Jr., Mary Hamilton Coolidge (Mrs. J. Randolph Coolidge, Jr.), J. Randolph Coolidge III, Julia Coolidge (soon to be Mrs. Henry H. Richards), Archibald Cary Coolidge, Helen Stevens Coolidge (Mrs. John G. Coolidge), John Gardner Coolidge, Harold Jefferson Coolidge, and Julian Lowell Coolidge. *Front row, from the left:* Eleonora Randolph Coolidge, Roger Sherman Coolidge, J. Gardner Coolidge II, Hamilton

Coolidge, Mary Eliza ("Elsa") Coolidge, Julia Gardner Coolidge (Mrs. Joseph Randolph Coo-
lidge), Joseph Randolph Coolidge, Lawrence Coolidge, Emily Fairfax Coolidge (held by her
mother, Edith Lawrence Coolidge, wife of Harold J. Coolidge), Jane Revere Coolidge (in
front of her father), Margaret Wendell Coolidge (held by her mother, Theresa Reynolds
Coolidge, wife of Julian Lowell Coolidge), and Archibald Cary Coolidge II. *Seated in the
foreground:* Oliver H. Coolidge and Harold J. Coolidge, Jr.

VIRTUTE ET FIDE

ARCHIBALD
CARY COOLIDGE
1866 — 1928
PROFESSOR·OF·HISTORY
AND·DIRECTOR·OF·THE
UNIVERSITY·LIBRARY
NON·SIBI·SED·NOBIS
SED·PATRIAE
M·D·C·C·C·C·X·X·I·X

The Coolidge Plaque by Joseph Coletti.

cepted, and on 25 March the Corporation approved the appointment. The same day Lowell wrote to T. Jefferson Coolidge, A.B. 1915, Chairman of the Library Visiting Committee,[293] urging that the Overseers give their consent at the next meeting, and confirmation followed on 9 April.

Whether or not he knew in advance of Mr. Lowell's choice of Blake — and it seems likely that he was not privy to it — the Library's senior officer, William Coolidge Lane, wrote on 19 March to offer his resignation, "to be accepted, if you so choose, at any time after April 1." Added Lane, "I shall cheerfully stand aside if you think best."[294] A week later the President and Fellows acted on Lane's "resignation," and upset Lane's sense of propriety. "I was surprised," he told Francis Hunnewell, "to learn that the resignation had been presented and acted upon on Monday [26 March], for I had expected to send in a formal resignation addressed to the President and Fellows at some date after April 1 as I proposed in my recent letter to the President."

Lane's well-merited recognition came on Commencement Day, when he received from President Lowell the diploma of an honorary Master of Arts with the citation, "William Coolidge Lane, Librarian of Harvard for thirty years, to whom scholars are grateful for the accessibility of its vast collections."

In the meantime, at Blake's recommendation, Alfred C. Potter was

---

my Harvard position than for one like this which very few people would want." Coolidge recorded that he "never got over my grief that your connection with [the Library] did not become permanent." Munn finally came to Harvard as Professor of English in 1932.

[293] Not only was this, nationally, the Coolidge era, but at Harvard with a Coolidge presiding over the Library, another Coolidge (Charles Allerton Coolidge, A.B. 1881, a distant cousin of Archibald Cary Coolidge, the University's architectural consultant and an Overseer 1922–1928) served as chairman of the Committee to Visit the University Library from 1924 to 1926. He in turn was succeeded by T. Jefferson Coolidge, A.B. 1915, the son of A. C. Coolidge's first cousin.

[294] To the last, the gentlemanly Lane could not conceal his hurt at having been supplanted in 1909. He suggested that Lowell would want to consider carefully "whether the same combination of Director and Librarian is advisable for the future" and he confessed to a hope that while the consideration was taking place and the search for Director under way, he be allowed "to continue in the Library service for another year." Further, he offered "with your support and with the help and advice of the Council, to carry once more the full responsibility of the Library to the best of my ability" and added that "it would be a great satisfaction to me . . . to be made Acting Director." (W. C. Lane to A. L. Lowell, 19 March 1928.) These suggestions Lowell appears to have passed by without comment or acknowledgement.

appointed Librarian, and Lane became Librarian *Emeritus*, as of 1 September 1928. Mrs. Rice financed the completion of the shelving for the lower two floors of the stacks, while arrangements were made to expand the Treasure Room into the Lower Reading Room and to move the reserved book collection (mainly history, government, and economics) that had occupied this room to Boylston Hall, together with the Chinese collection, and the bindery.

Finally, as the gift of John B. Stetson, Jr., A.B. 1906, in memory of his stepfather, the Count of Santa Eulalia, the Library received the great Fernando Palha collection (6,700 books and pamphlets on Portuguese history and literature), the acquisition of which had been one of Coolidge's chief concerns during his last year as Director. Also received during the year were "the Shakespeare quartos and allied literature" collected by William Augustus White, A.B. 1863, the gift of his heirs.

Among the monetary gifts of the year — indeed 15 percent of the year's total gifts for book purchases — was the $2,470 received for books on the French Revolution, French history, and Russian art, which was Coolidge's "final gift," Blake reported.[295] But it was not Coolidge's final gift. His will provided sufficient funds to endow a professorship "in modern European or Asiatic history," and to create a large endowment in the University Library "for the purchase of books or for administrative purposes." The several funds bearing his name had a market value of approximately $2,000,000 some forty years later, while the scholarly collections in the Library which — either with his personal funds or with money he was able to obtain — he acquired for Harvard at a time when they could be bought, are certainly nearly priceless.

Some sense of what Coolidge achieved for Harvard with relatively modest means can be gained by comparison with what Henry E. Huntington was spending to build his own library between 1890 and 1927, the very period during which Coolidge was active. Huntington in that time "accumulated a couple of hundred thousand of the rarest

---

[295] Coolidge's lifetime gifts to Harvard totaled nearly $100,000 according to the office of the Recording Secretary, Harvard University, but even this is understatement, for his advances to buy needed books (later offset by sales) and his anonymous charitable giving for people, projects, and things would further swell the account.

of rare books, and some millions of manuscripts." Huntington concentrated on buying the collections that other people had put together — more than a hundred of them in his collecting life. In seven years between 1911 and 1917 he bought seven major collections at an average cost of $750,000 and a total expenditure of $5,250,000. It was Huntington who competed with Harvard for Hoe items in 1912 and drove the prices skyward. When Huntington purchased the Church library in 1911 he obtained for $750,000 about 4,000 items, including the manuscript of Benjamin Franklin's autobiography, the Bay Psalm Book, Eliot's Indian Bible, twelve Shakespeare first folios, and thirty-seven Shakespeare quartos.[296]

Huntington had enough income to spend several millions a year on books without diminishing his assets. So did Henry Clay Folger in the same period. Coolidge could hardly compete in this kind of wholesale purchasing. Nor was there any Harvard alumnus — save perhaps J. P. Morgan — with the money and enthusiasm to expend such sums.

Coolidge's effort was pitched in a lower key with a consistent aim of strengthening the scholarly resources of his university for future scholars, a highly selective and informed kind of collecting, building on existent strength and on the past generosity of men and women of scholarly instinct.

Instead of the liberal sums which Huntington had available, the central Harvard library had less than $20,000 in 1893–94 to spend on books — and not just "rare" books but books of all kinds, as well as serial publications (newspapers, scholarly journals, and the like). This was at the time Coolidge began his active interest and first "signified his readiness to increase the Slavic department of the Library."[297]

Under the leadership of Jerome Greene, and with the Rices' "accord and sympathy," a small committee of faculty and graduates initiated in February 1928 an effort to raise $6,500 for a memorial tablet on the wall of the "main vestibule" of Widener, near the corridor leading to Coolidge's office, to record Coolidge's achievement. ("My wife's feelings are deep and intense for its fulfillment," Rice reported.) "While

[296] See James Thorpe [Director of the Huntington Library and Art Gallery, San Marino, Cal.], "The Magic Word in Building Collections Is . . . ," *AB Bookman's Weekly*, LII:13 (24 September 1973), 1027–1030.
[297] Eighteenth *Report* (1895) of Justin Winsor, Librarian of Harvard University, p. 10.

it was Mrs. Widener who provided the bricks and mortar," Greene declared, "it was . . . largely Archie Coolidge who made the Library what it is, both through his own services and through the services that he enlisted." [298] The bas-relief sculpture in white marble, executed by Joseph A. Coletti (1898–1973), A.A. 1924, was unveiled on Commencement Day, 20 June 1928. In accepting the tablet from the donors President Lowell hailed

. . . the great spirit of the man who moved silently through this hall in charge of the library. To him above all is due the growth of its collections. Seen only here, he would be thought a man of books, and so he was to an eminent degree; but he also knew the world and its peoples from the Atlantic to the Yellow Sea. In knowledge, in tact, in insight he had the qualifications for a statesman, and he devoted them to the service of the University.[299]

Non sibi sed nobis sed patriae, reads the legend on the tablet. Not for himself, but for us — for the nation.

In the eighteen-year period during which Coolidge headed the Harvard Library the total collection and the central library approximately doubled in size. The library numbered about 1,500,000 volumes and pamphlets when Coolidge became Director and had reached almost 2,800,000 by the end of his tenure. The annual growth of the whole library had more than quadrupled, from 36,500 to 152,000 volumes and pamphlets a year. The annual income and gifts available for book purchases moved from $31,500 in 1909 to just under $100,000 in 1928. In fact more new book funds (47 worth $839,000) were given to the Library in the Coolidge years than in all of Harvard history (42 worth $477,000) up to that time.

Looking back, Coolidge could say

A generation ago, whenever we had any money to spare over what was necessary to meet pressing current needs and to assist a few favored specialties, we looked through book catalogues to see what we could buy at small cost and hardly dared raise our eyes to the higher-priced items. Today, though we have a fondness for getting good things cheap . . . when we look at a title . . . our first question is apt to be — is it a work which a scholar would have a right to expect that the Harvard Library should possess? [300]

[298] A. Hamilton Rice to J. D. Greene, 18 February 1928; J. D. Greene to A. L. Lowell, 8 February 1928.

[299] *Harvard Alumni Bulletin*, XXXI:38 (27 June 1929), 1121–1122.

[300] *Report of Archibald Cary Coolidge, Director of the University Library*, 1924, pp. 1–2.

It remained for Robert Pierpont Blake to pay the ultimate professional tribute to what his notable predecessor had accomplished. "It is to [Coolidge], to his clarity of vision, comprehensiveness of outlook, tenacity of purpose and ability in handling men and measures that the University can attribute the position which its Library now holds among the collections of the world. The constructive work he performed endures and is his true monument; the problems that he has bequeathed to his successor are the problems that have arisen out of his own success." And Blake did not forget to include the "conscientious and faithful" Lane, who had so effectively complemented Coolidge's leadership, "unobtrusively guiding with a skilled hand the complicated technical aspects of the library administration."

"With the passing of these men from the active stage," Blake declared, "a remarkable epoch in the history of the Harvard Library has come to an end. The traditions they established, the foundations they laid, have made its continual growth and enrichment a certainty." [301]

The tradition of Archibald Cary Coolidge deserves admiration and nurture. He is rightfully to be regarded as the pioneer in establishing and developing Slavic studies in the United States. He was the mentor of a generation of scholars in international studies. He was one of the chief builders and supporters of a great library and always the tireless exponent of the principle that every venture into a new area of university scholarship has to be backed with books.

[301] *Report of Robert P. Blake, Director of the University Library*, 1928, p. 1.

Index

References which are *italicized* contain some biographical information.